CW01456225

COMPENDIUM

of

MARIAN DEVOTIONS

The Nativity, c.1490 (detail) / Costa, Lorenzo (1459/60-1535) / Bridgeman Images

COMPENDIUM

of

MARIAN DEVOTIONS

WRITTEN AND COMPILED BY
FR. ED BROOM, OMV

TAN Books
Gastonia, North Carolina

Compendium of Marian Devotions: An Encyclopedia of the Church's Prayers, Dogmas, Devotions, Sacramentals, and Feasts Honoring the Mother of God © 2022 Ed Broom

All rights reserved. With the exception of short excerpts used in critical review, no part of this work may be reproduced, transmitted, or stored in any form whatsoever, without the prior written permission of the publisher. Creation, exploitation, and distribution of any unauthorized editions of this work, in any format in existence now or in the future—including but not limited to text, audio, and video—is prohibited without the prior written permission of the publisher.

Unless otherwise noted, Scripture quotations are from the Revised Standard Version of the Bible—Second Catholic Edition (Ignatius Edition), copyright © 2006 National Council of the Churches of Christ in the United States of America. Used by permission. All rights reserved.

Scripture texts marked NABRE are taken from the New American Bible, revised edition © 2010, 1991, 1986, 1970 Confraternity of Christian Doctrine, Inc., Washington, DC All Rights Reserved.

Excerpts from the English translation of the *Catechism of the Catholic Church*, Second Edition, © 1994, 1997, 2000 by Libreria Editrice Vaticana—United States Catholic Conference, Washington, D.C. All rights reserved.

Cover Design by Caroline Green & David Ferris.
Interior design by www.davidferrisdesign.com.

Cover image: St Dominic receiving the Rosary from the Virgin Mary / Italian School, (17th century), oil on copper / Fitzwilliam Museum, University of Cambridge, UK / © Fitzwilliam Museum / Bridgeman Images.

Interior images: All images are under public domain in the United States of America via Wikimedia Commons unless otherwise attributed under the images. See list of public domain images on pages 265-266.

Library of Congress Control Number: 2022932614

ISBN: 9781505126853
Kindle ISBN: 9781505126778
ePUB ISBN: 9781505126815

Published in the United States by
TAN Books
PO Box 269
Gastonia, NC 28053
www.TANBooks.com

CONTENTS

The Heart of Mary by Leopold Kupelwieser

Who Is Mary?

Of all the women in the history of the created universe, in all the centuries of history, for all time as well as for all eternity, the greatest is Mary.

Mary, the Mother of Our Lord, the Immaculate Conception, is God's masterpiece, more beautiful and pure than any other creation. Numberless hearts have been captivated by her, devoting their time and talents to honor and venerate her in order that they might give glory to her Son, the final end of all Marian veneration.

In what arenas of life do we see Mary's influence? More than we may realize! As we will come to see, Mary has been the subject of countless pieces of literature, music, and art, and for centuries, parents have named millions of their daughters after her. Still more, cities, towns, countries, and provinces are also named after her. No woman in the history of the world has attracted more love and devotion than the Blessed Virgin Mary.

This is because of the role she has played in our salvation, her intimate relationship with the Trinity, the Church, and the saints, and her presence in the pages of Sacred Scripture.

In the Trinity

Mary has a central and intimate place, as well as role, in the very heart of the greatest mystery of Christianity—the Most Blessed Trinity: the Father, Son, and Holy Spirit. Mary is the Daughter of God the Father; Mary is the Mother of God the Son; Mary is the Mystical Spouse of God the Holy Spirit. In sum, Mary is the living tabernacle and sanctuary of the Blessed Trinity!

In the Church

The council fathers of the Second Vatican Council gave Mary a very special role. The Dogmatic Constitution on the Church *Lumen Gentium,* chapter VIII, presents the Blessed Virgin Mary as the Mother of the Church. Once pronounced in the assembly, there resounded an explosive applause that seemed to never end!

In the Lives of the Saints

The saints have a very deep, tender, and loving devotion to the Blessed Virgin Mary. For that reason, among her many titles in the Litany of the Blessed Virgin Mary is that of Queen of the Angels and Saints! However, as in seeing beautiful colors emanate from a diamond through the process of refraction, or a rainbow painting the sky as sunlight breaks through after a torrential downpour of rain, Mary radiates God's eternal beauty in the wide range of her various titles. Some of these are: Our Lady of Good Counsel (Saint Augustine), Our Lady of Perpetual Help (Saint Alphonsus Liguori), Our Lady Help of Christians (Saint John Bosco), Our Lady of Divine Mercy (Saint Faustina Kowalska), Our Lady, Queen of All Hearts (Saint Louis de Montfort). In other words, each and every individual saint loved Mary but was able to contemplate her beauty and majesty in a different dimension.

In the Bible

Biblical typology or symbolism abounds with respect to the person of Mary! She is seen as the conqueror of the ancient serpent, depicted as the second Eve, and viewed as the Ark of the Covenant. Mary also is the Daughter of Zion and can be seen as the Queen Mother in 1 Kings 2; still more, in Isaiah, Mary is the virgin who has conceived the child called Emmanuel—God with us!

But what has all this to do with us? Who is Mary to us?

Saint Thérèse of Lisieux, one of the most known and loved of the modern saints, asserted with respect to Mary: "It is true that Our Lady is Queen of Heaven and earth, but she is more Mother than Queen." We all need a mother. The qualities of a mother are many: she gives birth, nourishes, protects and defends, clothes, corrects, heals, educates, comforts and consoles, listens, and gives advice. But first and foremost, a true mother loves her child from the very depths of her heart! With respect to our mother Mary, it cannot be said with greater unction and eloquence than in these words of Saint Augustine, son of Saint Monica: "If you were to take all the love, of all the mothers, of all times and places together, the love that Mary has for you is much greater!" With these moving words of Saint Augustine, we should have a total, unreserved, unlimited, loving trust in the Blessed Virgin Mary, who indeed is the Mother of God, the Lord Jesus Christ, and the Mother of the Church; but most especially, your Mother and mine, in time and for all eternity!

In this *Compendium of Marian Devotions*, you will find a treasury of the many ways the Church has venerated Mary for the last two thousand years. Prayers, theology, artistic works, devotions, apparitions and mystical phenomena, sacramentals, liturgical feasts, hymns, and more fill these pages, drawing you into the heart of our heavenly mother. We hope and desire that all of you who read, reflect, and meditate on this humble work dedicated to Mary will fill your mind, heart, and soul with a tender, filial, confident, loving, and total donation of self to Jesus through the loving hands of Mary. Our hope, desire, and prayer are that your growing knowledge and love for Mary will set your heart on fire with a love for Jesus, her Son, so that when you die, you will be welcomed by Jesus and Mary into heaven. We pray that one day you will be a splendid jewel in the crown of Mary to contemplate the face of God—the Father, Son, and Holy Spirit—for all eternity!

The Virgin and Child / Master of Flemalle, (Robert Campin) (1375/8-1444) / Bridgeman Images

Madonna with child by Il Sassoferrato

CHAPTER 1

Mary, Our Mother

Saint Thérèse of Lisieux, a young Carmelite saint who died at the tender age of twenty-four, loved the Blessed Virgin Mary very much. She was known to have said: "It is true that Our Lady is Queen of Heaven and earth, but she is more Mother than Queen."

Before we examine Marian dogmas, teach Marian prayers, chronicle her apparitions, number her feasts, list her sacred titles, or reveal her many virtues, we must proclaim Mary's motherhood, for all of us understand the power of a mother's love. We begin with the heart, and from there, the rest will follow.

Indeed, Mary is first and foremost the Mother of God. It is from this role that she is also then the Mother of the Church, the Mystical Body of Christ, and by extension, our very own loving mother.

Up to this point, the Church has officially declared four Marian dogmas, a truth revealed by God through the Church that must be accepted. They are Mary's Divine Maternity, Mary's Perpetual Virginity, Mary's Immaculate Conception, and finally, Mary's Assumption into Heaven. Of these, the greatest and most sublime is Mary's Divine Maternity—which means that Mary was chosen by God to be His mother; we celebrate this every year on Christmas, as well as to start off the New Year on January 1.

Holy Mother Church declares this teaching of Mary's Divine Motherhood on the foundation of Sacred Scripture. We read that she gave birth to Emmanuel—*God With Us*—at the Nativity, and in the months before this, her cousin Elizabeth, filled with the Holy Spirit, called her "the mother of my Lord" (Lk 1:43). Later, at the feast of Pentecost, considered the birth of the Church, Mary is there praying with the apostles in the Upper Room when the Holy Spirit descends upon them like fire. By our baptism, we became members of the Church, the Mystical Body of Christ, and Mary is our mother in the order of grace.

To understand the importance of this motherly role that Mary plays, consider the role of motherhood in the natural order. Who could deny the importance of a mother in the life of her child? Why, then, would God, who calls himself "Our Father," and who gives us our Christian brothers and sisters to walk with in this life, leave us motherless in the spiritual order? What family is whole without a mother?

Archbishop Fulton Sheen posed this question once, asking, "Can religion do without motherhood? It certainly does not do without fatherhood . . . and since motherhood is as necessary as fatherhood in the natural order—perhaps even more so—shall the devoted religious heart be without a woman to love?"

Bishop Sheen went on to say, "If fatherhood has its prototype in the Heavenly Father, who is the giver of all gifts, then certainly such a beautiful thing as motherhood shall not be without some original Mother, whose traits of loveliness every mother copies in varying degrees."[1]

Let us return to the importance of mothers in the natural order. A mother has basic and innate qualities. First and foremost, the nature of a mother is to give life to the child that she carries in her womb and, second, to nurture the child once he has left the womb. Third, a mother is intent upon clothing her child to protect him from the cold and from sickness. Fourth, a mother protects her child from danger and the possibility of getting hurt. Fifth, a mother is intent upon educating her child, physically, intellectually, morally, and spiritually. Sixth, a mother will treat her child's wounds and tend to him when he falls ill. Seventh, a mother listens to her child whenever he wants to open up and express what is in the depths of his heart. Eighth, a mother has the courage to correct her child when he has made some error or is moving in a dangerous direction. Ninth, a mother comforts her child by her warmth, tenderness, concern, compassion, and care. And finally, tenth, the most important and characteristic note of an authentic mother is that she loves her child with all her heart. It is a love without limits, irrespective of where the child is and what the child has done—her love is as vast as the ocean!

All of these maternal qualities can be attributed to Mary our mother on a higher and more sublime plane. Let us now look at these motherly attributes and apply them to Mary as our heavenly mother.

---

[1] Fulton Sheen, *The World's First Love.*

The Immaculate Conception / Pinturicchio, Bernardino di Betto /
Photo © Fine Art Images / Bridgeman Images

Mary Gives Life

Mary is *full of grace* from the very moment of her Immaculate Conception in the womb of her mother, Saint Anne. Grace is the supernatural life of the soul. Mary prays for us so that we will attain grace beginning with our baptism. She prays for us so that this grace will grow and abound during our entire life. Finally, she prays for us to have the grace of all graces, and that is to die in the state of grace so that we will be saved for all eternity. Mary, my mother, attain for me life and life in abundance!

Mary Nurtures Our Spiritual Life

Through a fervent prayer life in which we speak often and confidently to Mary, our loving mother, she attains for us growth in our spiritual life. Once again, Mary, *full of grace*, attains for us special insights in our intellect and touches of grace in our soul so that we may grow and flourish like a healthy tree growing alongside an abundant and gushing stream.

Mary Helps to Clothe Us

Adam and Eve, after committing the original sin, recognized their nakedness. On a spiritual plane, when we are imbued with sanctifying grace through Baptism, we are spiritually clothed with the most exquisite garment. As our mother, Mary prays that we will always be clothed with this garment of grace, and if we lose it due to mortal sin, Mary prays that we will recover grace through a good Sacramental Confession.

Mary Watches Over Her Children to Protect Them

Mary is keenly aware of the many dangers that her children are exposed to from within and from without. The devil, the flesh, and the world are in constant pursuit of our attention, as well as our soul. Mary has her careful, attentive, and watchful eyes gazing upon us with love, and she warns us through grace and through inspirations of the dangers that encroach upon us.

Mary Educates Us

As a good mother strives to provide a good education for her children, so does Mary. Father Robert Fox, a true expert on Our Lady, most especially Our Lady of Fatima, pointed out that Our Lady of Fatima came in a very special way as a teacher. The words and messages of Our Lady of Fatima turn out to be a superb and excellent teaching, an excellent catechism, a clear and poignant signpost on how to arrive at what is most important—our eternal salvation. Jesus and Mary are the best of teachers; let us listen to them and obey their advice!

Mary Heals Her Wounded Children

If a child falls off a bike into a mud puddle and cuts his knee, his mother is the first one to run and succor the child. Lifting the child out of the mud, kissing the child, embracing the child, cleansing the child and changing his clothes, dressing the child's wound, and finally giving the child some hot chocolate—these are all gestures of a loving mother. When we are wounded, Mother Mary comes to us speaking words of wisdom: *Do not worry. I am here to bring you healing.* We should bring our gaping wounds to both Jesus, the Wounded Healer, and Mary, the mother of Jesus the Wounded Healer!

Mary Listens to Us

A true mother is ready to listen to what is in the heart of her child. On a much loftier plane, Mary is always ready to listen to us, to respond to our problems, to help us in our needs. The beauty of Mary as *listener* is the simple but all-consoling fact that Mary is never too tired, occupied, absorbed, or if you like, too busy to listen to us whenever we want to talk to her. We should get in the habit of talking to Mary as often as our heart desires. Mary's ears are always attentive to the supplication of her children. Moreover, she listens to us not only with her ears but also with her Immaculate Heart, and she understands us perfectly!

Mary Corrects Her Wandering Children

A loving mother is not bashful or slow to correct an errant child. If there is a wandering and hungry wolf outside, the mother will keep her child inside and lock the door, especially if that child is curious and tends to wander. Fraternal correction indeed is a dimension of the theological virtue of charity, which Saint Thomas Aquinas defines as "willing the good of the other." An example of Mary correcting her children comes to us, again, in the Fatima messages. Mother Mary warned that most souls are lost due to sins of the flesh and that many souls are lost due to a lack of prayer and sacrifice. Gently, but firmly, Mary exhorts us, her children, to intensify our prayer life, to be willing to live a more sacrificial life, and to strive to live a life of greater purity. This reminds us of the words of Jesus in the Sermon on the Mount: "Blessed are the pure of heart; for they will see God" (Mt 5:8).

Mary Comforts Her Children

In the midst of the many sufferings, trials, tribulations, afflictions, and setbacks in this short life on earth, which is merely a short pilgrimage on the highway to heaven, Our Lady ardently desires to comfort us as a loving mother. Among the many consoling titles of Mary is Our Lady of Consolation. Still more, the Marian prayer that we say to conclude the most Holy Rosary of the Blessed Virgin Mary is that of the Hail Holy Queen. This consoling prayer starts with these words: *Hail Holy Queen, Mother of Mercy, our life, our sweetness and our hope!* Beyond a doubt, these few words are like a gentle dew descending upon the dry and parched desert of our soul. Indeed, in the

My Mother, My Confidence!

O Mary Immaculate, the precious name of Mother of Confidence,
with which we honor thee,
fills our hearts to overflowing with the sweetest consolation
and moves us to hope for every blessing from thee.

If such a title has been given to thee,
it is a sure sign that no one has recourse to thee in vain.

Accept, therefore, with a mother's love, our devout homage,
as we earnestly beseech thee to be gracious unto us in our every need.

Above all do we pray thee to make us live in constant union
with thee and thy Divine Son, Jesus.

With thee as our guide, we are certain that we shall ever walk in the right way, in such wise that it will be our happy lot to hear thee say on the last day of our life those words of comfort: "Come then, my good and faithful servant; enter thou into the joy of my Lord." Amen.

My Mother, my Confidence!

sorrows, sadness, and failures that we all experience in this valley of tears, we should run to Mary as our mother to comfort us. She will come quickly to soothe our sorrows with the comfort and consolation of her loving heart!

Mary Truly Loves Us, Intensely!

A natural mother loves her children. However, human love has limits, and it often wanes, declines, and can even grow cold. This is a sad but true reality. Not so in the case of Mother Mary. The love of the most pure and Immaculate Heart of Mary never wanes, diminishes, or grows cold. It is a constant, intense, and faithful love. Mary loves

Deposition (1329) / Pietro Lorenzetti / Photo © NPL - DeA Picture Library / G. Roli / Bridgeman Images

us irrespective of where we are, what we have done, and what we have failed to do. Her love is most pure and perfect. Possibly the best way to understand to a limited degree the love Mother Mary has for you and for me would be by meditating upon the words of the Doctor of Grace, the great Saint Augustine: "If you were to take all the love, of all the mothers, of all times and places together, the love that Mary has for you is much greater!" In other words, it is impossible to fathom the inexpressible, sublime, and ineffable love that Mary has for you!

We hope and pray that starting now you will experience the extraordinary power of the presence of Mary in your life, most especially as your heavenly mother. As a mother, she will attain life—life in abundance—for you. As a mother, she will nurture and strengthen your spiritual life. As a mother, she will clothe you with the royal garment of sanctifying grace. As an attentive mother, she has her loving eyes fixed upon you at all times. As a good mother, she will educate you in the Gospel—the Good News of salvation that Jesus her Son taught. Wounded? Mary is also known as *Health of the sick,* and like Jesus, she will intercede as a physician. Never too busy, Mary will lend you an attentive ear; she is the best of listeners. If you are a wandering sheep from the fold, Mary, as mother of the Good Shepherd, and aware of the presence and danger of the wolves, will bring you back to the fold. In the midst of the sorrows and failures of life, Mary is "your life, your sweetness, and your hope." Finally, Mary loves you intensely with her Immaculate Heart and desires that one day you will be with her forever in heaven to praise the Father, the Son, and the Holy Spirit for all eternity.

The Four Marian Dogmas

A dogma of the Catholic faith is a truth declared by God which the Magisterium declares as binding. In simpler terms, this means it is a teaching of the Church we must believe to be true, without any doubt, and this belief must be reflected in our Christian witness and discipleship and the way we live our lives. A dogma of the faith is that Jesus is the Son of God, or that the Eucharist is truly His Body, Blood, Soul, and Divinity. Conversely, believing in certain miraculous events, like a Marian apparition, is not a dogma. Even though they can greatly aid our faith, we do not have to believe in these miracles to be a member of the Church.

Within the Church, as we will see, there are many Marian devotions, prayers, feasts, apparitions, and other spiritual practices, all of which are powerful and important, and greatly *encouraged*, but not mandated. But there are only four Marian dogmas that we must believe as Catholics.

1. Mary's Divine Maternity

This dogma was declared at the Council of Ephesus in 431. The council proclaimed Mary as the *Theotokos*—the God-bearer. There was a theological battle between the heretical bishop Nestorius and Saint Cyril of Alexandria. Nestorius said there were two separate persons, one human and one divine, in the incarnate Christ. But Saint Cyril affirmed that Jesus Christ was both God and man—His divine nature and human nature united in one Person, the Second Person of the Blessed Trinity. In this, of course, is the presence of Mary as the Mother of God, an honor we celebrate for her on January 1.

1. The Adoration of the Shepherds / Reni, Guido / Bridgeman Images   2. The Madonna in Sorrow by Giovanni Battista Salvi da Sassoferrato
3. The Virgin and Child with Saint Anne (circa 1503) by Leonardo da Vinci   4. Assumption of the Virgin by Guido Reni

2. Mary's Perpetual Virginity

This dogma states that Mary was a virgin before, during, and after the birth of Our Lord. Tradition tells us that Mary had taken a vow of virginity, and Isaiah tells us that "a young woman shall conceive and bear a son" (7:14). Following the birth, Joseph guarded Mary's virginity. Jesus did not have any other brothers and sisters, as some wrongly claim by misreading parts of Scripture. The Second Vatican Council affirmed Mary's virginity, saying, "Christ's birth did not diminish his mother's virginal integrity but sanctified it" (*Lumen Gentium*, no. 57).

3. Mary's Immaculate Conception

A dogma only recently promulgated in 1854 by Pope Pius IX, it states that Mary was preserved from sin when she was conceived in the womb of her mother and remained free from sin throughout the entirety of her life. She confirmed this shortly after the declaration by Pope Pius IX at her apparitions at Lourdes to Saint Bernadette, calling herself "the Immaculate Conception." Some point to a passage in Scripture that says all require salvation through Christ, therefore, if Mary was sinless, she would not need saving. The Church answers this objection by pointing out that Mary did need her Son to save her, but while we are saved from our sins, she was *preserved* from sin through the foreseen merits of her Son's saving death. The feast of the Immaculate Conception is celebrated on December 8.

4. Mary's Assumption

Another recent dogma defined in 1950, this time by Pope Pius XII, states that after the course of her earthly life, Mary was assumed, body and soul, into heavenly glory. This dogma is intimately tied to the Immaculate Conception, for if sin did not touch her, neither would death. We celebrate this feast each year on August 15.

Virgin in Glory with St. Gregory and St. Benedict / Pinturicchio, Bernardino di Betto (c.1452-1513) / Bridgeman Images

CHAPTER 2

The Queenship of Mary: Hail Holy Queen!

Mary is our mother, yes, but let us look at the words of Saint Thérèse of Lisieux again: "It is true that Our Lady is Queen of Heaven and earth, but she is more Mother than Queen."

This holy young woman stresses the motherhood of Mary, but she does not do so at the expense of denying her queenship, for Mary is both Mother and Queen!

Why do we call Mary our Queen? Let us explain.

One common source of confusion when we consider the queenship of Mary is that she was Jesus's mother, not wife. When we think of a kingdom, we think of the queen as the king's spouse. But this was not so in the Davidic kingdom because the king had more than one wife. This reality meant that the king's mother—not his wife—was the queen. She had the role of queen mother.

A powerful image that shows the relationship between the king and the queen mother can be found in First Kings when Bathsheba approaches King Solomon. We read that he "had a seat brought for the king's mother," and she says to him, "I have one small request to make of you." Solomon replies, "Make your request, my mother; for I will not refuse you" (1 Kgs 2:19–20). In this, we see a foreshadowing of the relationship between Jesus and Mary. Mary, as the true Queen Mother, sits beside the King of Heaven and makes intercessory petitions for us, her children. Because He loves His mother so much, He will not refuse His mother's requests.

It is vitally important to understand the structure and hierarchy of the Davidic kingdom if we are to understand how Christ's Church is meant to look here on earth.

The Coronation of the Virgin / Ridolfo Ghirlandaio / Photo © Photo Josse / Bridgeman Images

In the Davidic kingdom, as we noted, the king's throne was flanked by the queen mother's throne; then, the king sat surrounded by twelve elders of the twelve tribes of Israel, and the key-bearer assisted in the care of the kingdom as a kind of prime minister. For the Church to be the fulfillment of the Davidic kingdom, she must have the help of Mary of Nazareth, the Queen Mother, be governed by the twelve apostles and their successors (the bishops), and be headed by the key-bearer, the pope. (Saint Peter, the first pope, was given the keys. Keys were a symbol of an office, which meant a position that would have successors.) All these aspects are not complicated extras added to the gospel by the Catholic Church but rather are intricate and essential parts of the covenantal community of Jesus Christ!

Another clue from Scripture that proves Mary's royalty is the way the angel Gabriel greeted her, with the salutation of "*Hail* Mary." "Hail" is a way to greet royalty, the way we greet a queen.

Still more, in Revelation, chapter 12, we read about the woman "clothed with the sun, with the moon under her feet, and on her head a crown of twelve stars" (12:1). The Church teaches that this woman from Revelation is Mary, who wears her crown of stars as the Queen of Heaven. In the last Glorious Mystery of the Rosary, we meditate on Mary's coronation as Queen of Heaven, pointing to this passage in Revelation.

We know that heaven is a kingdom—this was how Jesus spoke of it on many occasions. It is only natural, then, for this kingdom to have a king and a queen. There is little doubt who the King is—Jesus—and He has total and absolute authority. His Queen is the woman by His side who helps Him rule, and who loves their subjects with a mother's heart. Mary is quite clearly this Queen. Her role as the Mother of God bestows this honor upon her, and so all of creation, not just us but the angels as well, call her their Queen!

The Church celebrates the feast of the Queenship of Mary every year on August 22. We must make every effort we can to attend Mass on this day and receive Holy Communion in honor of our Queen. Furthermore, we should find prayers to pray that honor her as Queen and give praise to her as Queen. One of the most popular is the Hail Holy Queen.

Hail Holy Queen, Mother of mercy, our life, our sweetness, and our hope!

To thee do we cry, poor banished children of Eve.

To thee do we send up our signs, mourning and weeping in this valley of tears.

Turn then, most gracious advocate, thine eyes of mercy toward us.

And after this our exile, show unto us the blessed Fruit of thy womb, Jesus.

O clement, O loving, O sweet Virgin Mary.

V. Pray for us, O holy Mother of God,
R. *That we may be made worthy of the promises of Christ.*

Mary, Queen of Heaven and Earth, pray for us!

Our lady of perpetual help. Photo by Immaculate / Shutterstock

CHAPTER 3

Mary's Two Greatest Desires

In Dante's *Inferno*, the devil informs Jesus that a certain soul is his, a soul that is destined for eternal damnation. Jesus responds by denying the devil's assertion. The devil insists, claiming that this soul, due to his many serious sins, is his property. Jesus then says with utter clarity and simplicity, "That soul is not yours because he invoked the holy name of my mother Mary!"

This literary masterpiece does not deny the serious quality of sin, especially mortal sin. However, it does highlight a hallmark and indispensable help on the highway to salvation: the presence of Mary, the power of Mary, the importance of invoking the holy name of Mary!

If Mary is our Mother whom we love, and our Queen whom we serve, we should ask what her greatest desires are. Do we not want to please our Mother and our Queen?

Our Lady has two constant and ardent desires. The first is to praise and glorify God. Any praise we give to her she passes on to the Blessed Trinity, and in doing so, she teaches us how to properly praise and worship God. All the Marian prayers and feasts and devotional practices we will explore in this text bear this same goal—to glorify God.

The Virgin Mary's second desire is the perseverance, sanctification, and salvation of immortal souls. All her prayers and hopes and efforts of intercession are directed to this second desire so that her first desire of glorifying God can be fulfilled.

And how do we fulfill these desires? How does she help us fulfill them?

In many of her apparitions, including both Lourdes (1858) and Fatima (1917), which we will talk about in more detail in later chapters, Our Lady expressed the clear call to conversion from sin and to pray for the conversion of poor sinners. Our Lady's message could be summed up in three words: sin, prayer, sacrifice. Let us explain these words.

Sin

Our Lady pointed out very clearly, especially in Fatima, the evil of sin. She prophesied to the three shepherd children to whom she appeared (Lucia, Jacinta, and Francisco) that as a result of sin, wars had broken out, and if people kept sinning, a worse war would explode. Twenty-two years after Fatima, the worst war in the history of the world crashed into human history—World War II—killing millions upon millions, estimated between fifty and fifty-eight million. Our Lady also pointed out that souls are lost to the eternal fires of hell due especially to the sins against the very demanding virtue of purity. The words of Jesus resound clear and with conviction: "Blessed are the pure of heart, for they will see God" (Mt. 5:8). Even the Immaculate Heart of Mary surrounded with sharp and penetrating thorns manifests sin in a very personal way—sin pierces the Immaculate Heart of our Heavenly Mother. Our Lady challenges each of us to look into our life, examine our conscience, and make a firm purpose of amendment once and for all to strive with all our energy to renounce sin in all shapes, colors, sizes, and forms! And that includes avoiding near occasions of sin—those persons, places, things, circumstances, or times of the day that draw us into sin!

Prayer

In all six of Our Lady's appearances to the three children of Fatima, she exhorts them to pray the Rosary daily. Truly, the Rosary is our ladder to heaven! The Rosary, another topic we will discuss in more detail soon enough, is biblical—following the lives of Jesus and Mary in Sacred Scripture. Pope Saint John Paul II in his apostolic letter on the Rosary, *Rosarium Virginis Mariae*, tells us that through the Rosary, we "contemplate the face of Christ in union with, and at the school of, his Most Holy Mother." He goes on to say, "We are remembering Christ with Mary, we are learning Christ from Mary, we are being conformed to Christ with Mary, we are praying to Christ with Mary, and we are proclaiming Christ with Mary!"

Sacrifice

In both Lourdes and Fatima, the Blessed Mother, concerned about the conversion and salvation of sinners, asked for frequent and fervent prayers to be offered. However, in addition to prayers, she noted that sacrifice was also required if souls were to be saved!

Detail of the Head of the Virgin, from The Virgin of the Rocks, c.1508 / Vinci, Leonardo da (1452-1519) / Bridgeman Images

Jesus reiterates the same message: "Unless a man deny himself and take up his cross and follow me, he cannot be my disciple" (Lk 14:26).

If this is the case, that Jesus and Mary want us to offer sacrifices for the salvation of souls, then what can we do? Lucia de Los Santos once asked Our Lady of Fatima what she, Francisco, and Jacinta should do with respect to sacrifices. Our Lady responded by telling her to offer up all to God as a sacrifice. As a guide or help, we would like to suggest ten distinct areas that you can offer to Jesus and the Blessed Virgin Mary as forms of sacrifice and, as such, collaborate with them in the salvation of many souls. Indeed, the harvest is rich, but the laborers are few. May you be among the harvesters with Jesus and Mary in the harvest of immortal souls for all eternity!

Morning Offering

Start off every day by offering all you are, all you have, and all you plan to do that day to the Sacred Heart of Jesus and the Immaculate Heart of Mary for the salvation of souls.

Weather Conditions

Instead of complaining about the heat, the cold, the rain, or the wind, simply accept the weather as it is and thank God you are alive! If it causes you discomfort, offer it for the salvation of souls.

Headache

When you experience a headache, unite it with the head of Jesus pierced by a crown of thorns for those many sinners whose minds are full of sin—in their memories, thoughts, or imagination. May their minds be purified by your willingness to accept your headache!

Traffic

Instead of giving in to both anger and impatience while stuck in traffic, say an extra Rosary for the conversion and salvation of sinners.

Being Ignored

If at home or at work you are forgotten, not taken into account, snubbed, or simply ignored, offer it in reparation for the many who treat Jesus the same way by ignoring Him or denying Him.

Dryness in Prayer

When you pray but don't experience strong feelings or emotions, and this may go on for some time, take advantage of this spiritual desert that you are traversing by offering it for the conversion of sinners who are far from God and who are living in a moral wasteland.

Humiliations

They can come in many shapes, forms, and sizes, and can be very painful! Accept them for the sake of the salvation of so many poor sinners who are on the very precipice of the eternal loss of their souls!

Upset Plans

Inevitably, life teaches us that our plans can easily be upset and overturned. Accept this and the suffering it entails in order to collaborate with Jesus and Mary in the conversion and salvation of many immortal souls.

Painful Waiting

You have an appointment, and the person arrives late. In the interim, offer your suffering by praying an extra Rosary or Chaplet of Divine Mercy. Even though waiting can be an annoyance, even painful, it too can be the means of the conversion and sanctification of lost sinners. God is willing to take whatever we are willing to offer Him with a sincere, pure, and generous heart to save souls!

Slip, Trip, Fall, and Bruise

It has happened to all of us. We forget to watch our step, we stumble, trip, fall, and end up bruising ourselves, if not worse. Instead of blurting out some vulgar word, offer it for the many souls who have slipped morally, who are bruised spiritually, who have fallen into the deep mud of mortal sin and are in danger of never getting up and out of their sinful condition. Perhaps your offering will help them to rise up and return to the loving embrace of the merciful Father.

To conclude, Our Lady has an ardent longing for God to be honored, praised, and glorified in this life and forever in heaven. Still more, Mary loves what God loves: the conversion of sinners and the salvation of an abundant harvest of souls. Let us work generously with Jesus and Mary!

Adam and Eve banished from the Garden of Eden by an angel, Illustration from the Dore Bible, 1866 / Universal History Archive/UIG / Bridgeman Images

CHAPTER 4

Old Testament Types for Mary

A biblical type is a person, event, object, or statement in the Old Testament that prefigures or foreshadows something we see in the New Testament. The study of these is called typology.

There are many Old Testament types for Mary. Knowing them and understanding who and what they are can give us a better understanding of who Mary is, which helps us to grow in love for her. Let us dive now into the pages of the Old Testament to discover the hidden places our heavenly mother can be found!

Mary as the New Eve

Adam and Eve were our first parents, created by God out of the abundance of His infinite love and created in His image and likeness. All that God created in the natural world, He created for the welfare and salvation of Adam and Eve.

Love demands a free response. Love cannot be coerced. To show their love for God, Adam and Eve had to obey Him, obey one simple command: they were not to eat from one tree in the Garden of Eden, the tree of the knowledge of good and evil.

Despite this command, Eve draws close to the tree and the forbidden fruit; she is placing herself in the near occasion of sin, so to speak, "playing with fire." How often have we placed ourselves in the near occasion of sin? Presumably, too many for our weak souls to sustain the weight of temptation!

Close to the forbidden fruit is the evil one, the one we call "the ancient serpent," the devil. Jesus called the devil a liar and a murderer from the beginning (see Jn 8:44).

Prayer to Mary, the New Eve

Dear Mother Mary, you are the true Mother of the Living. Help me to know and love you and Jesus more and more each day. Mary, Mother of the Living, help me to avoid the near occasions of sin, keep me away from the forbidden fruits in my life. In moments of temptation, come to my aid and crush with your heel the ugly head of the serpent, the devil. Amen.

The devil, a fallen angel, tempts Eve to eat the fruit, and even lies to her, saying that if she eats it, she will be like God. Eve lifts up her eyes and sees that the forbidden fruit looks good. How often does sin enter into us through our eyes! Eve lifts her hand, plucks the forbidden fruit from the tree, and bites into it. Then, Eve gives the forbidden fruit to Adam, and he also eats. Pope Saint John Paul II calls this the social effect of sin!

From that moment, Adam and Eve change. Instead of walking in the garden and talking with God as a friend, they now fear Him and hide in shame. Sin often causes within us fear and shame; we want to hide ourselves from God, like Adam and Eve.

Due to the sin of Adam and Eve, all of us are born with the stain of original sin. Baptism washes it away, but we still suffer *the effects* of original sin. The *Catechism* tells us: "As a result of original sin, human nature is weakened in its powers, subject to ignorance, suffering and the domination of death, and inclined to sin (this inclination is called 'concupiscence')" (*CCC* 418).

How does this story relate to Mary? Through her title as "the New Eve."

Eve's name means "mother of the living." Yet ironically, the first Eve brought us death. Whereas Mary, the New Eve, brings us back to life!

Mary was God's chosen instrument to carry out the greatest mission the world has ever known, and she received privileges commensurate with her high calling. Mary is a young woman at prayer when an angel of God, the archangel Gabriel, whose name means, *Strength of God*, appears to her and speaks these words: "Do not be afraid, Mary; you have found favor with God. You will conceive and give birth to a son, and you are to call him Jesus. He will be great and will be called the Son of the Most High. The Lord God will give him the throne of his father David, and he will reign over Jacob's descendants forever; his kingdom will never end" (Lk 1:29–33).

Upon Mary's "yes" to God, there is an explosion of joy among the angelic court. The power of the Holy Spirit overshadows Mary, and the Word, the Son of God, becomes flesh and dwells within her. He dwells among us still today in His holy Church, and through the sacraments, He dwells within us by sanctifying grace.

Eve, by listening to the advances of a fallen angel, and by saying "no" to God through her pride to be like him, introduces death and sadness into the world by eating the forbidden fruit from the tree. Sin always causes sadness in our minds, hearts, souls, lives, families, and the world at large, and brings death to our souls.

But Mary, the New Eve, unties the knot of Eve's disobedience. Through her humility, Mary receives the message not from a fallen angel but an archangel and says "yes" to God. Many years later, Mary would stand at the foot of a different tree—the cross—and when we eat of this "fruit of her womb" in the sacrament of the Holy Eucharist, we are brought back to life. The parallels are striking!

Mary is known as the Cause of Our Joy. Drawing close to her, we move away from sin through frequent confessions and Holy Communions. We live in joy and we become heralds of joy to our family, friends, and the whole world!

Mary as the Ark of Refuge

In the book Genesis, God presents a man whose name is Noah. This man Noah and his family are good people. They truly love God and try to serve Him. However, the other people of Noah's time have forgotten about God and are living sinful lifestyles.

Therefore, God decides to destroy these people with their many sins. He will carry this out by sending an enormous downpour of rain, a deluge for forty days and forty nights. But because of Noah's righteousness, He decides to save Noah and his family.

God speaks to Noah, telling him that to save himself and his family, he must construct an ark. The ark will be enormous, and it will demand much time, work, and sweat to finish such a huge undertaking. Just the same, Noah follows God's plan, despite all possible difficulties.

As Noah and his sons start to saw, hammer, and construct the ark, the people grow curious and ask him what he is doing. Noah tells the truth: he is

The Construction of Noah's Ark (circa 1675) by Französischer Meister

obeying God by building an ark so as to save himself and his family from the coming deluge. At this, the people ridicule Noah.

The day is approaching. The deluge is soon to descend from the skies. God tells Noah to take a pair of each of the animals into the ark, and then to enter it himself along with his family. With no sign of a storm approaching, the people continue to laugh at Noah.

Finally, the door of the ark is closed. The skies darken, and soon thereafter, the rains begin. It pours and pours for forty days and forty nights.

Where are the scoffers now? All of the people and animals outside the ark are drowned. They perish, almost all of humanity. Only Noah and his family and the animals inside the ark are saved.

Finally, the rain ceases to pour down upon the earth. "Then God said to Noah, 'Come out of the ark, you and your wife and your sons and their wives. Bring out every kind of living creature that is with you—the birds, the animals, and all the creatures that move along the ground—so they can multiply on the earth and be fruitful and increase in number on it'" (Gn 8:15–17).

Noah built an altar to the Lord, and taking some of the clean animals and clean birds, he sacrificed burnt offerings on it in thanksgiving. This was very pleasing to the Lord and he said: "Never again will I curse the ground because of humans, even though every inclination of the human heart is evil from childhood. And never again will I destroy all living creatures, as I have done" (Gn 8:20–21).

The simple reason why Noah and his family, as well as the animals, were saved, is because they obeyed God by seeking refuge in the ark.

Today, we are living in tumultuous times, times that are arguably even more sinful than those of Noah. Errant philosophies and lifestyles diametrically opposed to the Gospel of Jesus Christ are being spread far and wide around the globe!

For this reason, God, in His loving care, gave us Mary, our Ark of Refuge! She will keep us close to her Son, Jesus, in the Church and in the sacraments. We may get ridiculed and scoffed at by non-believers, like Noah, maybe even persecuted, but in the end, we will be saved, and we can only pray that our prayers and sacrifices can help save them as well.

Amidst the trials, temptations, perils, and dangers of life, we must run to our Ark of Refuge, the Blessed Virgin Mary!

Mary Became the New Ark of the Covenant

In the Old Testament, the Ark of the Covenant was built. The symbolic meaning of the ark was the desire of the Jewish people to have God present with them. They desired God to journey with them, to accompany them, to protect them, and to save

Joshua passing the River Jordan with the Ark of the Covenant (1800) by Benjamin West

them. Let us now read prayerfully the Word of God, Saint Paul's letter to the Hebrews, speaking about the Holy of Holies and the Ark of the Covenant with its sublime majesty and importance:

> Now even the first covenant had regulations for worship and an earthly sanctuary. For a tent was prepared, the outer one, in which were the lampstand and the table and the bread of the Presence; it is called the Holy Place. Behind the second curtain stood a tent called the Holy of Holies, having the golden altar of incense and the ark of the covenant covered on all sides with gold, which contained a golden urn holding the manna, and Aaron's rod that budded, and the tables of the covenant; above it were the cherubim of glory overshadowing the mercy seat. Of these things we cannot now speak in detail. (Heb 9:1–5)

The Ark of the Covenant was not God but a symbol of God. God's symbols are important. They are physical entities that point to a deeper spiritual reality. This symbol was important in helping the Chosen People be aware of God's all-abiding presence. It was constructed about a year after their exodus from Egypt and helped sustain them for the remaining thirty-nine years of wandering in the desert.

The Blessed Virgin Mary can be seen as the New Ark of the Covenant. The reason is clear. Mary carried not a symbol of God but God Himself within her very being. As a young woman, God the Father, through the message of an angel, invited Mary to say "yes" to conceiving His only begotten Son in her womb, and His name would be Jesus. At the moment Mary said "yes" to God's invitation, the Holy Spirit overshadowed her, just as we read in Exodus 34 how God came and "overshadowed" the ark when He entered it (came in a cloud), and the Son of God became flesh and dwelt within her.

Therefore, Mary had within her most pure womb Jesus, the Son of the living God, for nine months. Mary was the House of God, as well as the Temple of God—the New Ark of the Covenant!

Consider this further parallel. As we learned, Moses was given instructions on how to build this structure—this tabernacle—that would become the dwelling place of God in the Old Covenant. In it, three things were placed: the Ten Commandments, the manna from the desert, and Aaron's staff that miraculously budded.

In the New Covenant, Mary would now become the dwelling place for God. In housing Him in her womb, she held the Word of God not in stone like the Ten Commandments but in flesh. She held not the manna from the desert that Israelites lived off but the true Bread of Life which feeds us while we wander in exile here on earth. And she would hold the High Priest, a parallel to Aaron's staff which was a symbol for the priesthood.

Upon learning from the angel of the pregnancy of her elderly cousin, Mary went in haste to visit Elizabeth and assist her in her need. Mary traveled a long way to arrive at the home of Saint Elizabeth in the hill country. Reflecting in a deeply spiritual way, we can easily conclude that Mary, as the new and real Ark of the Covenant, with the baby Jesus in her womb, was a living Eucharistic procession. This is no metaphor!

Now take a few moments to enter into these ineffable mysteries of our faith! Imagine that you are traveling with Mary. It is a long way—about ninety miles—from Nazareth to Ain Karim, the little town in the hills of Judea where Zachary and Elizabeth live. In spite of the distance, Mary is filled with joy, and Jesus within her is the source of that overflowing joy! Accompany Mary in this journey. Look at her, what do you see? Beauty, peace, joy, youth, strength, enthusiasm, purity, and underlying all, gratitude, humility, and meekness—all of these virtues radiate resplendently from Mary, the New Ark of the Covenant!

Open up your heart and talk to Mary. She is already your mother, and Jesus is already your brother! She loves you very much. She is anxiously waiting for you to talk to her, spend time with her, share your joys with her, entrust your cares and worries to her, give yourself totally to her. Mary is the best of listeners; she never gets tired of listening to you, loving you, and giving you good counsel. Tell her what is on your heart right now.

Today, Jesus is present in the tabernacle in the Church where the consecrated Host—the Body, Blood, Soul and Divinity of Jesus, that we call the Blessed Sacrament—is reposed. That is why it is good to genuflect or bow your head when you pass before the tabernacle. Jesus is like us; He wants to be acknowledged and loved, not ignored. We should also acknowledge His divine presence when the consecrated Host is placed for exposition in a monstrance, whether on an altar or in a Eucharistic procession.

The modern classic *In Sinu Jesu* is written primarily for priests, but the author invites lay people as well to read and profit by it. In this work, Jesus is speaking to a priest in prayer, but Jesus is also saying these words to you: "I remain your Friend, the Friend of your heart. I am always present to you and My eyes are upon you at every moment. I desire your company. I long for the attention of your heart and for the consolation of your adoration, your reparation, and your love."[1]

Jesus, the fruit of Mary's womb, is really and truly present in all the tabernacles in all the Catholic Churches throughout the world. He is with us in His Eucharistic presence, *His Real Presence*, until the end of time! There is no place, time, or day that Jesus is not present to us, thinking of us, and loving us in the tabernacles of the world.

[1] A Benedictine Monk, *In Sinu Jesu: When Heart Speaks to Heart – The Journal of a Priest at Prayer* (Kettering, OH: Angelico Press, 2016), p. 20.

And we may look at Mary as the New Ark of the Covenant, the tabernacle, the monstrance, that holds Him, that gives Him a home in our world!

Now here is one of the greatest miracles that can occur while we live in time and space here on earth: receiving Jesus in Holy Communion! Pope Saint John Paul II compares Mary's "yes" to the archangel Gabriel, thus receiving Jesus into her heart and her womb, to you and me saying "Amen" to receiving Jesus in Holy Communion into our hearts, minds, and souls. In truth, like Mary, we have Jesus's real presence within us.

Prayer to Mary, the New Ark of the Covenant

Dearest Mary, mother of Jesus and my mother, I thank you for saying "yes" to God and bringing Jesus to be with us always, even until the end of time. Help me to be more aware of your presence in my life. Help me to be more aware of Jesus's real presence in my soul in Holy Communion. Help me to be more aware of Jesus's real presence in the tabernacle. Jesus, Mary, and Joseph, I love you! Amen.

There is still more typology that shows us Mary is the New Ark if we examine the story of her trip to visit Elizabeth, her cousin, and compare that to an important story from the Old Testament.

We read in the sixth chapter of 2 Samuel that when the ark came before King David, he was afraid because Uzzah had been killed after touching it. David said, "How can the ark of the Lord come to me?" (2 Sm 6:9). The ark was taken into the house of a man named Obed-edom for three months, who lived very near the hill country of Judea. After this time, David finally brought the ark into the city of David, and he danced with rejoicing before it.

Now we return to our mother, Mary of Nazareth. After she becomes the new dwelling place of God, she goes to visit her kinswoman, Elizabeth, who lives in the hill country of Judea, very near where Obed-edom lived. When Mary arrives, Elizabeth is filled with the Holy Spirit, and her greeting is very similar to David's when he stood before the ark: "Blessed are you among women, and blessed is the fruit of your womb! And why is this granted me, that the mother of my Lord should come to me?" (Lk 1:42–43).

Mary ended up staying with Elizabeth for three months, the same amount of time the ark stayed in the house of Obed-edom. Finally, while Elizabeth didn't dance before the New Ark like David did before the Old Ark, her babe, John the Baptist, leapt in her womb with joy! "For behold, when the voice of your greeting came to my ears, the babe in my womb leaped for joy" (Lk 1:44).

Other Old Testament Types for Mary

Mary's role as the queen mother was already discussed in chapter 2, but this is another important prefigurement of Mary and the queenship she would assume. Still more, we have the Daughter of Zion, the embodiment of the nation of Israel, and Old Testament prefigurements like Sarah and Hannah, who had unlikely and miraculous births of important sons in the story of salvation history. Many years later, Mary would give birth to *the Son of God* in a most miraculous fashion! Jael and Esther also foreshadow Mary, for they too had important roles in saving their people from wicked men plotting against them, the powers of evil at work, just as Mary helps battle the powers of darkness as our mother and queen. Finally, there are prophecies and psalms aplenty in the Old Testament that point to the coming of the Virgin Mary—too many to list here!

Let these Old Testament types serve as a reminder that God had Our Lady in mind long before she entered the world in Nazareth. Just as she lives on today in the life of the Church, she also has been a part of salvation history from the very beginning. We encourage all who are reading this to embark on a study of Marian typology in the Old Testament to learn more.

The Visitation (1643) by Philippe de Champaigne

CHAPTER 5

The Magnificat and Other Words of Mary from Scripture

"Out of the abundance of the heart his mouth speaks" (Lk 6:45).

These words were uttered by Jesus who is the Incarnate Word, the Logos, and the greatest of all the teachers that the world has ever known. The essential message in the interpretation of this short sentence is the following: we can get to know a person by the words that issue forth from his mouth because those words really issue forth from the center of his being—from his very heart. Ugly, profane, indecent, uncouth words all flow from a person's corrupt heart. On the contrary, noble, profound, pure, enlightening, and holy words emanate from a person whose heart is pure and holy.

The four Gospels mostly recount the words, actions, and gestures of Our Lord and Savior Jesus Christ. It should be an ardent pursuit of our lifetime to come to know, love, and put into practice the words of Jesus in the Gospels.

Also of great importance are the words of the Blessed Virgin Mary in Sacred Scripture. The words or sayings that we have from her are few, actually no more than seven ("word" here is used to express a series of words, or a "scene" in which she speaks). Nonetheless, the few words that we have of Mary most holy are words of great depth, holiness, and wisdom—words that we should come to know, love, memorize, and incorporate into our daily lives.

First Word

"How can this be, since I have no husband?" (Lk 1:34). This first word comes from the scene of the Annunciation. Mary is approached by the archangel Gabriel who

announces to her the good news that she is to be the Mother of God. Having taken a vow of virginity, Mary does not understand how she will bear a child. She asks, "How can this be, since I have no husband?" God's messenger states that the conception will be the work of the Holy Spirit, meaning Mary will remain a virgin. He also reveals that her elderly kinswoman, Elizabeth, once thought to be barren, is already in her sixth month carrying a child, for nothing is impossible for God. The message is clear: We should be faithful to our promises and try to live a life of great innocence and purity. This can be done through the example and prayers of the Blessed Virgin Mary!

The Annunciation (circa 1590-1603) by El Greco

Second Word

"Behold, I am the handmaid of the Lord; let it be done to me according to your word" (Lk 1:38). And the Word became flesh and dwelt among us! This second word of Mary, known in Latin as her *fiat* ("let it be"), resulted in the incarnation of the Second Person of the Blessed Trinity in the most pure womb of the Virgin Mary. We can derive many profound messages from Mary's *fiat*, her "yes" to God. First, Mary teaches us that true joy can only come from imitating her in saying yes to God in all times, places, and circumstances. Second, we owe eternal gratitude to Mary because as a result of her yes, Jesus came into the world as our Savior. In other words, we can be saved and go to heaven because Mary conformed her will to the will of God, accepting Jesus into her womb, into her life, and into the life of the world so as to save us from eternal sorrow, sadness, and separation from God.

Third Word

Mary's greeting to Elizabeth. This third word of Mary can be found in the context of the visitation of Mary to her cousin Saint Elizabeth. The biblical text simply states that Mary greeted Elizabeth (see Lk 1:40). We can surmise that the greeting consisted of the typical form of greeting of the Jewish people at this time, and that would be "Shalom," meaning *Peace be with you!* How does this word of Mary touch us? Hopefully in many positive ways. First, we should be kind enough to always greet other people, especially family members and friends, but even those whom we do not particularly like. Second, we should desire and pray to live in peace with God, in peace within our own hearts, and in peace with others. Third, we should desire that others experience the fruit of the Holy Spirit which is peace.

Fourth Word

The Magnificat. These words are a most sublime, profound, and inspiring hymn of praise that burst forth from the Immaculate Heart of Mary during her conversation with Saint Elizabeth in the Joyful Mystery of the Visitation. Mary's words are prayed by the Church every evening in Vespers, or Evening Prayer.

Mary teaches us immense lessons of wisdom in her *Magnificat*. First, she teaches us the great importance of prayer. Second, she teaches the importance of fearing and adoring God in His greatness. Third, Mary teaches us humility and reliance on God as our strength and our sustenance. Finally, Mary most Holy, in this prayer, can teach us how to worship Jesus after Holy Communion in Mass. Saint Louis de Montfort, in *True Devotion to Mary*, suggests that we pray Mary's *Magnificat* in thanksgiving after receiving Jesus into our hearts in Holy Communion.

The Magnificat

My soul proclaims the greatness of the Lord;

My spirit rejoices in God my Savior;

For He has looked with favor on His lowly servant.

From this day all generations will call me blessed;

For the Almighty has done great things for me, and holy is His Name.

He has mercy on those who fear Him in every generation.

He has shown the strength of His arm;

He has scattered the proud in their conceit.

He has cast down the mighty from their thrones,

and has lifted up the lowly.

He has filled the hungry with good things,

and the rich He has sent away empty.

He has come to the help of His servant Israel;

for He has remembered His promise of mercy,

the promise He made to our fathers,

to Abraham and his children forever.

Fifth Word

"Son, why have you done this to us? Your father and I have been looking for you in great anxiety." The fifth word of Mary can be found in the context of the fifth Joyful Mystery, the Finding of the Child Jesus in the Temple after three days of sorrowful search, anxiety, and anguish. Mary says to the Christ Child: "Son, why have you done this to us? Your father and I have been looking for you anxiously" (Lk 2:48). Once again, there is a treasure-house of wisdom contained in this short sentence, in these few words of the Blessed Virgin Mary. First, Mary teaches us to be constantly in search of Jesus. Second, Mary wants us to discover Jesus in the depths of our hearts. Third, Mary teaches us that if we have lost Jesus in the depths of our hearts due to serious sin, we should bring Him back through sorrow and the Sacrament of Confession. Lastly, we should discover who Jesus is by mediating often on the Word of God.

Sixth Word

"They have no wine." The sixth word of Mary can be found in the context of the second Luminous Mystery—the Wedding Feast of Cana (see Jn 2:1–12). Mary notices a serious and embarrassing problem for the newly married couple: the wine has run out! Mary says to Jesus: "They have no wine" (Jn 2:3). Even in just these four words, there is much depth to meditate upon. First, Mary's eyes and Immaculate Heart are always open and attentive to our problems and our needs. Second, Mary teaches us to turn and lift up our eyes to Jesus. Third, Mary cares for all, but especially those with problems. Fourth, Mary wants to bless marriage and the family which today especially are going through many crises and problems.

Seventh Word

"Do whatever he tells you." Aware of the shortage of wine and of the presence and power of Jesus the Lord, Mary says these few words as she turns to the servers: "Do whatever he tells you" (Jn 2:5). Once again, these words of the Blessed Virgin Mary, which are her last recorded in the Gospels, are jam-packed with infinite wisdom for all those who have a mind and heart open to God. First, Mary turns to Jesus in a time of trouble and anxiety; she wants us always to turn to Jesus as well. Second, Mary is keenly aware of the problems that we have in our lives, and she ardently desires to help us with them. This is symbolized by her being the one who noticed they ran out of wine. Third, Mary teaches us that she can help turn our water into wine—that is to say, through Mary's intercession with her Son, our problems can be resolved. Fourth, now Mary says, "Do whatever he tells you." Mediatrix of all graces is the title the Church gives to Mary, meaning all the graces that come to us indeed come from God but through the intercession of Mary.

These are the words of Mary in Sacred Scripture. Unlike today, when people talk much but convey little wisdom, she teaches us so much in just a few simple words. Let us meditate upon her words as much as possible, and let them to speak to our hearts!

The Marriage at Cana, Maerten de Vos (1596–1597)

Mary's Parents

"By their fruit you will know them. A good tree brings forth good fruit, but a bad tree brings forth bad fruit."

These are the words of Christ, found in Matthew's Gospel, chapter 7 (vv. 16–17), and how perfectly can they be applied to his grandparents, the mother and father of the Blessed Virgin Mary? Sacred tradition informs us that these holy souls were named Anne and Joachim.

This treatise on the Blessed Virgin Mary would be incomplete if nothing were mentioned about her parents. I believe that given the high estate of their daughter, it only makes sense that Saint Joachim and Saint Anne deserve our respect. They no doubt are powerful saints that we should pray to for intercession, but often they seem to be like forgotten saints. This is likely because there is no biblical data on the two of them. Nonetheless, tradition points out that this husband and wife were the vessels from which God sent into the world the greatest woman ever to be born and ever to live. Thus, we must highlight the great importance of this couple.

Like Abram and Sarai, like Hannah, like Saint Elizabeth and Zechariah, Saint Joachim and Saint Anne, despite their great desire and longing, were never able to have children. Furthermore, according to tradition, Anne, like Elizabeth, was beyond the normal childbearing age. This was a source of excruciating suffering for Joachim and Anne.

Despite this cross of barrenness which they bore, Anne and Joachim had very generous hearts. They were a devout Jewish couple, prayerful and humble. From the economic means they had for themselves, they preferred to give most of it away; one third they gave to the poor, and another third they donated to the Temple, keeping only a third for themselves.

How true the saying: "God cannot be outdone in generosity." God intervened in a most powerful way in response to the prayerful, humble, and generous hearts of Saint Joachim and Saint Anne. In seemingly impossible circumstances, God blessed them with a little girl, but of course she was no ordinary little girl but a little girl who would grow up to be the Mother of God and the Queen of Heaven! This little girl would transform the entire story of the human race!

In the womb of Saint Anne and through the seed of Saint Joachim, God performed one of the greatest miracles in the history of the world—the miracle of the Immaculate Conception, which means from the moment of her conception in the womb of Saint Anne, Mary was preserved from the stain of original sin that the rest of humanity suffers. God would not work such a mystery in the child of two people if they were not filled with tremendous holiness! Therefore, let us venerate these two holy souls, especially on July 26, the Church's feast honoring both of them, and thank them for giving us our spiritual mother. We must pray to them, asking them to help us practice the virtue of patience, as they were patient waiting on a child, and generosity, as they were generous with their material belongings. Parents and grandparents should especially carry a strong devotion to these saints considering the roles they played within the Holy Family.

Saints Anne and Joachim, pray for us!

The meeting of Joachim and Anne outside the Golden Gate of Jerusalem (1497) by Filippino Lippi

Saint Thomas Aquinas (1476) by Carlo Crivelli

CHAPTER 6

Mariology and a Defense of Marian Devotion

Mariology is the study of the Church's doctrines concerning Mary, the Mother of God. At its core, Mariology is Christology, for all things that pertain to the Virgin Mother lead to her Son. This is the final end of Marian devotion—to deepen our communion with Christ. She wants nothing else except for us to love Jesus, and this is what she teaches us to do—love Jesus—when we come to her.

In these times, in the fracturing of the Church following the Protestant Reformation, there is much confusion surrounding a Catholic's veneration of Mary. Let us clarify this confusion! Other parts of the text expand upon the study of Mariology, including an exploration of the Church's Marian dogmas, but here we will make a defense of the Church's devotion to Mary, the Mother of God.

If we truly love a person, then we want to defend that person when they are unjustly criticized or condemned. If someone launches unjust insults against our mom or dad, we will stand up to defend them. This also must apply in our loving relationships with Jesus and Mary, His mother and our mother in the order of grace. She who is called *full of grace* desires so ardently to attain for us grace, growth in grace, perseverance in grace, and the grace of all graces—to die in the state of grace so as to be with her in heaven for all eternity praising the Blessed Trinity.

One of the most common attacks against the person, power, and presence of the Blessed Virgin Mary comes from those who say Catholics have fallen into idolatry, in the sense that they claim Catholics actually *adore* Mary. To make matters worse, they assert that Catholics *worship* Mary by kneeling before statues of her. They assert that this goes directly against the first commandment, which commands us to worship only God.

So that we can refute these false claims and properly defend Mary, our mother, her privileges, and her place and prominence in the economy of salvation, we should get to know three key words: latria, dulia, and hyperdulia.

Latria

The word *latria* means that of praise or worship. It is true that as Catholics we adore only God—the Triune God: Father, Son, and Holy Spirit. The Father is worthy of all praise, glory, worship, and honor. When we pray the Lord's own prayer of the Our Father we say: "Our Father, who art in heaven, hallowed be they name." That is to say that God the Father and His holy name are worthy of all praise and worship.

Jesus is the Second Person of the Blessed Trinity. We adore Jesus and His holy name in all times, places, cultures, and circumstances. In the Letter of Saint Paul to the Philippians, we pray: "At the name of Jesus every knee should bow in heaven and on earth and below the earth" (Phil 2:10). This bending of the knee is an exterior sign of our recognition that Jesus is King of kings and Lord of lords and worthy of all honor, glory, and praise. For that reason, upon entering a Catholic Church and walking before the tabernacle—where Jesus is present in the consecrated Host—all are called to genuflect, bending one's knee to the ground. This was done in deference to a king in the Middle Ages. Jesus is the greatest King of all kings! He is God and we worship Him with all our heart, mind, soul, and even through corporal gestures.

Finally, the Holy Spirit is worthy of all worship, honor, and praise. He is the Third Person of the Blessed Trinity, the Consoler, the Sweet Guest of the Soul, and the life-giving principle or very soul of the Church. Praise, honor, and glory be to the Holy Spirit.

Dulia

This term applies to God's special friends whom we call the saints. These dear friends of God can help us immensely by their power of intercession, as well as by the good example they leave us to imitate and follow. We do not praise the saints, but we have great honor and respect for them. For this reason, Pope Saint John XXIII called the saints "God's masterpieces!"

Hyperdulia

Finally, we have arrived at the Blessed Virgin Mary's role in the economy of salvation, her role in the Church, and the very special place that she should have in each and every one of our hearts, our lives, and our eternal destiny.

The word that Mariologists—theologians who study Marian doctrine—give to our treatment of Mary is that of *hyperdulia*. This word, coming from Greek, actually means *"the highest form of veneration that can be given to a creature"*—and this is exactly what we give to the Blessed Virgin Mary! Mary is not praised and adored, like the latria attributed to the Blessed Trinity. However, the Blessed Virgin Mary is given the highest and greatest honor possible for a human creature.

The reason why Mary is truly in a class by herself, given the highest honor, is due to the office or sublime mission that God gave to her. She was chosen to be the instrument by which the Blessed Trinity would carry out the mystery of the Incarnation. In other words, Mary was invited by God to truly be the Mother of God. With total freedom, Mary gave her consent to God's invitation, and "the Word became flesh and dwelt among us" (Jn 1:14).

In addition to the sublime mission she freely fulfilled through her great humility, we must comment on Mary's supreme beauty.

Have you ever had a chance to contemplate a diamond exposed to the sun? Sunlight passing through a diamond refracts light into all the colors of the rainbow—God's wonderful, varied, unique, and illuminating presence breaking upon you. In fact, the beauty of all creation—the sun, the sky, the clouds, the stars, the meadows decked with countless flowers, the majestic mountains in their grandeur and magnificence, the soft and gentle rainfall, the morning dew on the grass, the silent descent of the first snowflakes, the brisk Autumn wind—all of these breathtaking creations are pale images of the God who is the Creator of all beauty!

Now call to mind some of the masterpieces of the world's greatest artistic geniuses in painting, sculpture, poetry, writing, and musical composition: Michelangelo, Leonardo da Vinci, Dante, Shakespeare, Bach, Beethoven; the list goes on.

God, as designer of all beauty, has far surpassed all of His created world, as well as all the works of human geniuses, in the creation of one person—the Blessed Virgin Mary! Indeed, Saint Louis de Montfort, with great zeal and enthusiasm, acclaims Mary as God's masterpiece of creation.

We must remember this the next time some person comes up to us claiming that Catholics are guilty of practicing idolatry in their relationship to Mary. Make sure to teach them the truth that all we are doing is honoring and loving our mother, and the role that God Himself gave her in asking her to bring us into the life of the Holy Trinity.

But we have not yet expressed all the many reasons we must love and honor our mother—far from it! Let us continue to manifest her beauty and perfection by turning next to her many virtues.

Detail of the Virgin Mary, from the Ghent Altarpiece (1432) Eyck, Hubert /
© Lukas - Art in Flanders VZW / Bridgeman Images

CHAPTER 7

The Ten Virtues
of Mary

Let us continue our journey by examining now the virtues of Mary. No one book could do justice in chronicling a full list of the Virgin Mother's virtues, so here we will focus on a specific few.

In his Marian literary masterpiece, True Devotion to Mary, Saint Louis de Montfort highlights ten of the most important virtues of the Blessed Virgin Mary: "True devotion to our Lady is holy, that is, it leads us to avoid sin and to imitate the virtues of Mary. Her ten principal virtues are: deep humility, lively faith, blind obedience, unceasing prayer, constant self-denial, surpassing purity, ardent love, heroic patience, angelic kindness, and heavenly wisdom."[1]

Let us humbly beg our Blessed Mother Mary for the grace to understand these ten virtues that she practiced always to a heroic degree of perfection, but also let us beg for the grace to be able to put these virtues into practice in our daily walk of life!

Deep Humility

A humble person recognizes that all the good they have done, and can do, is a result of the presence of God in their life. Mary was most humble, calling herself the servant or the handmaid of the Lord. Also, in her magnificent canticle of praise that we call the Magnificat (see Lk 1:46–55), Mary states that God has looked with favor upon

---

[1] St. Louis de Montfort, *True Devotion to Mary* (Charlotte, NC: TAN Books).

the humility of His handmaid. Let us beg Mary for a meek and humble heart so that like her, we will attribute our successes to God and our failures to ourselves.

Lively Faith

Faith is one of the three theological virtues—faith, hope, and charity. At its core, faith is believing in God and His Word without seeing with our eyes. Jesus gently reproved the doubting Thomas with these words: "Blessed are those who have not seen and yet believe" (Jn 20:29). Mary is the woman of faith par excellence. Therefore, when we are tempted to doubt, let us turn to Mary, the woman of faith, and beg for her most powerful intercession.

Blind Obedience

By giving her consent in the annunciation—"Behold, I am the handmaid of the Lord; let it be to me according to your word" (Lk 1:38)—Mary displayed an admirable attitude of obedience to the Word of God and trust in His holy will. When we are tempted to rebel and turn against God, let us, through Mary's prayers and example, obey God like Mary, and like Jesus, who was "obedient unto death, even death on a cross" (Phil 2:8).

Unceasing Prayer

Prayer can be defined as communication with God. There is no better example in the world, aside from Jesus, with respect to a life of constant prayer than that of the Blessed Virgin Mary. Scripture tells us, "Mary kept all these things, pondering them in her heart" (Lk 2:19). Perpetually, she thought of God in her mind and loved Him with all her heart; she maintained constant communication with the Blessed Trinity. The devil of laziness can attack us all. May Our Lady inspire us to be constant, fervent, and faithful in prayer! Indeed, prayer is the key to our salvation. What air is to the lungs, prayer is to the soul!

Constant Self-Denial

Another way of wording this is mortification—the ascetical life which leads to the mystical life of union with God. Mary denied and sacrificed herself in all times and in all places. By doing so, she gave full reign for God to work in the entirety of her life. In Mary's approved apparitions, both in Lourdes and in Fatima, she strongly encouraged the practice of prayer but also that of sacrifice. By making sacrifices, we are imitating Mary in the art of self-denial. Self-denial turns us towards God and away from self. Mary was always God-centered and never self-centered. May this be our style of life!

The Virgin Mary with the dove of the Holy Spirit above her, surrounded by six Saints
(1505) / Cosimo, Piero di / Luisa Ricciarini / Bridgeman Images

Surpassing Purity

One of the most sublime virtues that characterizes the Blessed Virgin Mary is that of her spotless purity. Mary is known as the Immaculate One. In Fatima, Our Lady sadly expressed that most souls are lost to the eternal fires of hell due to sins against the virtue of holy purity. Mary is the Perpetual Virgin. She was a virgin before, during, and after the birth of Jesus. True devotion to Mary can help us maintain our purity, and if we have lost it, to seek restoration through sacramental confession. Contemplating a beautiful picture, painting, or statue of Our Lady can instill in us noble aspirations for purity.

Ardent Love

Of all the virtues that we are called to practice, ardent love, sometimes called charity, is the greatest. Read the beautiful hymn of love by Saint Paul: 1 Corinthians 13. Our Lady practiced love to a sublime degree and in two ways, for love or charity has two dimensions. Mary at all times and in all places loved God first and foremost. However, Mary expressed concretely her love for God by ardent love for her neighbor. Think of the Annunciation. Through her unconditional "yes," Mary showed her total and unreserved love for God. Then, moving in haste to visit her cousin Elizabeth, Mary manifested great love for her neighbor. In imitation of Mary, may we say in the words of Saint Paul, "The love of Christ controls us" (2 Cor 5:14). May we learn this double commandment—love of God and love of neighbor—and strive to live it out on a daily basis. Saint John of the Cross states: "In the twilight of our existence, we will be judged on love."

Heroic Patience

Not one of us can say that we are patient at all times, in all places, and in all circumstances. This is unlike Mary, who manifested remarkable patience. We must not think of patience just as waiting for something to take place; it is more trusting in God's providence in all matters, that He has ordained events to unfold in our lives in a certain manner (and yes, at a certain time) according to His holy will. Consider her pregnancy, traveling the long trek to Bethlehem and then being rejected—what great patience! Losing the Child Jesus when He was twelve years of age for three long days before finding Him in the Temple—another manifestation of heroic patience! Most especially, in accompanying Jesus in His passion leading up to His brutal crucifixion and death, Mary manifested unequalled patience! She always trusted in God's plan. When our patience is put to the test, let us call out to Mary for her assistance. She will never fail us!

Angelic Kindness

The opposite of kindness is rudeness. Just try to imagine the way and manner in which Mary must have treated her neighbor! A warm welcome, a kind and winning smile, courtesy to the maximum, and an attentive ear to listen are all clear manifestations of kindness, angelic kindness, in fact. Mary did all this to the highest degree! On this virtue, Saint Francis de Sales commented: "One can attract more flies with a spoonful of honey than with a barrel full of vinegar." In other words, kindness attracts others to Christ, while rude and drastic measures repel them. May Our Lady teach us what it means to be kind and may we put it into practice!

Heavenly Wisdom

One of the sublime titles given to Mary in her glorious litany is "Seat of Wisdom." A wise person knows what is most important in life. Dynamic love for God and ardent desire for the salvation of immortal souls are hallmarks of true wisdom. Our Lady had a burning love for God and an ardent desire for the conversion of sinners and their eternal salvation. The Second Vatican Council document *Lumen Gentium* tells us, "The Blessed Virgin persevered in her union with her Son unto the cross . . . joining herself

Assumption of the Virgin / Titian (Tiziano Vecellio) / Cameraphoto Arte Venezia / Bridgeman Images

with his sacrifice in her mother's heart." King Solomon was once wise, but he gave into his weakness—that of lustful desires—and ended his life a fool. We beg for the intercession of Our Lady, Seat of Wisdom, to attain for us not only wisdom now, but perseverance in this sublime virtue until the very end!

In conclusion, may we ardently desire to know, love, and imitate our Blessed Mother Mary. May we be motivated with a firm decision to meditate frequently and fervently on the virtues of Mary most holy, and strive to live them out all the days of our lives!

Nature Reflects the Beauty of Mary

God is indeed the Creator of all that is good, true, and beautiful. The great mystics and saints are able to see God in all things, including in the beauty of creation. The pinnacle of God's creation—His masterpiece—was the Blessed Virgin Mary.

We must always be keenly aware of the fact that all the beauty of creation is a mere reflection of the beauty of God, and Mary's beauty far exceeds that of any other created being or thing.

Therefore, let us offer for your reading, reflection, meditation, and prayer some images in nature that can help us lift our gaze to Mary, and as a consequence, enter into communion with her and with God.

Stars

One of the most famous mystical poets of the Church is Saint Bernard of Clairvaux. We invite all to meditate carefully on his literary and mystical masterpiece entitled *Stella Maris*—meaning *Star of the Sea*. Sailors from centuries past lifted their gaze to the stars to lead them safely and securely to port. Likewise, we need to lift our gaze to Mary, the *Stella Maris*, trusting that through her guidance and inspiration, we will reach our eternal port, our heavenly home.

Rain

The abundant downpour of rain interpreted through a mystical lens can be viewed as graces that descend from on high through the intercession of Mary and enter into our soul thereby producing beautiful flowers in our soul. These flowers are virtues: faith, hope, love, purity, humility, patience, and obedience, to name a few.

Clouds

Traditionally, white points to the virtue of purity. Hopefully, this will engage you in a meditation on Mary's purity of heart, mind, body, and soul. As you look on high at those beautiful and pure white clouds, may this stir in your whole being a desire to imitate Mary—to be pure in heart, mind, body, soul, desire, and intention.

The Blue Sky

How can this not call to mind the blue mantle of Mary? How could this not cause to surge within our hearts a fervent appeal to Mary to protect us, to shield us, to envelop us in her heavenly mantle? Underneath Mary's mantle, we indeed can find a sure refuge!

The Moon

The moon reflects the light and beauty of the sun. So it is no surprise that the moon is symbolic of Mary, whose purpose is to reflect and glorify the light of her Son, the Light of the world

Flowers and Roses

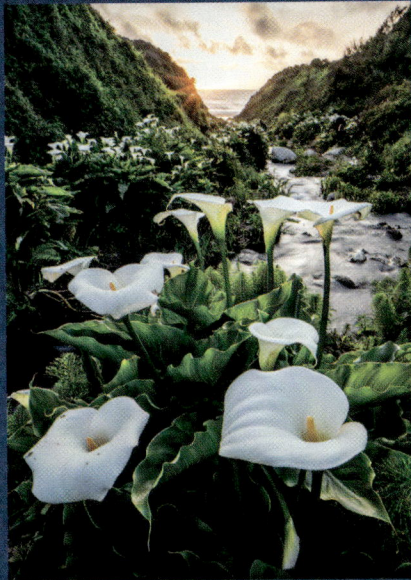

Calla lilies in spring. Photo by Fractal7 / Shutterstock

Flowers are both beautiful and fragrant. Therefore, in the course of your nature walk, as you come across a meadow with a variety of colorful and fragrant flowers, lift up your mind, your heart, and your affections to Mary, colorful and fragrant in her virtues. Reflect upon the beauty of Mary in her holiness. Beg Mary, known also as the Lily of the Field, to instill within your heart an ardent yearning to be holy as your heavenly Father is holy. She is in a special way tied poetically to the rose. Indeed, in the Litany of Loreto, Mary is invoked as the Mystical Rose. Dante, in his literary masterpiece *The Divine Comedy*, also writes about the Mystical Rose. And it is no great surprise that the Rosary we pray to Mary is related to the Mystical Rose, for the Rosary (meaning "crown of roses") is comprised of fifty prayerful roses offered to Mary. Every Hail Mary is a mystical rose that fills Mary's heart with unspeakable joy!

The Gentle Breeze

As the gentle breeze caresses your tired and weary face, remember Mary, who, though strong, is the essence of gentleness. Mary is the gentle woman who has won the heart of God. The gentle breeze also elicits a remembrance of the Holy Spirit. Mary has an intimate association with the Holy Spirit and, of course, with the Blessed Trinity.

Waves

Never do we go to the shore of the sea and fail to see the waves crashing on the shore. They are perpetual, dependable, and consistent. Likewise, Mary's love is perpetual, dependable, and consistent for her children. Waves return and return without ceasing, and so does our mother return to us time and again, even when we fall into sin.

The Annunciation, 1474-75 / Antonello da Messina (c. 1414-1493) / Bridgeman Images

CHAPTER 8

Our Lady Exterminator of All Heresies

Among the many roles of the Blessed Virgin Mary in the Church is that of helping to exterminate the heresies that crop up. The Protoevangelium, meaning the first proclamation of Good News, came after the fall of our first parents, Adam and Eve, which the Church defines as original sin. The Good News was this: "I will put enmity between you and the woman, and between your seed and her seed; he will bruise your head, and you will bruise his heel" (Gn 3:15).

The ancient serpent, also known as the devil, constantly tries to sow weeds in the wheat, sow division and destroy harmony, and sow lies so as to suffocate the truth. Jesus calls the devil "a murderer from the beginning" (Jn 8:44).

What then is heresy? It is nothing other than a perversion of the truth, the promotion of lies, prevarication, and falsification. Often, more pernicious and insidious is that of the half-truth, which is in reality a half-lie, and an offense against the fullness of the truth which we all have a right to know.

The founder of the congregation Oblates of the Virgin Mary, Venerable Father Bruno Lanteri, had a constant, dynamic, filial, and burning devotion to the Blessed Virgin Mary. For that reason, he named the congregation he founded after her. Among the many great works and accomplishments of Lanteri was his promotion of love for Mary. Moreover, he observed that during the course of history when the serpent lifted its head to attack through the poison of heresy, it was the Blessed Virgin Mary who intervened and was instrumental in crushing the ugly head of this primordial enemy of the truth and of the Church as "the pillar and bulwark of the truth" (1 Tm 3:15). Even now, when so many false ideas or heresies are disseminating far and wide, the powerful presence of Mary, the Conqueror of all Heresies, or if you like, the Exterminator of All Heresies, should be marshalled forth!

Examples in the course of history are numerous. We will mention just a few with the hope that today when the heresies are almost countless, we will lift our eyes, our minds, our hearts, and our souls to Mary, the Conqueror of all Heresies, the Exterminator of all Heresies, and beg her to lift her powerful heel to crush the ugly head and expel the venomous poison of the devil—the father of lies and the spreader of heresies.

Nestorianism

This was a pernicious heresy that denied the foundational doctrine of the Trinity. Most specifically, it denied that Jesus Christ was the Son of God and equal to the Father in divinity. The Council of Ephesus convened in Ephesus (present day Turkey) in 431. This council confirmed the Nicene Creed. But with respect to Mary, she was proclaimed as the *Theotokos*—the God-bearer. There was a theological battle between the heretical bishop Nestorius and Saint Cyril of Alexandria. Nestorius said there were two separate persons, one human and one divine, in the incarnate Christ. Saint Cyril affirmed that Jesus Christ was both God and man—His divine nature and human nature united in one Person, the Second Person of the Blessed Trinity. In this, of course, is the presence of Mary as being the Mother of God. It was through Mary's intercession that this heresy was conquered. Mary is truly the Mother of God. Of all of the Marian privileges or dogmas, Mary as the Mother of God is the most sublime.

Albigensianism

This was a particularly lethal heresy that was spreading in France and Italy in the twelfth and thirteenth centuries, wreaking havoc within the Church and causing many to leave the Church. It falsely promoted the teaching that the spirit is good and matter (the body) is evil. Whereas in the first book of the Bible we read: "God saw everything that he had made, and behold, it was very good" (Gn 1:31). The key figure that God used to conquer this pernicious heresy was the person of the great Saint Dominic of Guzman—the founder of the Order of Preachers, known as the Dominicans. The preaching of the saint against the Albigenses had no real effect until Our Lady appeared to him and told him that the heresy would only be conquered by preaching the most Holy Rosary. Therefore, Dominic changed tactics and began preaching the praying of the most Holy Rosary. Almost immediately, there were stupendous results! Many of those who were contaminated by the poison of Albigensianism returned

Our Lady of the Rosary / Dítě, Emanuel (1862-1944) / © Lubomir Synek / Bridgeman Images

to the true faith of the one true Church, the Catholic Church. In a word, it was a Marian victory — a victory that came about through Our Lady of the Rosary. Once again, Our Lady crushed the head of the ugly serpent!

The Battle of Lepanto

The Battle of Lepanto took place in AD 1571. This was a naval engagement where the fleet of the Holy League led by the Venetian Republic and the Spanish Empire inflicted a major defeat on the Ottoman Empire in the Gulf of Patras on the Ionian Sea. The Ottoman Empire, the Turks, intended to conquer the Catholic-Christians in a naval battle. By far, the Ottoman Empire had the most powerful fleet in the world, with ships, soldiers, slaves, arms, cannons, experience, and preparation; the mere number of their combatants far outnumbered that of the Christian fleet. Aware of this dire situation in the world and the peril facing the Church, in which the Muslims planned to conquer Rome and establish their supremacy in Rome, the Holy Father, Pope Saint Pius V, received an inspiration from on high. It was this: call on Mary to come and conquer this ugly Islam heresy that could devastate the Church. How? The pope was a Dominican—a son of Saint Dominic, the lover of the Holy Rosary. Therefore, the Holy Father told the people in Rome, far away from the battle of Lepanto, to implore the intercession of the Blessed Virgin Mary to intercede with her power before the throne of God.

In the initial phase of the battle, the Turks were dominant, as was to be expected. However, as the pope and large numbers of Catholics fervently prayed the Rosary, the winds changed, the tide turned. The Turks panicked and the Catholics got the upper hand. To make a long story short, the Catholic fleet won the battle, thereby saving Catholicism from invasion and penetration of the Islam religion into Rome. From afar and by divine inspiration, Pope Saint Pius V knew of the victory and humbly rejoiced,

Allegory of the Battle of Lepanto (1571) by Paolo Veronese

thanking Our Lady of the Rosary for having conquered the enemy. Once again it was Our Lady who conquered this ugly heresy that would have entered into the Church and caused total devastation. As a consequence, the pope instituted the feast of Our Lady of the Rosary, formally known as Our Lady of Victory, on October 7, to commemorate the decisive victory in 1571 of the combined fleet of the Holy League over the Ottoman navy at the Battle of Lepanto. On October 5, 1907, this feast was formally proclaimed by Pope Saint Pius X. For this reason, October is the month of the most Holy Rosary!

And what about today? Now more than ever, we must run to Our Lady and beg humbly and with much faith for the intercession of Mary. As children in danger, we want to run to Mary and beg for her help. There are so many dangers prevalent in our modern society, just to mention a few: materialism, consumerism, hedonism, agnosticism, militant atheism, subjectivism, rationalism, nihilism, and moral relativism. With the proliferation of so many systems that are diametrically opposed to the truth, now more than ever we must lift our gaze to Mary, who can help with her power of intercession to conquer the ugly head of the devil, to indeed be the Exterminator of All Heresies!

Rejoice, O Virgin Mary

Rejoice, O Virgin Mary, for thou alone hast destroyed all heresies in the whole world.

Mary Untier of Knots (1700) / Schmittner, Johann Georg Melchior / Artothek / Bridgeman Images

CHAPTER 9

Our Lady Undoer of Knots

One of the Marian devotions that is growing stronger in recent times is that of Our Lady Undoer of Knots. It was inspired by the famous Baroque painting of the same name that represents the devotion, which was painted by Johann Georg Melchior Schmidtner around the turn of the eighteenth century. The basic idea of this Marian devotion could not be simpler.

All of us have had experiences where we were working with a thread, a string, a rope, or even strands of Christmas lights, and we come to a knot. Consequently, we cannot move forward until the knot is undone. Usually, women have a knack for being able to untie those knots better than men—at least that is true in my case! Mom could untie and undo knots quicker than anyone in our family.

Just as with a thread or a rope, our lives constantly get tangled in knots of one kind or another. It is difficult to go through a day without being entangled in some form of a knot. If this knot is not undone, it becomes more entangled and difficult to undo. On the contrary, as soon as the knot is untied and undone, there is a real sense of relief; we can breathe more easily and peace is restored to our heart, mind, and soul.

Therefore, in this short chapter we would like to present typical examples of knots that many of us encounter in our daily walk of life. It is tempting to ignore them, hoping they will go away, but we know in our heart we must address them. However, let us not address them alone! Let us place the knots in the hands of the Blessed Virgin Mary, the true *Undoer of Knots*, and trust that these difficult situations will be undone, and you will experience a new sense of peace.

Family Knots

All of us struggle in our relationships in dealing with people on a daily basis, especially members of our own family. A cold relationship between a husband and wife, problems with alcoholism, past unfaithfulness, indifference in communication—these are thorny knots that we should bring to Our Lady to ask for her intercession. As Jesus turned water into wine at the wedding feast of Cana through Mary's intercession, so through her intercession there can be a breakthrough in a family knot.

A Child with Problems

Most parents have some form of problem with one or more of their children. Well, instead of worrying and even giving into despair, why not give these children to Mary and beg her to help them with their struggles? Mary is mother of the holy as well as the unholy; Mary is mother of the obedient children as well as the prodigal sons and daughters. Open up and tell Mary what is in your heart about these lost sheep of your flock. The mother of the Good Shepherd will not abandon those sheep.

Health Issues

As a result of original sin, sooner or later, something goes wrong with our health; the possible sicknesses and diseases are countless. However, it must be said that if we keep our problems to ourselves, especially with respect to our health, then interiorly we suffer more and can fall into depression. Why not give your whole self, and that includes your bodily ailments, to Mary, who is also known as Health of the Sick? On many occasions, Our Lady has interceded to heal incurable sicknesses and diseases—especially in Lourdes, France. Nonetheless, even if the sickness is not healed immediately or never healed, you will know that there is a loving and tender mother at your side to console you, comfort you, and support you in the physical cross that you must bear. When Our Lady intervenes with her powerful maternal presence, the cross becomes much lighter. For that reason, we cry out to Mary as "our life, our sweetness, and our hope!"

Moral Issues and Struggles with Sin

Not only do we struggle with physical sicknesses, but also with moral sicknesses—we call this sin! One of the great privileges that God bestowed upon Mary, which is a blessing for the whole human race, is that of the Immaculate Conception. By this great blessing, Mary was conceived without the stain of original sin and she was impeccable, meaning that Our Lady never once in her entire life committed even the smallest sin. She desires to share her purity, her holiness, and her great love for God with us,

Immaculate Conception, by Giandomenico Cignaroli / Mondadori Portfolio / Electa / Adolfo Bezzi / Bridgeman Images

her children. Therefore, one, if not many of the knots that we need untied is that of our sinfulness. By lifting up our gaze to Mary, she can help us overcome bad habits that we call vices. Mary can even help us conquer age-old bad habits that haunt us to this very day. Our Lady, Undoer of Knots, can help us to untie that knot of sin that is really binding us. Jesus calls sin slavery (see Jn 8:34). To help set us free from this slavery, He has given us many graces, most especially the grace of His mother, who wants to help her children break the bonds of sin, rend asunder this moral slavery, and experience the freedom of the sons and daughters of God! Turn to Mary and talk to her about your struggles with the sin or sins that you cannot seem to overcome. Mary is your ally; she will help you to be victorious!

Fears, Uncertainties, and Anxieties

In this world, many, possibly even you, experience on a daily basis some form of fear, anxiety, doubt, uncertainty, or stress. These fears are like ghosts that come out of the closet to haunt us. If we do not come to terms with these "ghosts," then we can go through life being almost paralyzed with unwarranted fears. This will prevent us from living our lives to the fullest extent possible, cultivating our talents and growing on a human and a supernatural plane. A little child who is absorbed and inundated with fears runs to their mother for safety and security. So should we run and seek refuge in Mary, our loving and tender mother, as well as the Undoer of Knots!

We all have many knots in our family life, social life, professional life, and moral life. Let us not keep these knots to ourselves, but rather let us place them in Mary's hands and she will undo the knots, and as such we will experience the true freedom of the sons and daughters of God and the true freedom of the sons and daughters of Mary, the true Undoer of Knots!

Virgin of the Rosary, late 17th-early 18th century / Holguín, Melchor Pérez de (c.1665-c.1730) /
© The Cleofas and Celia de la Garza Collection / Bridgeman Images

Prayer to Our Lady, Undoer of Knots

Mary, Undoer of Knots, pray for me. Virgin Mary, Mother of fair love, Mother who never refuses to come to the aid of a child in need, Mother whose hands never cease to serve your beloved children because they are moved by the divine love and immense mercy that exist in your heart, cast your compassionate eyes upon me and see the snarl of knots that exists in my life. You know very well how desperate I am, my pain, and how I am bound by these knots.

Mary, Mother to whom God entrusted the undoing of the knots in the lives of his children, I entrust into your hands the ribbon of my life. No one, not even the evil one himself, can take it away from your precious care. In your hands there is no knot that cannot be undone.

Powerful Mother, by your grace and intercessory power with Your Son and My Liberator, Jesus, take into your hands today this knot. (*Mention your request here*) I beg you to undo it for the glory of God, once for all. You are my hope. O my Lady, you are the only consolation God gives me, the fortification of my feeble strength, the enrichment of my destitution, and, with Christ, the freedom from my chains. Hear my plea. Keep me, guide me, protect me, o safe refuge! Amen.

Beautiful Titles of Our Lady

At various points in this work, we have discussed special titles of Our Lady, what they mean and the story behind them. But she possesses far too many glorious titles for each one to be discussed in detail. Thus, let us briefly mention a few more to acquaint you with the wonderful patronages, roles, and personalities our mother has.

Stella Maris

This Latin name means "Star of the Sea." It is symbolic of Mary being the guiding light that leads us to Christ. Saint Bernard of Clairvaux wrote, "If the winds of temptation arise; if you are driven upon the rocks of tribulation, look to the star, call on Mary. If you are tossed upon the waves of pride, of ambition, of envy, of rivalry, look to the star, call on Mary. Should anger, or avarice, or fleshly desire violently assail the frail vessel of your soul, look at the star, call upon Mary."

Cause of Our Joy

If our joy is to be with God, then, through her fiat, her "yes" to God, it is only through Mary that we are able to reach the kingdom of heaven. Thus, she is the "cause of our joy."

Theotokos

Greek for "the God-bearer," this title is tied back to the Marian dogma of Mary's Divine Maternity. In 431 at the Council of Ephesus, the heretical bishop Nestorius argued there were two separate persons, one human and one divine, in the Incarnate Christ. But Saint Cyril affirmed that Jesus Christ was both God and man—His divine nature and human nature united in one Person, the Second Person of the Blessed Trinity. In this, of course, is the presence of Mary as the Mother of God, an honor we celebrate for her on January 1.

Seat of Wisdom

Another title from the Litany of the Blessed Virgin Mary, Mary has been called Seat of Wisdom for many centuries by the saints and in the Church. In Scripture, we read about Wisdom personified in the Eternal Logos, the Word of God, the Second Person of the Blessed Trinity. Mary is the person who, through her most intimate relationship with God, was united with Him and bore Wisdom Incarnate in her womb, so we can rightly call her Seat of Wisdom.

The Immaculate Conception

This title refers to the miraculous conception of the Virgin Mary in the womb of her mother without the taint of original sin, which was proclaimed as a dogma in 1854 by Pope Pius IX. Several years later, Mary appeared to Saint Bernadette in Lourdes, France, and called herself "the Immaculate Conception." It is interesting to note that she did this only after the dogma had been promulgated by the Holy Father, as if bowing in humility to her Son's Church. The Church honors the feast of the Immaculate Conception on December 8.

Tower of David and Tower of Ivory

Still more titles taken from the Litany of the Blessed Virgin Mary, these two are powerful symbols. The Tower of David in Jerusalem stood prominently on the highest summit of the mountains. It was an integral defense fortress for the city. Mary is compared to this tower because her womb protected the Christ Child, and because through her intercession, she protects her Son's Church. Tower of Ivory can refer to her for similar reasons but with the additional symbolism of ivory being pure and strong, like Our Lady. The term is also found in the Canticle of Canticles (7:4).

Enclosed Garden and Mystical Rose

In the Canticle of Canticles, we read of a "garden locked" (Sg 4:12). This has been interpreted as a reference to Mary. Her virginity kept her Immaculate Garden "locked" for God. A similar title is Mystical Rose, taken from the Litany of the Blessed Virgin Mary. Flowers are an obvious symbol of beauty, which is fitting for the most beautiful woman in the world. The rose is especially tied to Our Lady since the word *rosary* comes from the Latin for rose. It is said that we are giving Mary a crown of roses each time we pray the Rosary.

Mother of Mercy and Refuge of Sinners

If Christ is Divine Mercy Incarnate, then Mary is the Mother of Mercy. We acknowledge her as such when we pray, *Hail Holy Queen, Mother of Mercy*. She called herself this in an apparition to Saint Bridget of Sweden, and Saint Faustina refers to Mary as the Mother of Mercy in her diary. She is our compassionate mother who will open her arms to us when we have fallen, and she will bring us back to her Son, where we can receive His grace in the Sacrament of Confession. For this reason, she has also been called the Refuge of Sinners.

Our Lady of Sorrows (18th century) by Carlo Dossi

CHAPTER 10

Our Lady of Sorrows

"If any man would come after me, let him deny himself and take up his cross daily and follow me" (Lk 9:23).

How true do these words from Our Lord ring? We all must carry crosses—crosses of sickness, addiction, shame, economic hardship, persecution, and natural disasters. Every day in this valley of tears seems to be a struggle!

Our Lord did not promise that this life would be easy. His words in the ninth chapter of Luke confirm this. He warned us that the crosses would come and be laid upon our shoulders. This is the sad reality of living in a fallen world plagued by sin and division. Some of our crosses are brought upon us through our own faults and transgressions, but many are not. No matter what burdens we carry, we are not able to survive them without our faith.

The Church gives us many gifts that sustain us during our earthly journey—chief among them, the sacraments. Yet one of the most powerful gifts we are given to bear times of agony is our Blessed Mother.

An important title for Mary is Our Lady of Sorrows, or Our Lady of Dolores. We remember her as the mother who stood at the foot of her Son's cross, remaining with Him until the bitter end. What pain and agony she must have felt watching the cruel torture and death of her only Son!

In life, when we have been through a traumatic event, it comforts us to find other wounded souls who have shared similar experiences. For this reason, it is fitting that we would go to Mary, who suffered so much, to find compassion. Compassion means "to suffer with," and this is what Mary did with Jesus, and what she does with us. She knows our pain and she comes to us at our times of great sorrow, standing at the foot of our cross.

It was at the foot of the cross that Jesus gave us Mary as our mother. We read: "When Jesus saw his mother, and the disciple whom he loved standing near, he said to his mother, 'Woman, behold, your son!' Then he said to the disciple, 'Behold, your mother!' And from that hour the disciple took her to his own home" (Jn 19:26–27).

John here stands in the place of all of us, Jesus's disciples. We are to take Mary into our hearts the way John took her into his home. And it was in this moment of her greatest sorrow that she was given to us. Let us meditate on this profound reality as we come to seek comfort and strength from Our Lady of Sorrows.

The Church honors the Sorrowful Mother during Passiontide and on the feast of Our Lady of Sorrows on September 15. Devotion to the Sorrowful Mother has been a common practice among Catholics for many centuries. It takes practical form in the Seven Sorrows Devotion. Just as we meditate on the mysteries of the life of Jesus and Mary while we pray the Rosary, so there are seven sorrows of Mary's life that we can meditate on during this devotional prayer:

1. The prophecy of Simeon (Lk 2:25–35)
2. The flight into Egypt (Mt 2:13–23)
3. The loss of the Child Jesus in the Temple (Lk 2:39–52)
4. Mary meets Jesus on the way to Calvary (Jn 19: 16–18)
5. Jesus dies on the cross (Jn 19:28–30)
6. Mary receives the dead body of Jesus into her arms (Jn 19:38–42)
7. Jesus is placed in the tomb (Mt 27:57–61)

While we meditate on each of these events, we accompany our meditation with short prayers that ask Mary to obtain for us specific virtues, ending each with a Hail Mary.

The First Sorrow: The Prophecy of Simeon

I grieve for thee, O Mary most sorrowful, in the affliction of thy tender heart at the prophecy of the holy and aged Simeon. Dear Mother, by thy heart so afflicted, obtain for me the virtue of humility and the gift of the holy fear of God.

Hail Mary, full of grace, . . .

The Second Sorrow: The Flight into Egypt

I grieve for thee, O Mary most sorrowful, in the anguish of thy most affectionate heart during the flight into Egypt and thy sojourn there. Dear Mother, by thy heart so troubled, obtain for me the virtue of generosity, especially toward the poor, and the gift of piety.

Hail Mary, full of grace, . . .

The Third Sorrow: The Loss of the Child Jesus in the Temple

I grieve for thee, O Mary most sorrowful, in those anxieties which tried thy troubled heart at the loss of thy dear Jesus. Dear Mother, by thy heart so full of anguish, obtain for me the virtue of chastity and the gift of knowledge.

Hail Mary, full of grace, . . .

The Fourth Sorrow: Mary Meets Jesus on the Way to Calvary

I grieve for thee, O Mary most sorrowful, in the consternation of thy heart at meeting Jesus as He carried His cross. Dear Mother, by thy heart so troubled, obtain for me the virtue of patience and the gift of fortitude.

Hail Mary, full of grace, . . .

The Fifth Sorrow: Jesus Dies on the Cross

I grieve for thee, O Mary most sorrowful, in the martyrdom which thy generous heart endured in standing near Jesus in His agony. Dear Mother, by thy afflicted heart, obtain for me the virtue of temperance and the gift of counsel.

Hail Mary, full of grace, . . .

Sixth Sorrow: Mary Receives the Dead Body of Jesus into Her Arms

I grieve for thee, O Mary most sorrowful, in the wounding of thy compassionate heart, when the side of Jesus was struck by the lance and His heart was pierced before His body was removed from the cross. Dear Mother, by thy heart thus transfixed, obtain for me the virtue of fraternal charity and the gift of understanding.

Hail Mary, full of grace, . . .

The Seventh Sorrow: Jesus Is Placed in the Tomb

I grieve for thee, O Mary most sorrowful, for the pangs that wrenched thy most loving heart at the burial of Jesus. Dear Mother, by thy heart sunk in the bitterness of desolation, obtain for me the virtue of diligence and the gift of wisdom.

Hail Mary, full of grace, . . .

V. Pray for us, O Virgin most sorrowful,

R. *That we may be made worthy of the promises of Christ.*

Let us pray:

Let intercession be made for us, we beseech Thee, O Lord Jesus Christ, now and at the hour of our death, before the throne of Thy mercy, by the Blessed Virgin Mary, Thy Mother, whose most holy soul was pierced by a sword of sorrow in the hour of Thy bitter Passion. Through Thee, O Jesus Christ, Savior of the world, who with the Father and the Holy Ghost lives and reigns world without end. Amen.

Fresco of the Seven Sorrows of the Blessed Virgin, by Tempesta and Circignani

To accompany the prayers of this devotion, there are beautiful artistic depictions of the Sorrowful Mother. These usually have seven swords puncturing her heart to represent her seven sorrows. It is recommended to obtain one of these, or a prayer card, and gaze upon her somber face as we pray the Seven Sorrows Devotion.

If we are unable to have these prayers in front of us, simply saying seven Hail Mary's while meditating on the seven sorrows is acceptable. In fact, according to the blessed word of Saint Bridget of Sweden (1303–1373), who was visited by the Blessed Virgin, seven graces are granted to the souls who honor her daily by saying seven Hail Mary's while meditating on her tears and dolors. These promises, from the mouth of our Lady, are as follows:

1. I will grant peace to their families.
2. They will be enlightened about the divine mysteries.
3. I will console them in their pains and I will accompany them in their work.
4. I will give them as much as they ask for as long as it does not oppose the adorable will of my divine Son or the sanctification of their souls.
5. I will defend them in their spiritual battles with the infernal enemy and I will protect them at every instant of their lives.

6. I will visibly help them at the moment of their death—they will see the face of their mother.

7. I have obtained this grace from my divine Son, that those who propagate this devotion to my tears and dolors will be taken directly from this earthly life to eternal happiness, since all their sins will be forgiven and my Son will be their eternal consolation and joy.

These promises should make our hearts leap and we should run straight away into the arms of Our Lady of Sorrows. And consider that this devotion is a source of great grace because it is pleasing to Our Lord. Who would not love a man or woman who comforts his mother in a time of great sorrow? Jesus loves those who love His mother and who wish to console her. In return, they both console us in our trials.

If you are going through some storm, turn to Our Lady of Sorrows! She will remain with you and deliver you into her Son's arms, where you will finally find peace.

Our Lady of Sorrows, pray for us!

Prayer to Our Mother of Sorrows for a Happy Death

O Mother of Sorrows, by the anguish and love with which thou didst stand by the Cross of Jesus, stand by me in my last agony. To thy maternal heart I commend the last three hours of my life. Offer these hours to the Eternal Father in union with the agony of our dearest Lord. Offer frequently to the Eternal Father, in atonement for my sins, the Precious Blood of Jesus, mingled with thy tears on Calvary, to obtain for me the grace to receive Holy Communion with most perfect love and contrition before my death, and to breathe forth my soul in the actual presence of Jesus.

Dearest Mother, when the moment of my death has come, present me as thy child to Jesus; say to
Him on my behalf: "Son, forgive him, for he knew not what he did. Receive him this day into Thy kingdom." Amen.

The Stations of the Cross and the Stabat Mater

We think in a special way of the Sorrowful Mother on Good Friday as we pray the Stations of the Cross. With Mary, we walk beside Jesus as he scales Calvary and is crucified between two criminals.

The *Stabat Mater* is a thirteenth-century hymn to Mary that sings of her suffering at the foot of her Son's cross. The title comes from its first line, "Stabat Mater Dolorosa," which means, "the sorrowful mother was standing." The hymn is sung on both the feast of Our Lady of Sorrows and Good Friday during the praying of the Stations.

Christ on the Cross with Mary and St John (circa 1512) by Albrecht Altdorfer

Stabat Mater

At the Cross her station keeping,
stood the mournful Mother weeping, close
to her Son to the last.

Through her heart, His sorrow sharing,
all His bitter anguish bearing, now at
length the sword has passed.

O how sad and sore distressed
was that Mother, highly blest,
of the sole-begotten One.

Christ above in torment hangs,
she beneath beholds the pangs
of her dying glorious Son.

Is there one who would not weep,
whelmed in miseries so deep,
Christ's dear Mother to behold?

Can the human heart refrain
from partaking in her pain,
in that Mother's pain untold?

Bruis'd, derided, curs'd, defiled,
she beheld her tender child
all with bloody scourges rent.

For the love of His own nation,
saw Him hang in desolation,
till His spirit forth He sent.

O thou Mother! Fount of love!
Touch my spirit from above,
make my heart with thine accord.

Make me feel as thou hast felt;
make my soul to glow and melt
with the love of Christ my Lord.

Holy Mother! Pierce me through,
in my heart each wound renew
of my Savior crucified.

Let me share with thee His pain,
who for all my sins was slain,
who for me in torments died.

Let me mingle tears with thee,
mourning Him who mourned for me,
all the days that I may live.

By the Cross with thee to stay,
there with thee to weep and pray,
is all I ask of thee to give.

Virgin of all virgins blest!
Listen to my fond request,
let me share thy grief divine.

Let me, to my latest breath,
in my body bear the death
of that dying Son of thine.

Wounded with His every wound,
steep my soul till it hath swooned,
in His very Blood away.

Be to me, O Virgin, nigh,
lest in flames I burn and die,
in His awful Judgment Day.

Christ, when Thou shalt call me hence,
be Thy Mother my defense,
be Thy Cross my victory.

While my body here decays,
may my soul Thy goodness praise,
safe in Paradise with Thee.

Saint Mary of Perpetual Help Church (Defiance, Ohio)
stained-glass, Immaculate Heart of Mary

CHAPTER 11

The Immaculate Heart of Mary

While the Church dedicates the month of May to Mary and October to the Most Holy Rosary, the month of June is dedicated to the Sacred Heart of Jesus. Along with the feast of the Blessed Trinity and Corpus Christi, the solemnity of the Most Sacred Heart of Jesus is one of several feasts immediately following Pentecost in the liturgical calendar.

But since the heart of Jesus is ever-united to the heart of Mary, the Saturday following the solemnity of the Most Sacred Heart of Jesus is the feast of the Immaculate Heart of Mary. How logical and consoling to celebrate these two liturgical feasts, one following the other, for their hearts beat as one!

The most Sacred Heart of Jesus is closely and intimately related to the Immaculate Heart of Mary in several ways. Biologically they are united because Jesus's heart was formed in the pure womb of His mother, and emotionally and spiritually, never were there two hearts so united. Their sentiments, goals, feelings, and desires harmonize perfectly! The purity, love, holiness, and humility in these two hearts radiate like the noonday sun!

But what exactly is the Immaculate Heart of Mary devotion? This is what we will try to answer here.

The Immaculate Heart of Mary devotion refers to the Catholic spiritual practice of focusing on the interior life of the Blessed Virgin Mary, both her joys and her sorrows, as well as her virtues and intimate connection with her Son. The goal of the devotion is to enter into her heart, into her interior life, to help us imitate her and unlock the mysteries of God's Word. In summary, the chief aim of the devotion is to journey to Christ through Mary's heart, to love God and Jesus better by uniting us to Mary, who is so united to the Blessed Trinity.

Why do we believe there are treasures stored up in Mary's heart? Scripture gives us our answer.

Twice in the second chapter of Luke's Gospel, Mary's heart (which we call "Immaculate" because she is most pure and free from all sin) is referenced. The first is when the shepherds visit in Bethlehem shortly after the birth of Christ. "And they went in haste, and found Mary and Joseph, and the baby lying in a manger. And when they saw it they made known the saying which had been told them concerning this child; and all who heard it wondered at what the shepherds told them. But Mary kept all these things, pondering them in her heart" (Lk 2:16–19).

The second is when Jesus is lost and found in the Temple. "'How is it that you sought me? Did you not know that I must be in my Father's house?' And they did not understand the sayings which he spoke to them. And he went down with them and came to Nazareth, and was obedient to them; and his mother kept all these things in her heart" (Lk 2:49–51).

What wonders we will find inside Mary's heart when Divine Revelation has told us that she, who was so intimately united to the life of Christ, pondered these mysteries and held them in her heart. We have only to ask our Mother Mary to help us meditate on and contemplate these mysteries through her eyes and heart, and she will open up to us the wisdom, sorrows, and joys of life with her son Jesus, both God and man.

At another point in the same chapter of Luke's Gospel, we have yet another reference to Mary's heart, or her soul, depending on which translation you read (but the point is the same, for the soul is of course a reality of the interior life). When Mary and Joseph present Jesus at the Temple, the holy and aged Simeon utters his famous prophesy of a sword piercing Mary's heart/soul. "And his father and his mother marveled at what was said about him; and Simeon blessed them and said to Mary his mother, 'Behold, this child is set for the fall and rising of many in Israel, and for a sign that is spoken against (and a sword will pierce through your own soul also), that thoughts out of many hearts may be revealed'" (Lk 2:33–35).

Simeon here spoke of the agony that would assail Mary at her Son's crucifixion. Though Jesus physically had the lance thrust through His heart, opening up His side and thereby spilling out His precious blood and water, seen as symbols for the Church's sacraments, so Mary would suffer a similar piercing of her heart, spiritually and emotionally. This means that within her Immaculate Heart, we will find the wounds of her Son's passion, and there are unspeakable treasures united with those who unite themselves to this event and console their sorrowful mother.

Devotion to the Immaculate Heart dates back to the Middle Ages, thanks in large part to saints like Anslem of Canterbury, Bernard of Clairvaux, Gertrude the Great, and Bridget of Sweden. In more modern times, Saint John Eudes (d. 1681) propagated the devotion and led a cause to celebrate Mary's heart with a feast on the Church's calendar. Though Saint John would not live long enough to see it, Pope Pius VII enacted the feast of the Immaculate Heart of Mary in 1805. Then, after the visions of Our Lady of Fatima in 1917, the devotion spread even further. (More can be read about the Immaculate Heart in our chapter on the Fatima apparitions.)

The crowd looking at "the Miracle of the Sun", occurred during the Our Lady of Fatima apparitions, 13 October 1917.

Mary's heart is honored in a special way in sacred art. For centuries, the Immaculate Heart of Mary has been depicted on fire, representing her love for Jesus and for mankind, with heavenly roses, usually red or white, wrapped around her heart to symbolize her beauty. Some depictions show the Immaculate Heart with a sword, or seven swords (for Mary's seven sorrows), piercing it, as a symbol of the sword that Simeon promised would pierce her.

But then how, we might ask, is this devotion carried out in practice? There are several simple things we can do to enter into the Immaculate Heart of Mary in our everyday lives. Let us list the ways!

Prayer to the Immaculate Heart of Mary

Try to cultivate the habit of praying this short Fatima prayer to enkindle your love for the Immaculate Heart of Mary: "Sweet Heart of Mary, be my salvation." Prayed frequently and fervently during the course of the day, this simple prayer enkindles our love for Mary's heart.

The Saints on the Immaculate Heart of Mary

"My heart will be your refuge and the way that will lead you to God."

–Our Lady of Fatima to Lucia

"Tell everyone that God grants graces through the Immaculate Heart of Mary."

–Saint Jacinta Marto

"Mother dear, lend me your heart. I look for it each day to pour my troubles into."

–Saint Gemma Galgani

"The Immaculate Heart alone has from God the promise of victory over Satan. She seeks souls that will consecrate themselves entirely to her, that will become in her hands powerful instruments for the defeat of Satan and the spread of God's Kingdom."

–Saint Maximilian Kolbe

Gospel Reflections

We must try, as much as we are able, to read and meditate on the passages previously mentioned in Luke's Gospel that reference the heart of Mary.

Enthrone or Consecrate Your Home to the Sacred Heart of Jesus and the Immaculate Heart of Mary

A wonderful practice and devotion that can serve to unite and fortify families in this modern, paganistic, materialistic, and atheistic world is to formally enthrone, or consecrate, your home to the Sacred Heart of Jesus and the Immaculate Heart of Mary. Consecration means to be set aside and given over for a sacred purpose, so by this practice, we offer our home, and our family, to Jesus and Mary to be used for their purposes. Begin by purchasing two beautiful images of their hearts and invite a priest into your home to bless it. Ask him then to carry out the formal process of consecrating your entire family to the Sacred Heart of Jesus and the Immaculate Heart of Mary. Make sure that the two hearts are enthroned in a prominent place so that all those who enter have no doubt that Jesus and Mary are the King and Queen of your home.

Family Prayer and Rosary In Front of the Two Hearts

Vatican II states very clearly that the family is the domestic church, the Church in miniature. Prayer is at times a struggle for all of us, both young and old. However, means or tools that can truly facilitate our growth and perseverance in our prayer life are these two spiritual gems: praying the Most Holy Rosary and praying in front of these beautiful images of the two hearts. Therefore, when you bring your family together to pray each evening, come before the two images of Jesus and Mary—the Sacred Heart of Jesus and the Immaculate Heart of Mary. Know that they are looking at you with love. In this way, distractions will be diminished and prayer will be more fervent and pleasing to these two loving hearts.

Sacred Heart of Jesus, oil on canvas, 19th-century Portuguese school

The Flame of Love of the Immaculate Heart of Mary, french print / PVDE / Bridgeman Images

Console the Immaculate and Sorrowful Hearts of Jesus and Mary through Reparations

In the Fatima message, we learn that it is our duty as Mary's children to console her sorrowful heart, which bore such pain in watching her Son be crucified and is outraged at how mankind offends God. We can console her heart by making small acts of reparation, which are sacrifices and penances we offer in atonement for offenses committed against God and the two hearts. These small acts could range from giving up dessert to giving up our free time to pray the Rosary to any other sacrificial act. But they must be done with the specific intention of making reparation. If we truly love the hearts of Jesus and Mary, let us do all we can to console them for the many sins of the world.

To expand upon this last aspect of devotion to the Immaculate Heart of Mary, there are specific sins that we should be aware of that especially wound her heart, as well as Jesus's heart. We can see these sins as the thorns that piece their hearts, and by making acts of reparation, it is as though we are removing those thorns one at a time. These include:

- **Abortion.** For the many sins that destroy human life even before it is born, we offer reparation and mercy to the loving hearts of Jesus and Mary.

- **Euthanasia.** For the efforts in many parts of the world to legalize and promote euthanasia—the assistance in killing the elderly and infirm—we turn to their loving hearts for the grace to respect life at all stages, from the moment of conception until natural death.

- **Sexual immorality and license.** We lift our gaze to the most pure hearts of Jesus and Mary begging pardon and mercy for the many sins against the true meaning of marital love.

- **Sins of despair.** For the many in the world who have given up all hope of living due to pain, suffering, and crosses, may the hearts of Jesus and Mary be their comfort, support, and consolation!

- **Bitterness, anger, and hatred.** For the many individuals who have been hurt in one way or another by others and thus are given over to bitterness, anger, and hatred, may the loving and merciful hearts of Jesus and Mary be their secure refuge of healing.

- **Priests, religious, and bishops.** May those who have failed in their promises and commitments as priests, bishops, and religious be drawn back to faithfulness, fervor, and zeal for the salvation of souls through the hearts of Jesus and Mary.

- **Cold, indifferent, and lukewarm hearts.** For the widespread coldness, indifference, and tepidity of so many would-be followers of Christ, may the fire of love that burns in the hearts of Jesus and Mary enkindle in these indifferent hearts a renewed vigor and enthusiasm for the desires and intentions of these two loving hearts.

- **Those dying and in moral danger.** For those poor souls who have abandoned the hearts of Jesus and Mary by embracing an immoral and sinful lifestyle and who are now in their last moments of life, may they seek refuge in the merciful and loving hearts of Jesus and Mary and thereby attain eternal salvation.

- **Those who are blind due to the fire of their passions.** May the fiery love of the hearts of Jesus and Mary surrounded by thorns purify their inner vision so they can contemplate the true beauty of heavenly realities over the false glimmer and glitter of the seductions of the flesh and the world with its empty promises!

- **The multitudes of Catholic-Christians who have left the practice of the faith.** Let us turn to the Sacred Heart of Jesus and the Immaculate Heart of Mary for the huge multitudes of Catholics who have abandoned the practice of their Catholic faith. May God's grace, through the intercession of the Immaculate Heart of Mary, bring them back to the harbor of salvation—the Catholic Church.

In our lives, we are attacked by so many dangers from within and from without. The devil, the flesh, and the world assault us daily. We must seek a sure refuge from these dark forces. In the midst of so much struggle, toil, uncertainty, and suffering, let us calmly and gently lift our eyes to the Sacred Heart of Jesus and the Immaculate Heart of Mary. Let us seek our refuge, our harbor of safety, our security, our peace, and our eternal salvation in these two hearts. May these short but powerful prayers resound frequently in the depths of our own hearts:

Sacred Heart of Jesus, I place all my trust in You.

Sweet Heart of Mary, be my salvation.

Act of Reparation to the Immaculate Heart of Mary

O Most Holy Virgin Mother, we listen with grief to the complaints of your Immaculate Heart surrounded with the thorns placed therein at every moment by the blasphemies and ingratitude of ungrateful humanity. We are moved by the ardent desire of loving you as Our Mother and of promoting a true devotion to your Immaculate Heart.

We therefore kneel before you to manifest the sorrow we feel for the grievances that people cause you, and to atone by our prayers and sacrifices for the offenses with which they return your love. Obtain for them and for us the pardon of so many sins. Hasten the conversion of sinners that they may love Jesus and cease to offend the Lord, already so much offended. Turn your eyes of mercy toward us, that we may love God with all our heart on earth and enjoy Him forever in heaven. Amen.

Mary in the Morning, Mary in the Evening

Statue of the Virgin Mary. Photo by MARI TERE / Shutterstock

All lovers of Mary should bookend their days with her!

Just as a baby cries for his mother to come get him in his crib each morning, so we should cry out to our mother in heaven—Mary—to come to us before we start our day. We should ask that she come to us and protect us and bring her Son into our day in whatever ways the Holy Spirit designs.

It is fitting that Mary should be a part of our morning routine, for one of her beautiful names is that of *Stella Matutina*—meaning the *Star of the Morning,* or *Morning Star.* Mary in fact is the Star of the Morning that precedes the sun, just as in life she preceded the birth of her Son, Our Savior.

A common practice in the Church is to make what is called a "morning offering." This is a morning prayer of intention for how you will live your day as you strive toward holiness. Consecrating yourself to Mary each morning, offering yourself to her so that she can give all your good works to Jesus, so that he may enrich them and use them for your salvation and for the salvation of others, is a sure way to reach the holiness you seek.

And just as a baby cries for his mother in the morning, so does a mother lay down her infant at night. Likewise, we must end our day with Mary, just as we started it with her.

Among the many times in which the devil can attack us is upon retiring for the night. God allows the devil to insert and plant bad images in our mind, most specifically in our imagination. Astute, wily, crafty, and insidious as the devil is with his legions of demons, he indeed uses our bedtime as well as our sleeping hours to tempt and draw many into sin. Equipped with this knowledge, we should equip ourselves with spiritual weapons to win the battle. The devil will launch his attack, and we must be vigilant in return, ready and willing to execute our counterattack. This we would like to carry out with the powerful intercession of the Blessed Virgin Mary.

Among the two most potent Marian weapons that we must use constantly, but especially as we retire for the night, are the wearing of the scapular and the practice of praying three Hail Marys. Each of these can be prayed for a different intention that buttresses the larger intention of purity.

The first intention that we place in the Immaculate Heart of the Virgin Mary is for *purity of thought*. There is a saying: "The thought is the father of the deed." The actions that we carry out are strongly influenced by the preceding thoughts in our mind, in our imagination. Therefore, in the first Hail Mary, we beg Our Lady to preserve as from any impure or ugly thoughts during the course of the night's repose.

The second intention is for *purity of heart*. The human heart can contain the most noble of desires and aspirations. However, it is also true that the human heart can imbibe, contain, and cultivate some of the most ugly and impure feelings. Therefore, we beg Our Lady upon retiring and in the dark hours of the night and early hours of the morning to take our unstable, weak, sinful heart and draw it close to her most pure and Immaculate Heart.

The third Hail Mary can be prayed for the intention of *purity of body*. Often, we must recall the words of Saint Paul that our bodies are temples of the Holy Spirit. Frequently, we should call to mind the dignity that flows from having received the sacrament of Baptism—that we are truly living temples of the Blessed Trinity! Therefore, in the third Hail Mary, we beg the most pure and Immaculate Heart of Mary to help us to be constantly aware of the presence of God in us, of our dignity as well as our destiny.

We hope and pray that this practice of beginning and ending your day with your mother will help you live a life pleasing to God, ensuring you have good intentions throughout the day and pure thoughts as you drift off to sleep.

Sweet Heart of Mary, be my salvation!

Daily Offering to the Blessed Virgin Mary

My Queen and my Mother, to you I offer myself without any reserve; and to give you a mark of my devotion, I consecrate to you during this day my eyes, my ears, my mouth, my heart, and my whole person. Since I belong to you, O my good Mother, preserve and defend me as your property and possession. Amen.

INVENTES ME IN CORDE GERTRUDIS

Saint Gertrude (1763) by Miguel Cabrera

CHAPTER 12

The Golden Hail Mary

One of the great women of the Catholic Church, Saint Gertrude the Great, born in Germany in the year 1256, was a Benedictine mystic, writer, and intellect, but most especially she was a great lover of both Jesus and Mary. Her literary masterpiece, *Herald of Divine Love*, is highly recommended to enrich your spiritual life and to put you on a sure path to holiness.

As a mystic, Gertrude was gifted by God with the grace of miraculous visions, including those of Jesus, Our Lord. Of course, a vision must have a proper interpretation for the benefit of individuals, as well as for the Church at large, for it to be worthy of our consideration. Gertrude's visions have had such an interpretation, as they have been studied at length.

One of the most renowned visions of Saint Gertrude the Great was that of Jesus in heaven. In this particular vision, Gertrude saw before Our Lord a tall pile of coins, golden in color, shining, glimmering, and glowing. This pile of coins radiated extreme beauty!

Saint Gertrude then observed Jesus deposit another shiny, glimmering coin on top of the pile. This most recent golden coin seemed to shine even more brilliantly than the others.

Curious, to say the least, Saint Gertrude wondered about the nature of the coins, most especially the last one that He deposited onto the pile. When she asked Jesus, He replied, "My daughter, every time you pray a calm, fervent, and loving Hail Mary to my Mother, I deposit a golden coin in the treasury of heaven for you." What a wonderful image!

But what is this prayer?

In the Gospel, Jesus exhorts us not to worry about things, not to focus on material things that come and go. Rather, Jesus says, "Seek first his kingdom and his righteousness, and all these things shall be yours as well" (Mt 6:33). This story shows us exactly what will be given to us if we seek the things of God.

The interpretation of this vision of Saint Gertrude the Great for us is not overly complicated. Mary is the Mother of God, the Mother of the Church, and the Mother of all of us individually. Mary has a great maternal love for us and desires our happiness in this life, but most especially in the life to come. As such, she watches over us and protects us from harm. In return, how can we show our love for her? Well, there is a prayer that causes the Immaculate Heart of Mary to rejoice, to leap with joy, and that is the Hail Mary!

Saint Ignatius of Loyola, in his spiritual classic the *Spiritual Exercises*, presents to us various modes, or forms, of prayer: mental prayer, contemplative prayer, the daily examen, and many more. In addition to these, the saint offers another form that can truly enrich our spiritual lives and our relationship with Jesus and Mary. He advises us to take a formal, vocal prayer that we have possibly prayed many times but may not have meditated upon in depth. Take this prayer, the Hail Mary, for example, and say it very slowly, pondering each word, *relishing* each word, really savoring it. You may be surprised what new meaning is derived from meditating on this prayer, which we sometimes pray flippantly during our ordinary and routine lives. The Hail Mary, which many of us have prayed thousands of times by reciting the Most Holy Rosary, is a spiritual gem, a spiritual masterpiece, if we would only stop to appreciate it.

Hail Mary

Hail Mary, full of grace,

the Lord is with thee.

Blessed art thou among women,

and blessed is the fruit of thy womb, Jesus.

Holy Mary, Mother of God,

pray for us sinners,

now and at the hour of our death. Amen.

The first part, sometimes called the Angelic Salutation, can be found in the first joyful mystery of the Holy Rosary—the Annunciation (Lk 1:26–38). These words were first uttered by the Archangel Gabriel—whose name means "power of God"—to the Virgin Mary of Nazareth: "Hail, full of grace, the Lord is with you!" (Lk 1:28). How much this should encourage us to pray the Hail Mary with greater fervor, attention, and devotion—that we would be repeating words expressed by an archangel sent from the throne of Almighty God! We should strive to imitate the Archangel Gabriel in our humble, reverential, and trusting attitude towards Mary, who approached her as one would approach a queen, using the dignified greeting, "Hail."

But let us break down these words still more, for there is rich meaning in them.

Full of grace. Of all women, Mary was by far the most beautiful, sublime, glorious, pure, laudable, holy, as well as the most endowed with grace! What then is grace? In the study of theology, the topic of grace is of paramount value and importance. A short catechetical definition tells us grace is "participation in the life of God" (*CCC* 1997). There we have it: grace is God's life within us! We are conceived with original sin and born without grace. Mary, on the contrary, was conceived without the stain of sin, so she was born "in grace"—she is the *full of grace.*

The great Doctor of the Church Saint Alphonsus Mary Liguori asserted that the grace of all graces is for us to die in the state of grace. If this happens, with the help of God's grace, we will be saved for all eternity. This is why we ask the woman who is "full of grace" to pray for us at the "hour of our death" in this simple prayer!

If we form the habit of praying the Hail Mary—and better yet, the Hail Mary fifty times in the Most Holy Rosary—then we will be constantly growing in grace. In fact, every time we pray the Hail Mary with faith, fervor, and love, we are augmenting sanctifying grace in our souls and preparing ourselves for an eternity in heaven!

By praying the Hail Mary to the Mother of God, Mary will attain for us extraordinary graces, or said another way, divine helps to stay close to God. These include:

1. **Protection.** The devil shoots fiery darts to wound and to kill us spiritually. Praying the Hail Mary is like a shield of protection against the fiery arrows of Satan and his minions.

2. **Joy. Grace communicates joy!** By praying the Hail Mary frequently, Our Lady attains for us a joyful heart, a radiant smile, and jubilant disposition that flows out abundantly upon all those we meet.

3. **Power to resist temptations.** Upon praying the Hail Mary, the great Mother of God intercedes for us before the throne of Almighty God, and she attains for us the grace (God's divine assistance) to resist temptations that can come often, powerfully, and insidiously.

4. **A clean heart.** By praying the Hail Mary often and fervently, the *full of grace* will obtain for us a pure and clean heart; actual purity of heart, mind, body, soul, intention, and life—a life pleasing to Almighty God!

5. **Peace of mind.** In the midst of a world beset by anguish, tensions, rivalries, envy, wars, and bloodshed, praying the Hail Mary frequently can attain for us great peace of mind, even in the midst of so much tension, turmoil, and conflict.

The Lord is with you. These essential words have great meaning and importance. From the very moment of Mary's Immaculate Conception in the womb of her mother, Saint Anne, God was with Mary. Never for even the slightest moment was Mary ever separated from God. As we said, Mary was and is the *full of grace.* Mary's whole being was imbued, absorbed, and penetrated by the presence of God. Mary's mind was filled with God's heavenly light. Mary's thoughts were focused totally on God and how God could be constantly glorified. Mary's eyes contemplated the beauty of God in all His glory and splendor. Mary's words proclaimed the greatness of God. Mary's whole body was a living and glorious temple of the Blessed Trinity—Father, Son, and Holy Spirit. And of great importance, Mary's Immaculate Heart constantly poured forth acts of fervent love for God. The heart is created especially to love, and aside from Jesus Himself, nobody ever loved more constantly and intensely than the Immaculate Heart of Mary!

But what about us? Is the Lord not always with us? Unfortunately, weak creatures that we are, the Lord may not always be with us! Why? Being free creatures, we can willingly choose to reject God through mortal sin. However, there is good news, and it comes through the presence and intercession of Mary. If we suffer the disgrace of losing grace by committing mortal sin, by beseeching the powerful intercession of Mary, she will attain for us the grace of heartfelt contrition and compunction, and the grace to return to God through a good sacramental confession. Indeed, Mary is the *full of grace* and God is always with her. But Mary loves sinners! She is the Mother of Mercy towards the fallen. If we turn to Mary, she will help us return to grace.

Now, let us move to the second part of the prayer, where we are given more words inspired by the Holy Spirit. After Mary greeted her cousin Saint Elizabeth, carrying John the Baptist in her womb, moved by the Holy Spirit, Saint Elizabeth proclaimed, "Blessed are you among women, and blessed is the fruit of your womb!" (Lk 1:42).

"Blessed are you among women" (Lk 1:42). Relishing these words, we meditate on the greatness of the woman, most especially reflected in the person of the Blessed Virgin Mary. Every woman on the face of the earth, as she prays the Hail Mary, should contemplate Mary as her model and guide on whom she patterns her whole life.

"And blessed is the fruit of your womb!" (Lk 1:42). Mary as this model, teaches women, as well as the world at large, the importance of maternity. One of the greatest gifts God can give to the world is through the instrumentality of the woman, that of a new life, a new person, a child whose destiny one day is the kingdom of heaven!

In the last part of this sacred prayer, we utter words given to us through the tradition of the Church: *"Holy Mary, Mother of God, pray for us sinners, now and at the hour of our death."* Here, we ask for Mary's intercession through her prayers, which we know with confidence her Son hears and cherishes, for He loves her as His mother. And we ask of her prayers at the two most important points of our lives: now and at the hour of our death!

Therefore, meditation and reflection on the Hail Mary should fill us with great reverence, awe, love, and devotion towards she who was, and is, *full of grace.* May she who is *full of grace* attain for us a constant appreciation of grace—the life of God within our soul. With the help and intercession of Mary, may we daily grow in grace. May we attain more abundance of grace, especially the grace of all graces for the human person—to die in the state of grace! If accomplished, we will be saved and rejoice in heaven with Mary and the Blessed Trinity for all eternity!

To conclude, we invite all of you to strive to be multi-millionaires in the spiritual life. You may not have a big bank account on earth, but you can have an enormous bank account in heaven! Remember the vision of Saint Gertrude and the golden coin—the Golden Hail Mary. In imitation of Saint Gertrude, every time you pray the Hail Mary, but especially when you pray it slowly, pondering the beautiful words in your heart, you store golden riches in heaven for all eternity!

Sub Tuum Praesidium

While the Hail Mary is easily the most well-known Marian prayer, it was not the first. The earliest known prayer to the Blessed Virgin Mary is the *Sub Tuum Praesidium* (Beneath thy Protection). It dates back to the third century and is a specific prayer asking for our mother's protection from danger and threats. This would have been a constant need in the early Church, when so many were martyred for their belief in her Son. Still today, we face many dangers, though they may look different than they did before. Therefore, whenever we are frightened or face storms, whenever threats lurk, whenever we feel we are in danger, let us pray:

We fly to thy protection,
O Holy Mother of God;
Despise not our petitions
in our necessities,
but deliver us always
from all dangers,
O Glorious and Blessed Virgin.
Amen.

The Angelus (1857-1859) by Jean-François Millet

CHAPTER 13

The Angelus

Any reflection on the Hail Mary should be followed by a reflection on the Angelus, for the two prayers are intimately linked, both tied as they are to the Annunciation.

The Holy Father, when he is not traveling but rather is present in the Eternal City, Rome, on Sundays at noon, has the beautiful custom of giving a short homily, which he concludes by praying the famous Marian prayer, the Angelus. Upon the conclusion of this beautiful prayer, he imparts his papal blessing upon all who are present. What a marvelous way to start off a new week—listening to a brief but inspiring message from the Vicar of Christ, praying to the Blessed Virgin Mary, and receiving the blessing of the Holy Father!

Let us talk now about this wonderful prayer so dear to the heart of the Blessed Virgin Mary, which we call "the Angelus." Well prayed with devotion, undoubtedly, this traditional Marian prayer will rain down blessings upon you, your family, and upon the whole world.

The structure of the Angelus is simple. It is composed of three short biblical phrases—how important it is for us to relish and love the Word of God, like Mary who meditated on the Word of God in her heart (see Lk 2:19)—after which follows the praying of the Hail Mary. This simple prayer can be prayed in less than two minutes. Short in duration, but of infinite value!

Here are the words of this beautiful prayer:

V: The Angel of the Lord declared unto Mary,
R: *And she conceived by the power of the Holy Spirit.*

Hail Mary, full of grace,

the Lord is with thee.

Blessed art thou among women,

and blessed is the fruit of thy womb, Jesus.

Holy Mary, Mother of God,

pray for us sinners,

now and at the hour of our death. Amen.

V. Behold the handmaid of the Lord.
R. *Be it done unto to me according to thy word.*
  (Repeat the Hail Mary)

V. And the Word was made flesh,
R. *And dwelt among us.*
  (Repeat the Hail Mary)

V. Pray for us O Holy Mother of God,
R. *That we may be made worthy of the promises of Christ.*

Pour forth we beseech thee, O Lord, Thy grace into our hearts, that we to whom the Incarnation of Christ Thy Son was made known by the message of an angel, may by His passion and cross, be brought to the glory of His resurrection. Through the same Christ Our Lord. Amen.

As we can see, the biblical passages this prayer calls to mind contain the two primary hinges of the history of our eternal salvation. First, the Angelus calls to mind the Incarnation of Jesus, the Son of God made man, through the consent and *fiat* of Mary. Her "yes" to God through the message of the angel resulted in Jesus becoming Incarnate in her most pure womb. Second, we jump from the beginning of

Jesus's human existence to the end. The Paschal Mystery refers to Jesus's suffering, passion, crucifixion, and death on the cross, before rising three days later in His glorious Resurrection from the dead. Indeed, our salvation came about through the passion, death, and Resurrection of Our Lord and Savior Jesus Christ.

Jesus is the Savior and Redeemer of the human race. All salvation comes about through Him, whose name means Savior. The archangel revealed to Mary His name: "You shall call his name Jesus" (Lk 1:31). However, the role of Mary is essential. Mary is the *mediatrix* of all graces, meaning that all the graces of

Annunciation (circa 1410-1430)

God pass through the Blessed Virgin Mary. It must be emphasized that Jesus chose His Blessed Mother Mary as His close helper, His advocate, His collaborator, in the mystery of our salvation. The Mellifluous Doctor of the Church, Saint Bernard, expressed this sublime truth in poetic and mystical language: "The whole earth awaits this [Mary's response.] . . . Answer quickly, O Virgin. Reply in haste to the angel, or rather through the angel to the Lord. Answer with a word, receive the Word of God. Speak your own word, conceive the divine Word. Breathe a passing word, embrace the eternal Word."[1]

Therefore, again, it is in the Angelus that we recall both the Incarnation of Jesus and our redemption through the Paschal Mystery—that is to say, the two primary and essential moments in the history of our salvation. And indeed, Mary was present and instrumental at both these events. In the Incarnation, she played her role through her generous offering of herself to God: "Behold, I am the handmaid of the Lord; be it done to me according to your word" (Lk 1:38). Still more, she was also present as Jesus suffered and died on the cross, shedding His Precious Blood, given to Him through the Blessed Virgin Mary, during His suffering on the first Good Friday. Valiantly, Mary stood at the foot of the cross, sorrowful but trusting in faith. In His

---

[1] Excerpt from a homily of Saint Bernard, Office of Readings for December 20 in the Fourth Week of Advent.

Immaculate Conception (circa 1618-1620) by Diego Velázquez

infinite wisdom, in the mystery of the economy of salvation, clearly, Jesus wanted His mother to play a prominent role.

For all these reasons, how important it is for us to form the habit of praying the Angelus. If we do this, we are constantly reminding ourselves of the great love that Jesus and Mary had, still have, and will always have for us. By praying it daily, we raise our minds to a higher realm and fortify our spiritual lives. Through the Angelus, we are lifted from the mundane to the sublime, all in the brief span of two minutes!

One might ask when and how often to pray the Angelus. The best answer is: as often as possible! But the most common time to pray it is at noon, in the middle of our day. There is a famous painting called *The Angelus* by French painter Jean-François Millet (d. 1875) which depicts a young couple pausing in their labor in the fields at noon, at the sound of the church bells, to pray the Angelus. This is a striking portrayal that shows the faith and devotion we must have to pause in the middle of our labors to pray and bring Jesus and Mary to mind, even today (especially today) in our faster-paced world.

In the very Catholic country of the Philippines, many commercial centers carry out this practice, briefly closing at noon to pray the Angelus. And as we already mentioned, the Holy Father prays the Angelus publicly at noon on Sundays.

But why not pray this beautiful Marian prayer three times a day, at 9:00 a.m., at the traditional time of noon, and then at 6:00 p.m.? This triple Marian homage and reminder can help us to sanctify, bless, and anoint three key times during the course of our day: the morning, the afternoon, and the evening. Even though this triple practice will not take up more than ten minutes a day from our busy schedule, these short reminders will call to mind Jesus and Mary in our lives, the purpose of our existence, and the two pillars of our faith and our salvation—the Incarnation and the Paschal Mystery. Also, the Angelus will be a breath of fresh air, the breath of the Blessed Virgin Mary upon us, our activities, and our encounters. Indeed, in the thrice daily praying of the Angelus, Mary will be our life, our sweetness, and our hope!

The Regina Caeli

During the Easter season and ending at Pentecost, in the place of praying the Angelus, it is common practice to pray the Regina Caeli ("Queen of Heaven"), a Marian antiphon that celebrates the Resurrection of Our Lord.

V. Queen of Heaven, rejoice, alleluia.
R. *For He whom you did merit to bear, alleluia.*

V. Has risen, as He said, alleluia.
R. *Pray for us to God, alleluia.*

V. Rejoice, and be glad, O Virgin Mary, alleluia.
R. *For the Lord is truly risen, alleluia.*

Let us pray:

O God, who gave joy to the world through the resurrection of Thy Son, Our Lord Jesus Christ, grant we beseech Thee, that through the intercession of the Virgin Mary, His mother, we may obtain the joys of everlasting life. Through the same Christ Our Lord. Amen.

The Virgin in Prayer (circa 1660) / Sassoferrato, Il /
Photo © The Courtauld / Bridgeman Images

CHAPTER 14

The Litany of the Blessed Virgin Mary

A litany is a common form of Catholic prayer consisting of a series of petitions directed toward members of the Blessed Trinity, saints and angels, or the Blessed Virgin Mary. The roots of the word in Latin and Greek are tied back to the word *supplication*, which is just a way to say we ask for something. Most litanies have a repetitive nature to them, with a combination of invocations alternating with petitions in a rhythmic pattern.

The practice of praying litanies can be traced back to early Christians in Rome and Asia. The *Kyrie Eleison* (Lord, have mercy) was likely the first litany, one we still pray today in the Holy Mass. Other litanies may be prayed during the Mass at certain times of the liturgical year.

While there are many litanies that can be prayed in private worship, only six are approved by the Church for public worship:

1. The Litany of the Sacred Heart of Jesus
2. The Litany of the Holy Name of Jesus
3. The Litany of the Most Precious Blood of Jesus
4. The Litany of the Saints
5. The Litany of Saint Joseph
6. The Litany of the Blessed Virgin Mary
    (also referred to as the Litany of Loretto)

Our concern is obviously this last litany, which was approved in 1587 by Pope Sixtus V. It is also called the Litany of Loretto because it is believed it was first prayed in the Northern Italian shrine of Our Lady of Loretto, the third largest Marian shrine in Europe (behind only Fatima and Lourdes). Tradition tells us that the home of the Virgin Mary, where Gabriel would have appeared to her at the Annunciation, was moved to Loretto, where it stands today at the shrine. Some say the house was moved there by angels, others say by crusaders returning from the region.

In any event, the Litany of Loretto is a beautiful prayer that helps us plumb the depths and greatness of this Masterpiece of Creation who is the Blessed Virgin Mary. It is a common custom and practice to pray the Litany of the Blessed Virgin Mary at the end or conclusion of the recitation of the most holy Rosary. However, it can be prayed at any time, in any place, and in any language.

This prayer has many positive fruits or effects in our lives. Through it, we come to see Mary in her virtues, actions, and gestures, and we give her cause to rejoice when we pray it. It also helps us come to know and love our heavenly mother, which of course leads us to know and love Jesus better, for the two are never separated. This litany is a great source of self-enrichment to our spiritual life. It would be wise for us to keep a copy of it handy and pray it daily.

Throughout the litany, we refer to Mary by a series of names. Many of these phrases are biblical, others are mystical, and still others are beautiful expressions of poetic imagery, inspiring to say the least! After you pray the litany, take one of the phrases that seems to have touched you the most and let it remain with you during the course of the day. Walk with Mary in her holiness and beauty, like taking a rose with you during the course of your daily activities. Indeed, one of the many striking titles of Mary is that of the Mystical Rose!

May the frequent recitation of the Litany of the Blessed Virgin Mary continually bring to mind Mary as a beautiful and glimmering diamond that you contemplate with the eyes of your soul as frequently as possible so as to bring to your mundane existence a perpetual heavenly presence, beauty, and fragrance!

The Immaculee / Francesco Mola / Photo © Mauro Ranzani / Bridgeman Images

The Litany of the Blessed Virgin Mary of Loreto

Lord, have mercy.

Christ, have mercy.

Lord, have mercy.

Christ, hear us.

Christ, graciously hear us.

God, the Father of Heaven, have mercy on us.

God the Son, Redeemer of the World,
    have mercy on us.

God the Holy Spirit, have mercy on us.

Holy Trinity, One God, have mercy on us.

Holy Mary, pray for us.

Holy Mother of God, pray for us.

Holy Virgin of Virgins, pray for us.

Mother of Christ, pray for us.

Mother of Divine Grace, pray for us.

Mother most Pure, pray for us.

Mother most Chaste, pray for us.

Mother Inviolate, pray for us.

Mother Undefiled, pray for us.

Mother most Amiable, pray for us.

Mother most Admirable, pray for us.

Mother of Good Counsel, pray for us.

Mother of our Creator, pray for us.

Mother of our Savior, pray for us.

Virgin most Prudent, pray for us.

Virgin most Venerable, pray for us.

Virgin most Renowned, pray for us.

Virgin most Powerful, pray for us.

Virgin most Merciful, pray for us.

Virgin most Faithful, pray for us.

Mirror of Justice, pray for us.

Seat of Wisdom, pray for us.

Cause of our Joy, pray for us.

Spiritual Vessel, pray for us.

Vessel of Honor, pray for us.

Singular Vessel of Devotion, pray for us.

Mystical Rose, pray for us.

Tower of David, pray for us.

Tower of Ivory, pray for us.

House of Gold, pray for us.

Ark of the Covenant, pray for us.

Gate of Heaven, pray for us.

Morning Star, pray for us.

Health of the Sick, pray for us.

Refuge of Sinners, pray for us.

Comforter of the Afflicted, pray for us.

Help of Christians, pray for us.

Queen of Angels, pray for us.

Queen of Patriarchs, pray for us.

Queen of Prophets, pray for us.

Queen of Apostles, pray for us.

Queen of Martyrs, pray for us.

Queen of Confessors, pray for us.

Queen of Virgins, pray for us.

Queen of all Saints, pray for us.

Queen conceived without Original Sin,
    pray for us.

Queen assumed into Heaven, pray for us.

Queen of the most Holy Rosary, pray for us.

Queen of the Family, pray for us.

Queen of Peace, pray for us.

The Coronation of the Virgin / Veronese / Cameraphoto Arte Venezia / Bridgeman Images

*Lamb of God, Who takes away the sins
of the world,*
spare us, O Lord!
*Lamb of God, Who takes away the sins
of the world,*
graciously hear us, O Lord!
*Lamb of God, Who takes away the sins
of the world,*
have mercy on us.

V. Pray for us, O Holy Mother of God.
*R. That we may be made worthy of the
promises of Christ.*

Grant, we beg you, O Lord God, that we your servants may enjoy lasting health of mind and body, and by the glorious intercession of the Blessed Mary ever Virgin, be delivered from present sorrow and enter into the joy of eternal happiness. Through Christ Our Lord. Amen.

The Little Office of the Blessed Virgin Mary

Another spiritual practice that can fill Mary's heart with joy, and thus Jesus's heart as well, adding to the many prayers and devotions we have already mentioned, is the recitation of the Little Office of the Blessed Virgin Mary, also known as the Hours of the Virgin.

What exactly is this practice? It is a liturgical devotion dedicated to honoring God and the Blessed Virgin Mary in imitation of the Divine Office, also known as the Liturgy of the Hours, or, as commonly called today, the Breviary. The Divine Office breaks up the day into periods of prayer throughout the day: the major hours of Matins, Lauds, and Vespers, and the minor hours of Prime, Terce, Sext, and None, and finally, Compline (night prayer). It is a way to add a healthy routine to our daily prayer while at the same time meditating on the sacred Word of God.

Like the Divine Office, the Little Office of the Blessed Virgin Mary consists of Psalms taken from the Old Testament, a series of hymns or songs, Sacred Scripture, and other sacred readings. If you have ever prayed the Liturgy of the Hours, you will see a resemblance and similarity.

Most likely, the Little Office of the Blessed Virgin originated as a monastic devotion around the middle of the eighth century. Pope Zachary commanded the Benedictine monks of Monte Casino to pray the Little Office of the Blessed Virgin Mary under strict precept. The Office may have originally been composed in connection with the Votive Mass of Our Lady on Saturday, as Saturday has traditionally been the day of the week on which Marian devotion is promoted.

Though the Little Office is too long to reproduce here, one can find many books and sources online that lay out the various prayers. Making a daily habit of spending time with Mary through her Little Office is sure to enkindle in your heart a deep love for God and His Word.

There are many lessons that can be learned from undertaking the practice of praying of the Office of the Blessed Virgin Mary. Chief among them is an appreciation and love for the Psalms. There is no doubt that the Holy Family would have prayed the Psalms, as they were the official prayers of the Jewish people during the time of Jesus, and still are to this day. They likely would have prayed them together as a family, as well as every Saturday—on the Sabbath—in the synagogue. Still more, in heading towards the Temple of Jerusalem for the major feasts, they would have both recited and sang some of the Psalms on their pilgrimage. Following these Jewish customs, the Church now prays the Psalms in the Liturgy of the Hours, as well as in the context of the Mass (the Responsorial Psalm) and in the Little Office of the Blessed Virgin Mary.

St Joseph at Work (1887-1890) / Faustini, Modesto / Mondadori Portfolio / Electa / Sergio Anelli / Bridgeman Images

Through these prayers, we learn the basic gamut of sentiments or affections that we should express in authentic prayer. They are (1) praise and worship, (2) thanksgiving, (3) supplication and petition, (4) contrition and reparation, (5) wonder and awe before the majesty of God, and (6) the expression of fears, doubts, and sufferings to the Lord, who knows us and desires to help us. All of these sentiments and many more are embodied in the Psalms, and of course, the Little Office of the Blessed Virgin Mary.

In the Little Office, we are spending time with the Holy Family. They are delighted by your presence and, no doubt, you will relish spending time with them. What a glorious sight—you sitting at the hearth next to Jesus, Mary, and Saint Joseph, praying the Psalms and thanking, glorifying, and praising God, the Father and Creator, for all of His bountiful blessings.

Our Lady of the Holy Rosary by Simone Cantarini

CHAPTER 15

The Most Holy Rosary

All the great men and women of the world who had a dream, an ideal, a clear goal that they believed was worth attaining, exerted incredible time, effort, energy, and if you like, blood, sweat, and tears in realizing their dream. Be it artistic beauty, literary genius, defending life, liberty, and the pursuit of happiness, creative inventions, or athletic prowess—all men and women of greatness were motivated by noble goals and by the pursuit of excellence.

This pursuit of noble goals and achievements on a natural plane should be applied all the more fervently to the spiritual life. Our natural life on earth, beyond the shadow of a doubt, has great importance. However, the pursuit of spiritual excellence, the desire for holiness, the quest to be a saint and arrive safely at our eternal destiny, far supersedes all natural goals and enterprises.

Having said this, we should call to mind frequently the purpose of our existence—why we are here, where we are headed, and how we are to arrive there. Expressed with the utmost clarity and simplicity, *we are here on earth to know God, to love God, and to serve God, so that we will be happy with Him forever in heaven.*

Our Lady, known as the Ladder to Heaven, can help us immensely in reaching our heavenly goal. This entire text has sought to show this, but perhaps no other chapter outlines a better form of Marian devotion than this one on the most holy Rosary.

No one book, much less one chapter, can convey the power and beauty of the Rosary and how effective it is in aiding our spiritual life. Nonetheless, we will try here, in a condensed form, to show you that the recitation of the Rosary is one of the most powerful spiritual armaments that we can and should utilize and wield on our winding journey to heaven.

A Brief Explanation and History

To understand the power of the Rosary, one must first understand what it is and how it came to be. (We will be brief here but there is also a guide to praying the Rosary found in the prayers in the back.)

Let us start with the word *rosary*, which is derived from the word *rose*. It is said that with each Rosary you say, you are giving our Blessed Mother in heaven a crown of roses. What a beautiful image to keep with us as we learn about this powerful prayer!

To begin praying the Rosary, one starts with the Sign of the Cross, similar to any other Catholic prayer. Following this, comes the Apostles' Creed, followed by an Our Father, three Hail Marys (prayed for the virtues of Faith, Hope, and Charity), and a Glory Be, a prayer of devotion to the Holy Trinity. Then comes the "meat" of the prayer, which consists of five sets of ten Hail Marys (called a "decade"); before each decade, the Our Father is prayed, and after each decade, the Glory Be and the Oh My Jesus prayer given to us through Our Lady of Fatima. One's progress through this parade of sacred prayers is kept by using a string of beads.

The tradition of the Rosary dates back many centuries. Monks used to chant the 150 psalms, counting pebbles to keep track. But the lay people, either without Bibles or unable to read, found it too difficult to remember all 150 psalms, so they began to replace them with Hail Marys. (You pray 50 Hail Marys one time around the beads, but a full Rosary at this time meant going around three times, which gets you to 150.) Over time, a more formal pattern developed, with stringed beads replacing the counting of pebbles, and the other aspects of the Rosary fell into place.

Our Protestant brothers and sisters may point here to the Scripture passage found in Matthew 6:7, where Jesus tells us to avoid "vain repetition" or "empty phrases" in our prayers. But the Rosary is anything by vain and empty! Yes, it is repetition, but it is *fruitful* repetition. Let us show you why!

In a sense, the repetition of prayers is merely a means to an end. They are meant to, if you like, serve as background music for our dialogue with Jesus and Mary. There is something mystical about repeating the sacred words of the Hail Mary, Our Father, and Glory Be, words that are tied back to Sacred Scripture, as all the prayers of the Rosary are. With the repeating of these words, which the mind can do without conscious thought, our souls are free to contemplate the particular mystery of each decade. Archbishop Fulton Sheen used to compare the Rosary to a runway that allows the soul to take flight. Let us put it another way. It is difficult to speak with God using our own words for more than a minute or two, but when the Rosary gives us the sacred words to say, the mind is not burdened with finding the right words to speak. This allows for deeper meditation and thought to be given to pondering the sacred mysteries in the lives of Jesus and Mary and their meaning for us, as well the various petitions we wish to send up to heaven.

On this note of meditation, let us turn now to discuss the mysteries of the Rosary.

Meditating on the Mysteries

As we pray the Rosary, we can of course speak to Jesus and Mary about whatever burdens, sufferings, aspirations, or fears lie within our own heart. These may concern things happening in our own life or in the world at large. This aspect of personal prayer is an integral part of praying the Rosary.

But in a more formal sense, as we pray the prayers of the Rosary, we are taught to meditate on the most important events in the lives of Jesus and Mary. These events are divided into three parts, each having what we call five "mysteries." These events are called *mysteries* because while we can read the literal accounts of each in Sacred Scripture, the deeper, spiritual significance of them reaches beyond our full understanding. Thus, we must meditate on them intensely, reliving them in our minds through the gift of our imaginations, to receive the grace needed to fully comprehend their contribution to the economy of our salvation.

These three sets of mysteries are the Joyful Mysteries, the Sorrowful Mysteries, and the Glorious Mysteries. It is in praying all three of these sets of mysteries—three times around—that we get to the 150 Hail Marys, tying it back to the Psalms. Then in 2002, in his apostolic letter *Rosarium Virginis Maria* (The Rosary of the Virgin Mary), Pope Saint John Paul II proposed a new set of mysteries, which he called the Luminous Mysteries. Thus, a full Rosary is four times around, though it is perfectly acceptable to just focus on one set of mysteries per day.

The *Joyful Mysteries* begin with the most important moment in all of human history—the Annunciation, the announcement of the angel Gabriel to Mary that she has been chosen to be the Mother of God. Upon Mary's consent, the Incarnation took place—the Son of God was made flesh in the Immaculate womb of the Blessed Virgin Mary. So of course we call these mysteries joyful! The rest of these mysteries take us through the early years of the Christ Child.

The *Luminous Mysteries*, the "mysteries of Light" introduced by Pope Saint John Paul II, concern the public life of Christ in which He proclaims the Gospel of the Kingdom. In the second mystery, the Wedding Feast at Cana, we encounter Jesus's first public miracle through the powerful intervention of Mary, the first among believers, and because of this, "his disciples believed in him" (Jn 2:11). These mysteries culminate in the sublime mystery of the institution of the Most Holy Eucharist, and the Holy Priesthood—"Do this in remembrance of me" (Lk 22:19)—necessary to perpetuate Christ's august and sublime Gift of Self in the Eucharist!

The *Sorrowful Mysteries* walk us through the Way of the Cross and Christ's passion with our Sorrowful Mother Mary. Pope Saint John Paul II tells us in *Rosarium Virginis Maria,* "The sorrowful mysteries help the believer to relive the death of Jesus, to stand at the foot of the Cross beside Mary, to enter with her into the depths of God's love for man and to experience all its life-giving power."

The *Glorious Mysteries* begin with the Resurrection of Jesus and end with the Assumption of Mary into heaven and her coronation as Queen of the Angels and Saints! With Christ's Resurrection comes the promise of the resurrection of the faithful. Therefore, the grace of all graces is to die in the state of grace! In praying the Rosary, we beg Mother Mary's intercession to obtain for us this grace of all graces.

With these broad comments made, let us now dive deeper into each mystery. In this section, you will see the exact biblical passage where you can find the mystery in the Bible. This gives evidence to the statement that the Rosary is a very biblical prayer, a prayer that hopefully non-Catholics will be able to appreciate due to its rich scriptural content. Also listed is the "fruit" of each mystery, or if you like, the lesson or virtue we can take from each as we meditate on the scene.

The Joyful Mysteries

The Annunciation (Lk 1:26–38)

As stated a moment ago, this mystery calls to mind the announcement of the Angel Gabriel to Mary that she was to become the Mother of God, and upon her consent, the Incarnation took place. One of the key virtues that Mary teaches us in this first Joyful Mystery is the importance of silence so as to listen to the voice of God in our hearts. The next is the fact that true joy can be achieved only when we say *yes* to God in imitation of Mary.

The Visitation (Lk 1:39–56)

This mystery calls to mind Mary's journey to visit her cousin, Elizabeth, soon after the Annunciation. Scripture tells us she went "with haste" after hearing that Elizabeth was with child. In this mystery, the youthful and energetic Mary, who has just conceived Jesus in her womb, points out to us the importance of not putting off inspirations but rather being docile to the inspirations that come from the Holy Spirit. Also, filled with the Holy Spirit, Mary teaches us the primary role that fraternal charity—service to our neighbor—should take in our lives, as she went to serve her cousin. Finally, Mary shows us what it means to be a Christian missionary—once she received the Word, she brought Him to others.

The Annunciation (1859) / Pichon, Auguste / Bridgeman Images

The Baptism of Christ (circa 1655) by Bartolomé Esteban Murillo

The Nativity (Lk 2:1–20)

This mystery, commonly known as Christmas, chronicles Mary and Joseph's journey to Bethlehem and the Christ Child's birth in the stable. Countless lessons fill this narrative, but we will offer two here. One is that we should learn the importance of detachment from material things so that our hearts will be attached to God as our primary source of true happiness. The second is that Jesus is born every day in the hands of the priest as he consecrates the bread that becomes Our Lord in the Eucharist. "O come, let us adore Him."

The Presentation of the Child Jesus in the Temple (Lk 2:22–40)

When the infant Jesus was forty days old, Saint Joseph and Mary, following the custom of their people, brought Jesus to be presented at the Temple, where the holy Simeon delivered his now famous prophecy. In this mystery, we learn the virtue of obedience through the example of the obedience of Mary and Saint Joseph to the Law of Moses. We too must obey God's commandments if we want to be pleasing to Him. Still more, in Simeon's prophecy that Mary's heart will be pierced with a sword of sorrow, we come to know that Mary promises to be with us in the sorrows of our life.

The Finding of the Child Jesus in the Temple (Lk 2:41–52)

After losing Jesus for three days, Mary and Saint Joseph rejoice at finding Him in the Temple. Mary teaches us the importance of searching for Jesus after we have lost Him.

The Luminous Mysteries

The Baptism of Jesus (Mt 3:13–17)

This first of the Mysteries of Light calls to mind Jesus's baptism in the River Jordan by John the Baptist. It invites us to renew our own baptismal commitment—to renounce sin, the devil, and all the temptations that surround us. Also, the mystery reminds us that through our own baptism, we became living tabernacles of the Blessed Trinity!

The Wedding Feast at Cana (Jn 2:1–12)

At Cana, we bear witness to Christ's first public miracle, the changing of water into wine at Mary's prompting, giving birth, as it were, to His public mission and teachings. This was the event that allowed His disciples to believe in Him. And here, Mary shows us the intercessory role God has given to her between us and her Son. We may invite her to take pity on our worries and anxieties and bring them to Jesus so He may transform them. Our minds here are also given a foreshadowing of the cross, for as Venerable Fulton Sheen tells us, "He turned the water to wine, so that one day the wine could be turned to blood." Finally, the Wedding Feast at Cana invites us to pray fervently for the institution and the sacrament of Holy Matrimony and the sanctification of the family.

The Proclamation of the Kingdom of God (Mk 1:15)

This mystery serves to call our attention to the preaching of Jesus about the Kingdom of God, which can be found in many places in Scripture but is best summarized in Mark 1:14–15: "The time is fulfilled, and the kingdom of God is at hand; repent, and believe in the gospel." Note that in this proclamation is the call to conversion—"Repent!" Among the many fruits that can be gathered from this orchard is that of begging for our own daily conversion and the conversion of all sinners. Next, we beg for the grace of frequenting the sacrament by which we undergo a conversion every time we receive it worthily—the Sacrament of Confession!

The Transfiguration (Mt 17:1–13)

In this mystery, we relive the moment Jesus was transfigured on the mount before Peter, James, and John, when he was flanked by Moses and Elijah. Pope Saint John Paul II calls this the mystery of light *par excellence*, for it was here that the apostles were witnesses to Christ's vibrant light! In union with them, we beg for the grace of a growing intimacy in friendship with Jesus. Second, we beg for the grace to climb, to ascend the mountain of holiness, and to never give up!

The Institution of the Holy Eucharist (Mt 26:26–28 / Jn 6:47–59)

Entering into the sublime Easter Triduum with Holy Thursday, we contemplate the sublime moment that Jesus gave us the Gift of gifts—the most Holy Eucharist—at the Last Supper. We beg for a greater faith, love, devotion, and appreciation for the Holy Eucharist. Next, we beg for vocations to the priesthood and that priests will be holy and faithful, giving a good example to the whole world!

The Sorrowful Mysteries

The Agony in the Garden (Mt 26:36–46)

In this first mystery of the passion of Our Lord and Savior Jesus Christ, as we enter Gethsemane with Him, there is much to be learned and many graces to beg for. First, we beg the Lord Jesus for the gift of fervent prayer—not tepid, lukewarm, and mediocre prayer but a prayer of fervor and passion. Second, we beg for the grace to be faithful in prayer, to pray even when we do not feel like praying. This is not hypocrisy; this is heroic virtue and very pleasing to Jesus and Mary. Finally, we pray for resignation to God's holy will, as Jesus taught us: "Father, if you are willing, remove this cup from me; nevertheless, not my will, but yours, be done" (Lk 22:42).

The Scourging at the Pillar (Jn 19:1)

In this mystery, when Our Lord was scourged at the ordering of Pilate, we beg for very special and much needed graces and virtues. We beg for the virtue of purity of

INRI

Crucifixion with Madonna and Sts Paul, Mary Magdalene,
John and Francis (circa 1530) by Bernardino Luini

mind, of thought, of affections, of body, of soul, and even of intentions. Still more, we beg for the virtue of modesty in dress, manner, and speech, which as the *Catechism of the Catholic Church* teaches us, is the custodian of purity.

The Crowning with Thorns (Mt 27:28–31)

The Lord's sufferings continue. This was utterly humiliating for Jesus, pressing on His Sacred Head a mock crown of sharp thorns. Not only was it excruciatingly painful, but it was also derisive and demeaning. Therefore, by contemplating this mystery, we beg to grow in the virtue of humility. Also, we beg Our Lord Jesus for the purification of our mind so that we may, as Saint Paul commands us, "have the mind of Christ" (1 Cor 2:16).

The Carrying of the Cross (Jn 19:17)

Our Lord is loaded down with a very heavy cross—pressing down on His shoulders are all the sins of humanity. This cross He carried willingly for love of you and me. The first fruit to be derived is begging for the virtue of patience as we carry our own crosses. Next, we beg for the grace, like Simon the Cyrene, to help others carry their heavy crosses. Let us pray with Saint Francis of Assisi: "We adore You, O Christ, and we bless You, because by Your holy cross You have redeemed the world."

The Crucifixion (Jn 19:25–30)

In this last sorrowful mystery, as we contemplate our loving Savior hanging from the cross, there are countless lessons and graces that flow from our crucified Lord. First, we should beg for the grace to die daily to sin, to put to death the old man, as Saint Paul reminds us. Next, we should beg Mary and Jesus for the grace of all graces: to die in the state of grace so as to be saved for all eternity!

The Glorious Mysteries

The Resurrection (Mk 16:1–8)

In this first of the Glorious Mysteries, we meditate on the resurrection of Jesus on Easter. We beg here for an ever-deepening faith in Jesus, in the Church, and in heaven. Second, we beg for the grace to live out the Paschal Mystery in our own lives: to die to sin and to live in holiness.

The Ascension (Mk 16:15–20)

As we contemplate Jesus's ascension into heaven, where He takes His place at the right hand of God the Father, we beg Mary and Jesus for two special graces. First, we beg for the all-important virtue of hope. By this we mean to have a firm and total trust in God and His ways at all times. Next, we beg Mary and Jesus for an ardent longing for heaven, our true and eternal home.

The Holy Women at the Tomb of Christ, (1890) / Bouguereau, William-Adolphe / © Lukas - Art in Flanders VZW / Bridgeman Images

The Descent of the Holy Spirit (Acts 2:1–11)

In this fiery and dynamic mystery, where we remember the feast of Pentecost, when the Holy Spirit descended on Mary and the apostles, seen now as the birth of the Church, we beg for constant docility and openness to the Holy Spirit. Next, we beg, in imitation of the apostles praying with Mary, for a zealous missionary zeal, a real desire to labor zealously for the salvation of immortal souls.

The Assumption (Rv 12:1)

As we contemplate Our Lady, who was taken up to heaven in body and soul at her glorious Assumption, we beg for the grace to use our own bodies to glorify God in this life so as to be with Our Lady in the next life. Next, we pray for our beloved deceased and for our loved ones here on earth so that we will be united with them and with Mary and Jesus in heaven forever.

The Coronation (Rv 12:1)

We have arrived at the last of the twenty mysteries of the Holy Rosary. Here we meditate upon Our Lady being crowned the Queen of Heaven. We beg our Queen for the gift of perseverance until the end. Even though we are weak sinners prone to fall, we can always turn to Jesus and be received lovingly through the prayers of Mary. Finally, we beg that one day we will all be a jewel in the crown of Mary so as to contemplate the glorious and radiant beauty of the Blessed Trinity for all eternity.

These are the mysteries of the Rosary. In them, we find the most significant events in the story of our salvation. Let us meditate on them and ask for all these graces we have outlined, for with these graces, we are sure to reach heaven!

More Fruits of the Rosary

In the previous section, we outlined specific fruits, or graces, that can be meditated upon and asked for during each mystery of the Rosary. But there are, of course, more general graces that flow to us from praying the Rosary in full, hopefully each day of our lives.

Let us list just a few.

Extended Fruitful Prayer

Any prayer that we pray well is pleasing to Almighty God and will produce abundant fruits that we will only see upon our entrance into eternity. However, prayer can be a difficult thing to engage in for a long period of time. If we speak using our own words, we can scarcely muster up a few minutes. But praying the Rosary gives us the opportunity of (at least) twenty minutes of intense prayer, up to an hour or more if we choose to pray the full Rosary. What a gift this is!

Familiarity with the Word of God

We should never forget that the most holy Rosary is essentially a biblical prayer, for the mysteries, as we just outlined, are centered on the life of Jesus and Mary from Sacred Scripture. Meditating on them gives us a familiarity with the Word of God.

Vocal Prayer

The Rosary is a wonderful prayer that we can express vocally, including with a prayer group, and it is a most efficacious tool to help children learn the art of prayer. God gave us senses, including the sense of hearing, as a way to glorify Him. Speaking and hearing sacred words repeated over and over again mysteriously draws our souls to a higher plane.

Mental Prayer

The Rosary also introduces us to the art of mental prayer, sometimes called meditation. Many saints—such as Saint Alphonsus Liguori, Saint Teresa of Avila, and Saint Ignatius of Loyola—insist that mental prayer or meditation is absolutely indispensable to arrive at deeper spiritual growth. Again, when else are we given a personal tool that can help us engage in deep mental prayer for up to an hour?

Ignatian Contemplation

Furthermore, the Rosary prayed well introduces us to another form of prayer termed "Ignatian contemplation." By this is meant, the proper use of the imagination in which you apply yourself to one of the scenes (mysteries) and imagine you are part of the scene itself, living and interacting with Mary, with Jesus, and in the Joyful Mysteries, even with good Saint Joseph.

Transformation

It is a wise saying that we become like those with whom we live or associate. In other words, we tend to imitate those we live with or those we call friends. As the proverb says: "Show me who your friends are, and I'll tell you who you are!" Applying this to praying the most holy Rosary, if we are constantly thinking about Jesus, Mary, and Saint Joseph, talking to them, imagining interacting with them in their lives in contemplative prayer, then most likely we will start to imitate them. Until we can finally say in the words of the great apostle Saint Paul: "It is no longer I who live, but Christ who lives in me" (Gal 2:20).

Discipline

What is lacking in the lives of many, and that might be us, is discipline, order. Saint Ignatius states that one of the primary purposes of the Spiritual Exercises is to "order the disorder" in our lives. If the Rosary is prayed well, prayed regularly, prayed with love and devotion, then it can serve as an indispensable tool to order the many disorders that characterize our lives. What training does for the athlete's body, the Rosary does for our soul.

Our Lady of Guadalupe and Ordering

There is an interesting detail in the apparition of Our Lady of Guadalupe in Mexico to Juan Diego on December 12, 1531. At one point, Our Lady told Juan Diego to cut the roses that were growing on the top of Tepeyac Hill. When he came down the hill, Our Lady actually ordered the roses in Juan Diego's tilma with her own hands. This is symbolic of what Our Lady wants to do with us by our faithful recitation of the Holy Rosary. She wants to order the disorder in our lives. Often this means detaching us from our attachment to sin!

Peace of Heart, Mind, Body, and Soul

Another positive fruit of the faithful recitation of the holy Rosary is that of peace of heart, mind, body, and soul—in other words, our total person! We all desire peace in our lives. Saint Augustine defines peace as "the tranquility of order." As mentioned a moment ago, the recitation of the holy Rosary brings about interior, as well as exterior, order. Consequently, the fruit will be peace. One of the many beautiful titles of Mary is Queen of Peace!

A Gift for Mother—Bringing Joy to the Immaculate Heart of Mary

It must be said that every time we pray the Rosary individually, or in the family, or in the parish, or wherever the holy Rosary is recited with love, fervor, attention, and devotion, this homage paid to Mary, as well as to Jesus, for the two are never separated, fills her Immaculate Heart with immense and overflowing joy! A gesture of attention and love shown to Mary, a gift for Mother Mary like this, will never be forgotten. She will surely repay you with abundant graces here and forever in eternal life!

The Rosary as a Weapon

We all know the story of David and Goliath, how the little boy took down the giant with his slingshot. Often, in the face of the terrible evils in our world, we can feel like David standing before Goliath. And unlike the first Goliath, many of the modern enemies we face are insidious, deceptive, and can easily be camouflaged. But our little slingshot—our rosary—can bring down giants! Let us list just a few.

Materialism

The false god of wealth and possessions is so dangerous! Many are easily trapped into believing that money and possessions are the true keys to happiness.

Hedonism

This is the false god of pleasure. Live it up! You've only got one life to live! If it feels good, do it!

Atheism

God does not really exist. God is just a figment of your imagination, a relic from the Middle Ages. God is for the uneducated.

Moral Relativism

An all-too-common heresy asserting that each person is their own authority on truth, without any reference to the absolute authority whom we call God.

Lack of Hope—Despair

Many today, confronted with what they believe to be insurmountable problems or challenges in their lives, simply give up, throw in the towel, and live sad and dismal lives.

Therefore, confronted with these modern and ferocious Goliaths, not to mention countless others, we are like the small and almost insignificant David. We have a dire and urgent need for a modern slingshot. That modern slingshot is indeed the holy Rosary.

Like the slingshot, the rosary is small, seemingly insignificant in the eyes of many. Like the stones in the slingshot, the rosary's composition is that of small round objects—not stones, but beads. Like the slingshot in the hand of David to defeat Goliath, we are the modern David with the rosary in our hand to defeat the modern Goliaths. Like the slingshot aimed at the enemy to disarm and kill, in a parallel sense the Rosary is the spiritual slingshot that must be used to disarm and kill our enemies—the devil and his many minions—so as to claim victory for our soul and our eternal salvation!

Let us name just a few victories the Rosary has brought about.

Saint Dominic Guzman

The founder of the Dominicans conquered the pernicious Albigensian heresy through preaching and praying the most holy Rosary.

The Battle of Lepanto

Catholic Christians conquered the Muslim Turks in a famous naval battle in a place called Lepanto. The reason? Pope Saint Pius V pleaded with Catholics to pray the Rosary around-the-clock for the Catholics to win the battle. At first, the wind was against the Catholics, and it was feared the Turks would attack before they could form their line. However, the wind changed its course in favor of the Catholics, resulting in a total and humiliating defeat for the Turks.

Our Lady of Fatima

Finally, Our Lady of Fatima, who encouraged the world to pray the most holy Rosary for the sake of the salvation of the family, no doubt had a hand in the fall of Communism, for she predicted that her Immaculate Heart would triumph over the "errors" infecting the world out of Russia. Soon after Pope Saint John Paul II carried out a consecration of the world to the Immaculate Heart of Mary, the walls of Communism began to crumble.

And how many battles have been won in the individual hearts of men and women through this spiritual weapon? Too many to count!

We are in constant spiritual combat, day and night, until the end of our days. Our enemies are like the ferocious and malicious Goliath who intended to kill young David and throw his corpse to the birds of the air and the wild beasts. David wielded his slingshot, lodged the stone, aimed it, and boom! Goliath fell. Then with speed and graceful ease, David appropriated the sword that Goliath planned to use for David's demise and turned it into an instrument of victory for David.

You must pull out your spiritual slingshot, which is the most holy Rosary, not just occasionally, but constantly, and beg the Blessed Virgin Mary, the general of the Catholic army, that under her guidance and powerful intercession, the many dangerous Goliaths in your life will be conquered!

Our Lady of Victory, pray for us!

Words from the Saints on the Rosary

The saints, who help guide us to heaven, have all encouraged the faithful in the praying of the most holy Rosary. Many saints prayed the Rosary; many saints preached the Rosary; many saints propagated the recitation of the Rosary as a sure means of overcoming sin and attaining peace in this life and eternal salvation in the next.

Therefore, we will offer a few of the sayings of the saints and their love for Mary through the recitation of the most holy Rosary.

1. **Our Lady of Fatima to Lucia.** *"Continue to pray the Rosary every day."* Our Lady of Fatima requested the daily recitation of the holy Rosary in every one of her six apparitions in 1917.
2. **Saint Louis de Montfort.** This French saint gave to the world one of the greatest means of consecration to Jesus through Mary in his classic *True Devotion to Mary*. Saint Louis had this to say about the power of the most Holy Rosary: "Never will anyone who says the Rosary every day be led astray. This is a statement that I would gladly sign with my blood."
3. **Blessed Alan de la Roche.** This true man of God was a zealous promoter of the most holy Rosary. He stated that the eternal salvation of our soul can be related to the Rosary: "If you persevere in reciting the Rosary, this will be the most probable sign of your eternal salvation."
4. **Saint Frances de Sales.** This great saint was delivered from a profound state of desolation through the intercession of Mary under the title of Our Lady

of Victories. Saint Frances de Sales asserted, "The greatest method of praying is to pray the Rosary."

5. **Saint Dominic.** This great saint founded the Order of Preachers, known as the Dominicans, from which came forth Saint Albert the Great, Saint Thomas Aquinas, Saint Raymond, and Saint Catherine of Siena. Saint Dominic used the Rosary to conquer the Albigensian heresy. Dominic said of the Rosary, "One day, through the Rosary and the Scapular, Our Lady will save the world."

6. **Blessed Pope Pius IX.** We are in spiritual combat, spiritual warfare. An army has to be well prepared and well equipped to win the battle. This is what the great Blessed Pope Pius IX had to say about his choice of weapon in combat: "Give me an army saying the Rosary and I will conquer the world."

7. **Saint Bernardine of Siena.** A Franciscan Doctor of the Church and highly gifted preacher who glowed in his love for Mary, Saint Bernardine made this fascinating comment: "You must know that when you 'hail' Mary, she immediately greets you. Don't think that she is one of those rude women of whom there are so many—on the contrary, she is utterly courteous and pleasant. If you greet her, she will answer right away and converse with you."

8. **Pope Saint Pius X.** Many of the popes overflowed in their love for Mary, especially in their love and devotion to the holy Rosary. One of these was Pope Saint Pius X. Many graces, blessings, and peace upon the family are attained through the Rosary. "The Rosary is the most beautiful and the most rich in graces of all prayers; it is the prayer that touches most the Heart of the Mother of God . . . and if you wish peace to reign in your homes, recite the family Rosary."

9. **Our Lady to Saint Mechtilde.** With clear and penetrating words, Our Lady spoke to this German mystic about the words that she loves most, and those are the words we pray in every Hail Mary. "'Hail Mary, full of grace, the Lord is with thee!' No creature has ever said anything that was more pleasing to me, nor will anyone ever be able to find or say anything that pleases me more."

10. **Saint Pio of Pietrelcina.** This Italian mystic and stigmatist is one of the most popular saints of these modern times. Concerning the Rosary and spiritual warfare, he once said, "The Rosary is the weapon for these times."

These are just a few fiery proverbs or sayings from the holiest souls to walk the earth. We hope and pray that you will be convinced of the importance of the most holy Rosary in your life. Moreover, we hope and pray that not only will you cling to your Rosary every day as a sign of your deep union with and love for the Blessed Virgin Mary, but that like the saints, you too will promote the importance of the daily recitation of the Rosary for the salvation of your soul, and so many others!

Our Lady of the Rosary, pray for us!

The Battle of Lepanto

Did you know that October is considered the month of the Rosary? This is because October 7 is the feast of Our Lady of the Rosary. The origin of this feast reaches back to one of the most important naval victories in the history of the Church.

In the sixteenth century, Ottoman Turkish forces were expanding into the Mediterranean, threatening the very life of Christendom as they conquered or killed everything in their path. Ottoman fleets were sailing west from their naval station in Lepanto when they were met in the Gulf of Patras by the fleet of the Holy League, an army of soldiers from several nations sent to defend Christian lands. The Turks far outnumbered the Christian fleet, and the battle seemed as though it would be a swift victory for the Islamic forces. But heaven had other plans!

Back in Rome, Pope Pius V, now Pope Saint Pius V, sat on the Chair of Peter. Before rising to the papacy, he belonged to the Order of Preachers—that is to say, the Dominicans. Their founder, Saint Dominic, wielded the most holy Rosary and preached it fervently and faithfully against the heresy of Albigensiansim. As a result, this pernicious and erroneous religious sect was conquered, and many who were contaminated by its errors returned to the Catholic Church.

Pope Pius V followed the lead of Dominic and called for a Rosary crusade in Europe, encouraging the Catholics of the world, far and wide, to pull out their spiritual weapon, their spiritual sword—none other than the Rosary—and use it as the weapon of victory. Thousands upon thousands of Catholics answered the Holy Father's call and prayed the Rosary for victory, and as a result, a miracle occurred! Despite being dramatically outnumbered, the Holy League won the battle! The tide then turned in the greater battle against the Islamic forces, and many today say all of Christendom was saved because of this naval victory.

To commemorate the victory, Pope Pius V instituted a new liturgical memorial—Our Lady of the Rosary, celebrated on October 7.

Today we face similar battles where our chances of success seem just as futile. These are not always military battles but rather spiritual ones against the rise of militant secularism. If we want to defeat these enemies, we must, like the Christians of the sixteenth century, pick up our weapon—the most holy Rosary—and wield it confidently. We must use it like the slingshot David used to take down Goliath! Let us especially during the month of October be dedicated to promoting, praying, and loving this great gift to the world—the most holy Rosary of the Blessed Virgin Mary.

Battle of Lepanto, painting by Venetian school, late 16th century, Detail / © A. Dagli Orti / NPL - DeA Picture Library / Bridgeman Images

Holy Family Catholic Church (North Baltimore, Ohio)
stained glass, Miraculous Medal front and back

CHAPTER 16

The Miraculous Medal

One of the most renowned Marian apparitions approved by the Church was to a humble, unknown French Sister in a Paris convent in the year 1830. Her name was Catherine Laboure.

While in bed, a child, whom she later discerned to be her guardian angel, awoke Catherine and told her to go to the convent chapel. Someone important was waiting there, said the angel. To many, this would have been quite astonishing, but Catherine had already at this point experienced other miraculous visions.

Dressing quickly, Catherine hurried into the chapel. Waiting there, sitting in the presider's chair—that of the priest—was the Blessed Virgin Mary. She had a joyful countenance and was more beautiful than Catherine could describe. Our Lady invited the young Sister Catherine to approach. As the nun obeyed, Our Lady beckoned her still closer, then closer, until finally Catherine could actually touch Our Lady, placing her hands in the Queen of Heaven's lap.

Sister Catherine had prayed fervently to Jesus to see the Virgin Mary, and now her prayer was being answered. When she was nine, her earthly mother died. It is said that after the funeral, she picked up a statue of the Virgin, kissed it, and said, "Now you will be my mother."

Now here she was, many years later, talking to her mother. Catherine opened her heart and spoke. The conversation between mother and daughter was calm, simple, and intimate. Our Lady inspired in Sister Catherine great trust and confidence. Therefore, Catherine was totally at peace, with total assurance that she could open up

Chapel of Our Lady of the Miraculous Medal, Catherine Labouré and Virgin Mary / Godong / UIG / Bridgeman Images

and talk to Mary about everything that was on her mind, knowing that Mother Mary knew her, loved her, and was ready to help her.

A second visit followed several months later, and it was then that Our Lady gave Catherine what has come to be known as the Miraculous Medal. Mary appeared within an oval frame, resting upon a globe and crushing a serpent, with rays of light emanating from her hands. Around the margins of the frame were the words "O Mary, conceived without sin, pray for us who have recourse to thee." The oval then began to rotate so that she understood she was looking at the back, where twelves stars were spread out in a circle, and within them a large *M* was surmounted by a cross, resting above the Sacred Heart of Jesus and the Immaculate Heart of Mary. Mary then instructed Catherine to take the image to her confessor so that they could be put onto medallions, and all who wore them would "receive great graces." Although it would take two years, many medallions were created, and eventually millions began to wear them around their necks, still to this day.

It must be said that simply wearing a medal like this is not sufficient; otherwise the wearing of the Miraculous Medal could be transformed into a mere superstition. Religiosity not explained can very easily be transformed into superstition. Therefore, let us offer a brief explanation, a catechetical teaching, on the medal itself.

The Front of the Miraculous Medal

"O Mary, Conceived Without Sin, Pray for Us Who Have Recourse to Thee."

Encircled around the front side of the medal is this prayer. These are simple words but have great profundity of doctrinal and spiritual meaning. They point first of all to the Immaculate Conception ("conceived without sin"), a dogma that was proclaimed in 1854 by Pope Pius IX. This dogma proclaims that Mary was given a unique privilege from the infinite goodness of God: that from the very moment of her conception she was preserved from the stain of original sin. The Church celebrates this as a solemnity every year on December 8. It is said that the visions of Saint Catherine gave support to the Holy Father's decision to promulgate the dogma.

But the prayer goes on: "pray for us." This points to the Church's teaching on Mary's intercessory role: that we ask our mother to pray for us so that God will give us graces. This is something we ask in the Hail Mary as well: "pray for us sinners, now and at the hour of our death." We firmly believe that Mary will pray for us and beg God—the Father, the Son, and the Holy Spirit—for the special graces that we need to attain the eternal salvation of our soul. Knowing that Mary, the Immaculate One, the Mother of God, is praying for us, is on our side and is interceding for us, should fill us with enormous consolation as we struggle in our battle to attain the prize of eternal life. The one who was "conceived without sin" will help us overcome sin through her prayers.

Mary's Open Arms and Hands

This artistic depiction is worth a million words! Mother Mary has her arms and hands open for all of us. They are welcoming us; they are ready to embrace us. In other words, in your sufferings, run to Mary; in your fears, entrust yourself to Mary; in your cloudy and even stormy days, seek the light and warmth of Mary's Immaculate Heart! Her posture is one of refuge, waiting to embrace us. She is a haven of safety in the midst of the moral bombs exploding all around us!

The Rays Emanating from Mary's Open Hands

The abundant rays emanating from the hands of Mary, like rays from the sun, symbolize what she so ardently desires to attain for us. Remember, she is *full of grace*! As such, she desires to communicate to us this grace. We must be in a state of grace when we die, or we will not enter the kingdom of heaven. Mary wants all her children to enter this kingdom, and so she wants to shower down graces upon us. Not graces that she herself generates, but rather God does, and sends them through His mother.

Chapel of Our Lady of the Miraculous Medal

Today you can visit the chapel where the Virgin Mary appeared to Saint Catherine Laboure. The Chapel of Our Lady of the Miraculous Medal is located in Paris and receives millions of pilgrims each year.

The chapel of Our Lady of the Miraculous Medal in Paris

Mary's greatest desire for us is to receive grace, grow in grace, fortify our souls with grace, persevere in grace, and if we have lost grace, return to the state of grace so as to finally die in the state of grace!

In one of the conversations that Our Lady had with Sister Catherine, there was an element of sorrow. Catherine asked why some of the rays leaving Mary's hands did not reach earth. The beautiful lady responded, "Those are graces for which people forget to ask." Therefore, my friends in Jesus and Mary, starting right now, as we meditate upon the meaning of Our Lady and the Miraculous Medal, let us humbly but fervently beg for those many graces Our Lady wants to attain for us and that are never asked for! May the words of Jesus from the Sermon on the Mount encourage us: "Ask, and it will be given you; seek, and you will find; knock, and it will be opened to you. For every one who asks receives, and he who seeks finds, and to him who knocks it will be opened" (Mt 7:7–8).

Our Lady Standing on the Top of the Globe and Crushing the Serpent

This takes us back to Genesis. After Adam and Eve ate the forbidden fruit in the garden, tempted to do so by the serpent, sin entered the world. But this original sin was followed by the *Protoevangelium*—meaning, "the First Gospel," the first Good News of the Bible: "I will put enmity between you and the woman, and between your seed and her seed; he will bruise your head, and you will bruise his heel (Gn 3:15). This was the first announcement that God would send a Savior. But still, it warned us that this life will be one of warfare! Our life on earth is a perpetual battleground between good and evil, light and darkness, truth against the father of lies. But fear not! Our Lady, like a general in battle array, is on our side! She is always ready and willing to help us, protect us, and defend us against the deadly assaults of the devil, who is the enemy of our salvation. Christ came into the world through her, and so she helps to crush the serpent from Genesis, the devil. Let us stand beneath the banner of Jesus and Mary as their noble soldiers, and with them at our side, the victory is surely ours!

The Back of the Miraculous Medal

The Twelve Stars

Encircling this side of the medal are twelve stars. This image points us to Scripture. In Revelation, chapter 12, we read: "And a great portent appeared in heaven, a woman clothed with the sun, with the moon under her feet, and on her head a crown of twelve stars" (12:1) The Church teaches that this woman from the last book of the Bible is the Blessed Virgin Mary. The crown with twelve stars obviously points to Mary as Queen of Heaven, and so the Miraculous Medal confirms this. Stars are a symbol also closely associated with Mary. She is known as *Stella Maris*—the Star of the Sea.

The Cross and the Letter M Intertwined

At the foot of the cross and actually attached to the cross is the letter *M*. This reminds us that Mary stood at the foot of the cross, staying with her suffering Son until He breathed His last. Likewise, she stands with us as we carry our own crosses. She cannot be separated from her Son's cross, nor can she be separated from our suffering. She is our mother who is always there with us, most especially at times of pain.

The Two Hearts

Below the letter *M* and the cross, we find the Sacred Heart of Jesus and the Immaculate Heart of Mary. His heart is surrounded by thorns, a symbol of the sins of the world that prick and stab His pure heart, and a reference to the crown of thorns He wore during His passion. The Immaculate Heart of Mary, meanwhile, is punctured by a sword. This points us to the devotion of the Seven Sorrows of Mary. (The sorrowful mother is usually depicted with seven swords through her heart, but of course the medal is too small for that. Please see our chapter on the Seven Sorrows devotion for more information.) Atop both hearts are flames, symbolizing their intense love for one another, but also for us. It is fitting that these two hearts are next to one another, for they are ever united and beat in unison. The Heart of Mary formed the Sacred Heart of Jesus within her womb. Mary will always lead us to Jesus!

With the history of the medal recounted, and the symbolism explained, we hope and fervently pray that you will consider wearing the Miraculous Medal around your neck, and over your heart, as well as give out as many medals as you can. We also hope to engender in you a devotion to Saint Catherine Laboure, the saint of the Miraculous Medal. Through her intercession, and that of the Blessed Virgin Mary, you will be the recipient of untold graces that will lead you to heaven!

Virgin and child statue Senora del Carmen, Our Lady of Mount Carmel /
Photo © Godong / UIG / Bridgeman Images

CHAPTER 17

Our Lady of Mount Carmel and the Brown Scapular

Every year on the July 16, the Church celebrates Our Lady of Mount Carmel. She is the patroness in a very special way of the Carmelite Order, the male and female branches, as well as the lay associates.

Our Lady can be honored in many different ways, as we have seen throughout this text, but in a very special way, we honor her on July 16 under the title of Our Lady of Mount Carmel. Therefore, let us offer key information to foster our devotion to Mary under this wonderful name, and in a most special way with respect to the scapular of Our Lady of Mount Carmel.

According to tradition, on July 16, 1251, Our Lady appeared to a religious priest of the Order of the Carmelites, Saint Simon Stock. During this miraculous visit, she handed to him a brown woolen scapular. She said to him, "This shall be the privilege for you and the Carmelites, that anyone dying in this habit shall not suffer eternal fire." In the course of history, the investment, wearing, and love of the scapular of Our Lady of Mount Carmel has spread far and wide.

The actual meaning of the word *scapular* (*scapula*) is "shoulder," because the scapular is worn over one's shoulder. The scapular is made of brown wool with a string or cord, which actually connects two scapulars—one to be worn in front and a second to be worn in back. Moreover, this scapular is to be worn at all times—except when taking a shower or bath.

Simon Stock (circa 1690) by Marc Arcis

The brown scapular is known as the *Garment of Grace*. A wonderful little booklet has been composed and is published by the Slaves of the Immaculate Heart of Mary under this title of *Garment of Grace*. Hopefully, you will purchase this little gem and read it. Not only does it explain the meaning and history of the scapular of Our Lady of Mount Carmel, but at the end of the pamphlet, there is a short but very clear catechesis on the scapular.

We can better understand the meaning of the scapular of Our Lady of Mount Carmel by means of an analogy. A soldier wears his uniform, with each branch of the armed services donning their own specific attire; a baseball player wears the uniform of his team and that differentiates him from the other teams; policemen, firemen, and medical personnel are identified by the garb they wear. In a parallel sense, Mary has her followers. They distinguish themselves by the wearing of the scapular of Our Lady of Mount Carmel.

If you like, giving the concept a different twist, those who wear the scapular of Our Lady of Mount Carmel belong to the school of Mary and to the family of Mary. Even more profound and intimate, those who wear the scapular belong to the Heart of Mary and are embraced by the most pure Immaculate Heart of Mary. In a real sense, they are seeking the heart of Mary as their refuge, their haven, their sure place of security amidst the many trials and temptations in life.

Our Lady of Fatima appeared six times to the little children of Fatima—Lucia, Francisco, and Jacinta. During these visits, Our Lady promised a miracle in October. This was the miracle of the sun spinning in the sky like a fiery kaleidoscope. In addition to this, the children saw a vision in the sky of the Child Jesus in the arms of Saint Joseph, as well as Our Lady of Sorrows and Our Lady of Mount Carmel. This noteworthy appearance of Our Lady of Mount Carmel speaks very eloquently about the fact that she wears the scapular and ardently desires that those who really love her should also wear the scapular as their sign of devotion and consecration to her.

For many years, it was the custom in parishes on the day of First Holy Communion to invest the children with the Scapular of Our Lady of Mount Carmel. The priest would impose the Scapular over the shoulders of each child, and then enroll the child in the Confraternity of the Scapular, a lifelong appointment!

The following are the words said by a priest enrolling a person in this confraternity: "Receive this blessed habit, praying to the most holy Virgin that by her merits you may wear it without stain, and that she may guard you from all evil and bring you to eternal life." Then the priest continues with the following words in which one becomes an official member and part of the Religious Order of Mount Carmel: "By the power granted to me, I admit you to participate in all of the spiritual goods, which through the gracious help of Jesus Christ are performed by the religious Order of Mount Carmel. In the name of the Father, and of the Son, and of the Holy Spirit. Amen."

Scapular with holy pictures / SSPL / UIG / Bridgeman Images

Then, there is the concluding prayer, which indeed is worthy of deep meditation: "May the Creator of Heaven and earth, Almighty God bless you; who has deigned to unite you to the confraternity of the Blessed Virgin of Mount Carmel. We beseech her, in the hour of your death, to crush the head of the ancient serpent, so that you may in the end win the everlasting palm and crown of the heavenly inheritance, through Christ our Lord. Amen."

How then should we live out the investiture and wearing of the scapular? There are various gestures or actions we can carry out:

Wear the Scapular with Pride

Always wear the scapular of Our Lady of Mount Carmel with great love, pride, and trust. You truly belong to Mary; you are a noble member of her family.

Consecrate Yourself to Mary

Upon arising every morning, make it a habit to consecrate your whole self, your whole being, to Mary—your heart, mind, body, and soul, your past, present, and future. Please see our chapter explaining Marian consecration for more on this topic, but here is a consecration prayer repeated for your convenience:

Mary, my Queen and my Mother, I give myself entirely to you. To show my devotion to you, I consecrate to you this day my eyes, my ears, my mouth, my heart, my whole being without reserve. Since, loving Mother, I am your own, keep me and guard me as your property and possession. Amen.

Kiss the Scapular

The kiss is a universal symbol of love. By kissing the scapular of Our Lady of Mount Carmel, you are like a little child kissing his mother with tenderness and love.

Indulgence

The Church is so pleased with the gesture of kissing the scapular that it offers a partial indulgence every time it is kissed. You can offer this for the poor souls in purgatory to alleviate their suffering and facilitate their speedy entrance to heaven.

Mary's Embrace

The scapular is worn over your shoulder, as well as over your heart. It should be a constant reminder of Mary's presence in your life and of her loving and maternal embrace, as if she is giving you a hug.

Imitate Mary

If truly we love Jesus and Mary, then we should strive to imitate Mary. We will be more inclined to do so if we feel her embrace around us through the scapular throughout the day.

Cultivating Virtue

The wearing of the scapular will help us cultivate the same virtues Mary possesses, that of profound humility, untarnished purity, and ardent charity—love for God and neighbor! We must practice these virtues if we wish to be worthy to wear the scapular.

Defeating Temptation

In times of temptation, it is important to call on Mary, and if possible, to kiss the scapular, begging Mary to ward off the evil spirits in your life.

Apostle of Mary

If we really love Mary, then we should do all in our power to make her known. Try to be an apostle of Mary by getting people to pray the holy Rosary and to wear the brown scapular of Our Lady of Mount Carmel.

Die with the Scapular

Beg for the grace to die in the state of grace with Mary's scapular surrounding you, and especially with Mary's scapular over your heart! She promises that the soul who dies wearing the brown scapular will never suffer the fires of hell.

The wearing of the brown scapular is so simple, and yet it offers profound graces. We pray you will take advantage of this gift from our mother and engender in your life a strong devotion to Our Lady of Mount Carmel!

Prayer to Our Lady of Mount Carmel

O most beautiful flower of Mount Carmel, Fruitful Vine, Splendor of Heaven, Blessed Mother of the Son of God, Immaculate Virgin, assist me in this necessity. (Mention your petition.) O Star of the Sea, help me and show me in this that thou art my Mother.

O holy Mary, Mother of God, Queen of Heaven and earth, I humbly beseech thee, from the bottom of my heart, to succor me in this necessity; there are none that can withstand thy power. Oh, show me in this that thou art my Mother!

O Mary, conceived without sin, pray for us who have recourse to thee. (three times)

Sweet Mother, I place this cause in thy hands. (three times)

(It is suggested to offer three times the Our Father, Hail Mary and Glory Be in thanksgiving.)

The Assumption of the Virgin, Poussin, Nicolas (1594-1665) /
Photo © Bridgeman Images

CHAPTER 18

The Month of Mary

Traditionally, May has been designated as the month of Mary. In point of fact, as Catholics, we should always honor Mary, venerate her with the most special of devotions, have recourse to her powerful intercession, and call upon her as our heavenly mother.

Nonetheless, May has been specially set aside as Our Lady's month in such a way that we should, so to speak, increase our love for her during these thirty-one days, just as we place a special emphasis on our mom during Mother's Day, which, providentially, also falls during the month of May.

Why is May the month of Mary? Like many traditions in the Church, the origins stem from multiple sources and have been guided by the Holy Spirit into what we practice today.

Perhaps the clearest reason May is Mary's month is the symbolism of new life that occurs during this first full month of spring (at least in the Northern Hemisphere). The Ancient Greeks and Romans both honored their own goddesses during May for this reason—Artemis, the goddess of fecundity, and Flora, the goddess of blooms, or blossoms. Throughout history, Christians have turned pagan practices to the purpose for which God intended before the fall of Adam and Eve—to reflect supernatural truths that lift our minds and hearts to God's salvific intervention in the history of mankind.

Mary is the New Eve who brought Life itself into the world after the first Eve brought death to man. In the resurrection of nature after a long winter, we see a symbol of the fertility of Mary bringing us the God-man who came to save our humanity by saving our souls. Additionally, May is a beautiful spring month in which the Risen Lord is celebrated—that is to say, it is the Easter Season. Flowers are blooming and the fragrance of their scent is in the air. Birds are singing their joyful melody. Often the skies are blue and the gentle spring breeze refreshes mind, body, and soul. How could this time of beauty not remind us of our beautiful life-giving mother, as well as the promise of our resurrection from sin in every good confession, and our hope of final resurrection to new life in heaven!

Finally, in the early Church, there is strong evidence that a major Marian feast was celebrated on May 15, giving rise to Marian devotions around this time. Still more, there existed in the Middle Ages a tradition called *Tricesimum*, also known as "Lady Month," where Mary was honored for a period of thirty days; though this was not originally in May, the practice was carried over and moved into May. Finally, since 1917, when Our Lady of Fatima first appeared on May 13, this time of the year has been strongly associated with Mary. It was in 1945 that Pope Pius XII solidified May as a Marian month after establishing the feast of the Queenship of Mary on May 31 (it has since been moved to August 22, while May 31 has become the feast of the Visitation of Mary).

As you can see, the Holy Spirit has worked hard to ensure His spouse is honored during this springtime month!

And what practices, then, should we carry out to honor our mother and show our love for her during this time? We will mention thirteen here and hope that with good will and a growing and tender love for Mary, you will strive to implement as many of these practices as possible!

May Flowers at Home
Given that May indeed is in the springtime in which flowers abound, why not honor Mary in your home by decorating her images and statues with beautiful bouquets of flowers? Such a floral decoration done with love will certainly delight the heart of your heavenly mother!

May Flowers at Church
An attractive statue or painting of the Blessed Virgin Mary captivates the mind and elevates the heart. However, embellishing the images of Mary with beautiful floral arrangements indeed enhances the awareness and the beauty of God's Masterpiece of Creation! Such gestures done with love delight the hearts of Jesus and Mary.

Marian May Processions

Many popes have encouraged Marian popular devotion, and this can become manifest in a public fashion by returning once again to the beautiful and inspiring Marian May processions so prevalent in the past. This can be done in or outside of the church, in a public manner to manifest externally our faith, love, and devotion to Mary. This can also be executed by carrying a beautiful statue of Mary, with the followers walking in procession behind her, including the children, who are so very dear to the heart of Mary. With peace and calmness, the procession can be done while praying the holy Rosary interwoven with Marian hymns.

Marian Hymns or Songs

Saint Augustine stated, "He who sings, prays twice." Lovers of Mary should learn a series of Marian hymns and sing them with overflowing joy and love. Just to mention a few: *Immaculate Mary, Hail Holy Queen, Sing of Mary* and *O Sanctissima.* Not only should we sing these songs with overflowing joy, but we should teach them to others, especially the children. Why not incorporate singing a Marian hymn each time you pray the family Rosary?

Marian May Crowning

In conjunction with the Marian procession can be added the Marian May crowning. At the end of the procession and after the statue of Mary has been enthroned in its proper place—often within the church itself—then it is time for the Marian May crowning. It is beautiful to allow a little child, usually a little girl, to have the honor and the privilege of crowning Mary as Marian hymns are sung. The meaning of this should be explained. That is to say, by crowning the statue of Mary with a beautiful crown, we are saying to the Blessed Mother, who is the Queen of heaven and earth, that we desire her to be the Queen of our home, Queen of our family, Queen of our very person, and Queen of our heart.

May 13

Also in the month of May, on the thirteenth, the Church has a very special feast in honor of Our Lady of Fatima to commemorate the day she first appeared to the shepherd children. As we recall her messages of prayer and penance (sacrifice) for the salvation of souls, let us prayerfully consider how we can incorporate one prayer and one act of penance into our daily routine for the salvation of souls. Every day, like the children of Fatima, let us do our part with Jesus and Mary to save poor sinners from the reality of hell.

May Novena

Make a novena to Mary sometime in May. This could consist of the Rosary or the Mass for nine consecutive days, or both! The novena can be for any intentions dear to your heart for yourself, your family, the Church, or the world at large.

May 31

The last day of the month of May is a day very special to Our Lady. It is the Feast of the Visitation to her cousin Elizabeth, who was with child, Saint John the Baptist. At the same time, Mary carried within her womb Jesus, the Son of God made man and conceived by the power of the Holy Spirit. This feast honors the second joyful mystery of the Rosary. Let us learn from our Mother Mary to bring Jesus to others whom we encounter each day through our good thoughts, words, or deeds on their behalf.

Receive Communion in Honor of Mary

On these Marian feasts in May, both on May 13, the memorial of Our Lady of Fatima, as well as on May 31, the Feast of the Visitation of the Blessed Virgin Mary to Saint Elizabeth, we should honor Mary by attending the Holy Sacrifice of the Mass—participating actively and fervently in the Mass and receiving Jesus in Holy Communion with great love, thanksgiving, and joy. What a splendid way to honor both Jesus and Mary. Actually, it is the best way!

Read About Mary

It will be very pleasing to the Blessed Virgin Mary if you find a good book on her and begin reading it during the month of May. *The Glories of Mary* by Saint Alphonsus Liguori is delightful and inspiring, and it can be read over time. A chapter per day can be read in fifteen to twenty minutes for busy people. Knowledge of Mary generates love for her. Then continue the practice of good spiritual reading.

Marian Movies

During the month of May, choose one or more Marian movies to watch with your family: older movies and newer ones. *The Song of Bernadette* and *The Passion of Bernadette*; there are several films that tell the story of Our Lady of Fatima, both older and newer versions; and *Mary of Nazareth* and *Full of Grace* are wonderful movies as well.

Family Rosary

Of course, our reflection would be incomplete if we did not encourage the recitation of the most Holy Rosary of the Blessed Virgin Mary in the month of May. It is true that October is the month of the most Holy Rosary. Still, Our Lady of Fatima insisted upon the recitation of the Holy Rosary *every day*, irrespective of time or place.

Our love for the Blessed Virgin Mary should always lead us to the faithful recitation of the Holy Rosary and a desire to spread this practice far and wide, even to the ends of the world, and until the end of time.

Maria Cogita, Maria Invoca

The Blessed Virgin Mary appeared six times to the three shepherd children of Fatima beginning May 13. This short Latin phrase, known and loved by the Oblates of the Virgin Mary, the religious congregation of the author, were spoken by the Fatima children daily. The words mean: *Think about Mary and Invoke Mary*. What better way to honor and love Mary than to think about Mary's loving and maternal presence as we go through our day and invoke her name in all our needs.

One of the great lovers of the Blessed Virgin Mary was Saint John Bosco, who believed in entrusting all to Mary. This towering giant of a saint lived most of his life in the Northern Italian city of Turin, where he founded an oratory for abandoned boys living in the time of the Industrial Revolution.

Saint John Bosco, excellent educator, lover of Mary, and patron of the youth, was convinced of the importance of the young cultivating a loving, tender, and filial devotion to Mary—Our Lady Help of Christians. So as to conquer their imperious passions, so violent at times in the prime teen years, Bosco insisted on frequent confession, frequent and fervent reception of Holy Communion, and a strong devotion to Mary. Parents could take note of this and follow in his footsteps with their teenagers.

So ardent and fervent was the devotion Saint John Bosco had for Mary, especially in the month of May, that the youth educator encouraged the boys in his oratory to offer some special gift, sacrifice, or prayer to Mary *every day* in the month of May. Indeed, love is measured by our willingness to sacrifice for the loved one. Jesus on the cross and Mary underneath the cross are our most transparent and sublime examples. We can repay them with small sacrifices every day, perhaps putting a fast of our choosing in place.

In conclusion, every year when the calendar ushers in the month of May, may we be joyful and enthusiastic in paying honor and tribute to the Blessed Virgin Mary in a very special way. We hope that the above ideas and suggestions will motivate you and your family to love Mary even more, and to crown her as the Queen of your family and the Queen of your hearts!

The Juggler of Our Lady

Le Jongleur de Notre Dame (The Juggler of Our Lady) is a fictitious religious story of a miracle that occurred in a monastery. Written in the 1890s by the French author Anatole France, Mary's Juggler has been compared to the Christmas carol *The Little Drummer Boy*.

It tells of a young juggler turned monk who struggles to adjust to his monastic life. At one point, he wishes to give a gift to a statue of the Virgin Mary, but he has nothing to offer except for his ability to juggle well. When the other monks witness him juggling before her statue, they disapprove and accuse him of blasphemy, but the statue comes to life, smiles, and blesses the juggler.

Another story that bears a similar theme is a charming image taken from Saint Louis de Montfort's *True Devotion to Mary*. In this masterpiece, teaching us how to consecrate ourselves to Jesus through Mary, he gives us the story of a pauper, unknown to the king, who ardently desires to offer his majesty a simple gift, that of an apple. But he does not have access to the king. To solve this problem, he approaches the queen and explains his situation, telling her about the gift he wishes to give the king. He asks if she will present it to him, and she agrees, polishing the apple and placing it on a silver platter alongside a beautiful flower.

The queen then presents the pauper's gift. As a result of the person who is offering the now attractive apple—his dearly beloved wife, the queen—the king gladly receives the apple with joy. He takes it, bites into it, and then thanks and praises the queen for that most succulent and delicious apple. The real reason the king received and ate the apple was not for the apple in its essence but because of the person who gave it to him.

In a parallel but very real sense, this little story can be applied to you and to me. We are the pauper—that is to say, we are poor sinners. We have very little to offer. Not only do we have very little to offer, but what we do have to offer is both imperfect and, in the eyes of the world, of very little value. However, if we offer it with good will to the queen, and this queen is the Blessed Virgin Mary, then she will give it to the King of the Universe, Jesus, her son, and He will receive our poor and insignificant gift from Mary's hands with great joy! It is not so much the gift but the dignity of the person offering the gift that makes the gift pleasing.

Ask yourself: what do you have to offer to the Blessed Virgin Mary? Perhaps you are not aware of talents that you have; maybe you feel your talents are few and insignificant. However, in the eyes of Mary, and of course Jesus, what is most important is your purity of heart, your good will, and your desire to offer them your best. When a little child offers her mother a birthday gift of a big fist of

The Juggler / Philpot, Glyn Warren / Photo © The Fine Art Society, London, UK / Bridgeman Images

dandelions—really weeds—it is received with much love by the mother not due to any economic worth or inherent beauty of the dandelion-weeds; rather, she receives them with great joy because she sees in them the love in the heart of her little child.

In the eyes of Jesus and Mary, holiness depends not so much on what we offer but on the purity of our intention and the love in our hearts. Saint Thérèse of Lisieux expressed this concept in these words: "Holiness consists in doing the ordinary things of daily life with extraordinary love." So let us become like the juggler of Notre Dame, let us become the pauper. Let us bring Jesus and Mary our prayers and our works, small in the eyes of the world, but with pure hearts full of love, knowing Jesus and Mary will receive them with great love and they will indeed have infinite value in their eyes!

Virgin with Child appearing to St. Francis de Sales (1691) / Carlo Maratta /
G. Dagli Orti /© NPL - DeA Picture Library / Bridgeman Images

CHAPTER 19

The Memorare

He was going through a terrible interior storm. There seemed to be no light at the end of the tunnel. It seemed hopeless; there was no way out! Doubt plagued him. He suffered loss of appetite, loss of sleep, and loss of desire for anyone or anything. Life seemed to be insupportable. As if he was hanging from a steep precipice, his life seemed precarious to say the least!

This was the interior state of one of the most known, most loved, and most admired saints in the Catholic Church. This was the interior state of the great Saint Francis de Sales!

When all seemed bleak, obscure, dark, almost beyond hope, the young man Francis de Sales entered a Church. One of his prayers was: "Lord, even if my destiny is hell, at least grant me the grace to love you even there!" Such was his interior condition! However, neither God nor the Blessed Virgin Mary ever abandon their children. Dawn grows and the sun breaks through in souls that entrust themselves to Jesus through Mary.

Though he entered a Church dedicated to the Blessed Virgin Mary, *Notre Dame de la Victoire*—Our Lady of Victory—it seemed lost on young Francis. However, there in this beautiful Church that was dedicated to Our Lady who wins victories, especially in the souls of her beloved children, Francis found a statue of Mary and a prayer dedicated to her.

This prayer was titled the *Memorare*. According to tradition, it is attributed to the Mellifluous Doctor, Saint Bernard. Kneeling down in front of the statue of Mary, young Francis opened up his mind and heart and prayed with all the fervor of his soul:

Memorare

Remember, O most gracious Virgin Mary, that never was it known, that anyone who fled to your protection, implored your help, or sought your intercession was left unaided. Inspired with this confidence, I fly to thee, O Virgin of virgins, my Mother; to thee do I come, before thee I stand, sinful and sorrowful. O Mother of the Word Incarnate, despise not my petitions, but in thy mercy hear and answer me. Amen.

After reciting this Marian prayer attributed to Saint Bernard, Francis experienced what seemed to be a miracle. That dense, impervious, dark cloud that had totally enveloped him, that had immersed and submerged him in hopelessness, suddenly dissipated! The sun broke through the clouds; light beamed at the end of the tunnel; his gloom and depression were transformed into peace and joy. He could hear the chirping of the birds and smell the fragrant scent of the flowers. God had finally lifted Francis out of the sinking quicksand of hopelessness!

God's plans are not our plans, and God's designs are very mysterious. The Lord willed to rescue the young Francis through the intercession of the Blessed Virgin Mary and the prayer of the Memorare.

God was preparing young Francis for an extremely important role in the Church, as well as the world at large. Priest, bishop, founder, writer, missionary, spiritual director—these were the roles that Saint Francis de Sales would assume and occupy in the heart of the Catholic Church. However, first he had to conquer the powerful enemy that tempted him to discouragement and almost to despair.

Thereafter, when tempted to discouragement, Francis de Sales would pray the Memorare. The devil, the enemy of our salvation, a liar and murderer from the beginning, cannot conquer the presence of the Blessed Virgin Mary. Even the holy name of the Blessed Virgin Mary causes the enemy mortal fear and panic, and he takes to flight.

Francis de Sales went through a very powerful state of desolation. What is desolation? It is when we have a lack of faith, lack of hope, lack of charity—we feel this! It is when we feel sad, discouraged, depressed, drawn to lowly things, and sensuality. In other words, we want to simply throw in the towel and give up! Life is useless! What is the meaning and purpose of it all?

Therefore, having learned in one short lesson the reality and meaning of desolation, we must counter it, and conquer it, through fervent prayer. We suggest and encourage praying to the Blessed Virgin Mary. We recommend the prayer of Saint Bernard that pulled Saint Francis de Sales out of the near pit of despair, the Memorare!

Therefore, prepare yourself for spiritual battle. We are all called to be soldiers of both Jesus and Mary in this very short life that God has given to us so as to attain eternal happiness in heaven. When all seems gray, bleak, obscure, dark, and meaningless, without any real hope, then lift up your mind, heart, and soul to the Blessed Virgin Mary, and she will never fail you. She will stretch out her gentle but firm hand and pull you out of the quicksand of your helplessness! *"Remember, O most gracious Virgin Mary, that never was it known, that anyone who fled to your protection, implored your help, or sought your intercession was left unaided."* Like Saint Francis de Sales, God is calling you out of darkness and into His wonderful light through the intercession of the Blessed Virgin Mary. Entrust your whole being to her; she will never fail you in life or in death.

Pentecost (1630) / Giovanni Lanfranco / © A. Dagli Orti /
© NPL - DeA Picture Library / Bridgeman Images

CHAPTER 20

Marian Novenas

A powerful wind, an event similar to an earthquake, and the descent of fire in the form of tongues—these and more phenomena—culminated with the coming of the Holy Spirit on the apostles that Pentecost day.

All of these events were preceded by the novena—a word that means "nine." The apostles, as well as the Blessed Virgin Mary, spent nine days and nine nights in the Cenacle (the Upper Room where Jesus had celebrated the Last Supper) before the Holy Spirit descended upon them. During these nine days, they engaged in deep prayer, silence, and fasting.

Of the greatest importance in the coming of the Holy Spirit was the presence of the Blessed Virgin Mary. The Holy Spirit, her mystical spouse, delights in her presence. For that reason, Saint Louis de Montfort claims, "The soul that loves Mary, the Holy Spirit flings Himself into that soul." In other words, He is drawn to souls where Mary is present. It is also fitting that Mary would be there that day of Pentecost because this was when the Church was born, and she is the Mother of the Church.

In imitation of the apostles and the Virgin Mary, the Church encourages the faithful to pray novenas. These are certain prayers prayed in nine successive days for specific intentions. We would like to invite all lovers of Mary to get into the habit of praying novenas. They are efficacious ways of deepening our prayer life.

In Saint Faustina's Diary, *Divine Mercy in My Soul*, Jesus strongly encourages Saint Faustina to offer novenas. This is where we get the powerful Divine Mercy Novena which starts on Good Friday and terminates on the Sunday after Easter, known as

Divine Mercy (1934) by Eugeniusz Kazimirowski

Divine Mercy Sunday. In addition to this novena to Divine Mercy, Faustina prayed other novenas, especially to the Blessed Virgin Mary.

While we can pray a Marian novena any time we wish, it is customary to pray them in the nine days leading up to a Marian feast, such as the feast of the Immaculate Conception, celebrated on December 8, and the Assumption of the Blessed Virgin Mary, celebrated on August 15. When we carry out novenas to honor Mary, her heart is filled with joy. In addition to honoring her, we ask for her intercession for a particular intention. Often, the Blessed Virgin Mary will grant special graces through these powerful prayers.

There are many different kinds of Marian novenas, too many to list here (a simple search on the internet will bring up dozens). The key to making a successful novena is simply to carry out and to remain faithful to whatever practices you decide to undertake for those nine consecutive days. Here are a few suggestions:

Find a Marian Novena

As we just noted, we can find many Marian novenas on the internet or in Catholic prayerbooks. These novenas may be dedicated to a specific apparition, such as Our Lady of Lourdes, or to some other Marian title, such as Our Lady of Sorrows. Find one that suits you or one that can be tied to an important intention you have in your life, something that is weighing down your heart, and pray that novena for nine days. Remember, the novena you choose is not nearly as important as your faithfulness in carrying it out.

Rosary

We should try to pray the Rosary every day. But if this is not currently a part of your prayer life, one

Novena to Our Lady of Hope

On January 17, 1871, Our Lady of Hope appeared in the French village of Pontmain. There she revealed herself as the "Madonna of the Crucifix." She gave the world her message of hope through prayer and the cross. A basilica was built in Pontmain by the Oblates of Mary Immaculate and has become one of the great French pilgrimage sites, noted for its miracles of grace.

Devotion to Our Lady of Hope is one of the oldest Marian devotions. This novena, to be prayed in nine successive days, is just one example of the many Marian novenas the Church gives us.

In the Name of the Father, and of the Son, and of the Holy Spirit.

I am the mother of fair love, and of fear, and of knowledge, and of holy hope. In me is all grace of the way and of the truth; in me is all hope of life and of virtue. Come to me all that desire me and be filled with my fruits (Sir 24:24–26).

O Blessed Virgin Mary, Mother of Grace, Hope of the world.

Hear us, your children, who cry to you.

Let Us Pray

O God, who by the marvelous protection of the Blessed Virgin Mary has strengthened us firmly in hope, grant we beseech You, that by persevering in prayer at her admonition, we may obtain the favors we devoutly implore. Through Christ Our Lord. Amen.

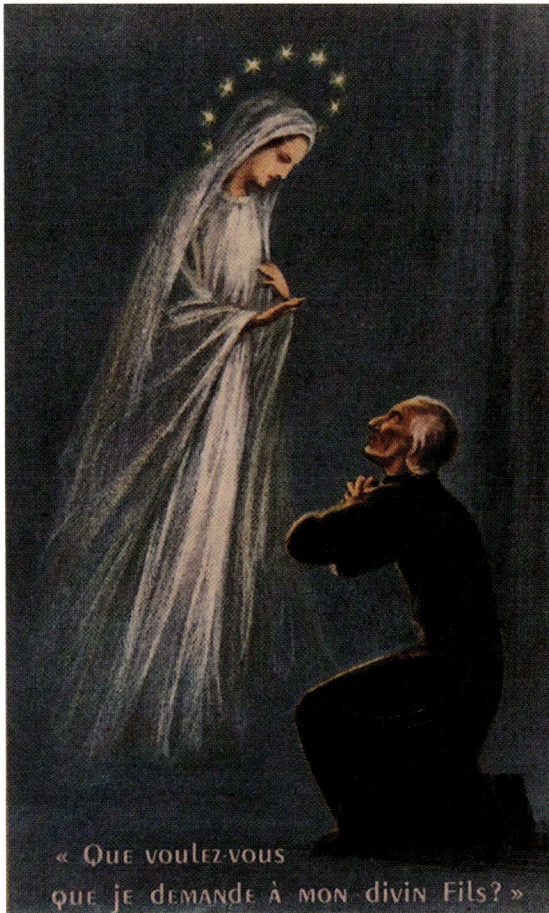

« Que voulez-vous que je demande à mon divin Fils? »

19th century novena painting from France

way to get in that habit is to begin praying a Rosary novena. By praying the most holy Rosary for nine consecutive days, you have a specific goal to reach that can help keep you disciplined. Then, hopefully, you will see the power of the Rosary and continue praying it thereafter!

Marian Litany

Another way that you can make a novena is to pray one of the litanies in honor of the Blessed Virgin Mary for nine consecutive days. Pray it with great fervor and love!

Mass and Holy Communion

Of course, of all the spiritual practices, the greatest is to receive Holy Communion in the Mass properly and reverently. Receive your Holy Communion through the Immaculate Heart of Mary; that will be a well-received Holy Communion! Doing this for nine consecutive days is a most fragrant offering to our Blessed Mother, who bore our Eucharistic Lord in her womb for nine months.

Fasting or Sacrifice

In addition to prayers, the Rosary, Mass, and Holy Communion, you might decide to offer some form of fasting or sacrifice in honor of the Blessed Virgin Mary. Jesus said very clearly that some devils "cannot be driven out by anything but prayer and fasting" (Mk 9:29). Your fast does not have to be intensely vigorous. Give up something small but do it with great love. Mary can take your little sacrifice offered with great love and use it for the eternal salvation of souls. Jesus and Mary, more than anything else in the world, desire the conversion and salvation of souls—as many as possible!

If you are feeling especially generous, you may decide to combine some of these practices—for example, praying a novena while also fasting and attending Mass for nine days. Just remember that whatever goals you set, you are faithful to them. The power of the novena lies in our faithfulness to it.

Prayer to Our Lady of Hope

O Mary, my Mother, I kneel before you with heavy heart. The burden of my sins oppresses me. The knowledge of my weakness discourages me. I am beset by fears and temptations of every sort. Yet I am so attached to the things of this world that instead of longing for Heaven I am filled with dread at the thought of death.

O Mother of Mercy, have pity on me in my distress. You are all-powerful with your Divine Son. He can refuse no request of your Immaculate Heart. Show yourself a true Mother to me by being my advocate before His throne. O Refuge of Sinners and Hope of the Hopeless, to whom shall I turn if not you?

Obtain for me, then, O Mother of Hope, the grace of true sorrow for my sins, the gift of perfect resignation to God's Holy Will, and the courage to take up my cross and follow Jesus. Beg of His Sacred Heart the special favor that I ask in this novena.

(*Make your request*)

But above all I pray, O dearest Mother, that through your most powerful intercession my heart may be filled with Holy Hope, so that in life's darkest hour I may never fail to trust in God my Savior, but by walking in the way of His commandments I may merit to be united with Him, and with you in the eternal joys of Heaven. Amen.

Mary, our Hope, have pity on us.

Hope of the Hopeless, pray for us.

Conclude with three Hail Marys.

The Virgin of the Navigators (1531–36) / Alejo Fernández / G. Dagli Orti / © NPL – DeA Picture Library / Bridgeman Images

Marian Consecration

Consecration means to be set aside and given over for a sacred purpose. Religious live a "consecrated life" because they are set aside to live a holy life in service to the Church and to the spreading of God's kingdom. Consecration has its source in Scripture, as the sacrifices made by the Israelites to God were consecrated or given over to Him (offered to Him), and figures like King David were anointed, a ceremony similar to consecration, to fulfill the roles God bestowed upon them.

Jesus was the first to be consecrated to the Blessed Virgin Mary when He was conceived in her most pure and virginal womb by the power of the Holy Spirit. Let us state this from the very beginning of our conversation on Marian consecration, for this is of central importance in discussing this devotion.

This is further explained in this excerpt from the dogmatic constitution on the Church *Lumen Gentium*.

> Predestined from eternity by that decree of divine providence which determined the incarnation of the Word to be the Mother of God, the Blessed Virgin was on this earth the virgin Mother of the Redeemer, and above all others and in a singular way the generous associate and humble handmaid of the Lord. She conceived, brought forth and nourished Christ. She presented Him to the Father in the temple, and was united with Him by compassion as He died on the Cross. In this singular way she cooperated by her obedience, faith, hope and

burning charity in the work of the Saviour in giving back supernatural life to souls. Wherefore she is our mother in the order of grace. (61)

The purpose of this chapter is to talk about the consecration of our lives and, more specifically, consecrating ourselves to Jesus through the Blessed Virgin Mary to be put at His service according to His Divine Providence. In Marian consecration, we give ourselves to Jesus through her hands. Indeed, in the words of Saint Louis de Montfort: "Mary is the quickest, easiest, and most secure path to Jesus." We ask her to take possession of us and mold us to be like Christ, just as she molded Him in her most pure womb, so that we are a worthy gift. We give her all we have and are so we can offer our lives to Christ in a more holy way.

Saint Louis de Montfort could be called the "Father of Marian Consecration." His book *True Devotion to Mary* teaches us what it means to consecrate our lives to Jesus through Mary and how to go about doing it. In his seminal work, he compares Marian consecration to a story where a poor peasant wishes to give a gift—a humble apple—to the king. But he does not know how to approach the king, and he knows his gift is unworthy of a king. So he approaches the queen and asks that she give it to him, knowing the king has a great love for her and will receive any gift from her with great joy. The queen receives the gift and takes the liberty of polishing it and putting it on a silver platter, thus presenting it to the king in a more honorable fashion than the peasant could do on his own.

This is what Marian consecration is. Yes, we can approach the King, Jesus Christ Our Lord, and offer ourselves to Him, but when we offer ourselves to Him through His Mother, whom He loves so dearly, she presents us in a more worthy fashion. Even when we have the best intentions, our prayers and actions can be tainted by self-interest and self-love. Mary purifies our hearts of these things and then presents us to

Saint Louis de Montfort. Founder Statue by Giacomo Parisini, 1948

her Son. When we come to the King alongside the Queen, His heart will be all the more touched.

The act of making a consecration can vary. Usually, there is a period of preparation, which might involve the reading of a book (like *True Devotion to Mary*) and the praying of certain prayers over the course of several days or weeks, perhaps a Rosary each day, or a Marian novena. After the preparation period is complete, the consecration is carried out with a consecration prayer, where we give ourselves over to Jesus through Mary's hands. We can pray this prayer alone; however, it is recommended, if possible, that we carry out the consecration with a church group, and a priest can oversee the consecration prayers.

Finally, it is a common practice to make a consecration to Jesus through Mary annually. In addition to de Montfort's classic, *True Devotion to Mary*, there are other books available on consecration to Jesus through Mary, one of which is by the author of this book.

Hail Mary...

My Queen, my Mother! I give myself entirely to you, and to show my devotion to you, I consecrate to you this day my eyes, my ears, my mouth, my heart, my whole being without reserve. Since, loving Mother, I am your own, keep me and guard me as your property and possession. Amen.

This consecration prayer is prayed on the day of consecration to Mary. It should then be prayed every morning as soon as we wake up for the rest of our lives. In this way, our consecration to Mary becomes the very heartbeat of our lives!

A Consecration to Mary

Consecrations can be done at any point, but generally it is good practice to time your preparation so that the consecration takes place on a Marian feast day. That will help us remember to renew our consecration annually.

But there are other key moments in which we can consecrate ourselves to Jesus through the Blessed Virgin Mary, especially key moments in our pilgrimage towards heaven. Like Jesus, we would like Mary to walk with us, to accompany us from the beginning of our lives to the end, in anticipation of reaching our heavenly home.

The most efficacious means is through the sacraments instituted by Christ and administered to us by His representatives on earth in the ordained priesthood and deaconate. Consider that through the sacraments, the priest accompanies us in every stage of our natural and spiritual life, all the important moments in our lives, for grace builds on nature!

Baptism (Birth)

After the baptism of a child, there is an optional ceremony in which the recently baptized child can be presented and consecrated to the Blessed Virgin Mary, as is my customary practice. This can be done in a very simple way, in which the child is brought before an image, painting, or statue of Mother Mary and presented through a prayer to Mary such as the Hail Mary, the Hail Holy Queen, or the Memorare.

First Communion (Nourishment to sustain us)

The most important moment in our lives, for most of us when we were children, is the day of our First Holy Communion, the day that for the very first time we received the Body, Blood, Soul, and Divinity of Jesus into the depths of our heart. At the end of the First Communion Mass, there is a common practice which I fully embrace and carry out—the priest can consecrate all of the children to Mary through the blessing and imposition of the brown scapular of Our Lady of Mount Carmel. The children can then be given this consecration prayer to pray:

> Hail Mary, my Queen and my Mother! I give myself entirely to you, and to show my devotion to you, I consecrate to you this day my eyes, my ears, my mouth, my heart, and my whole being without reserve. Since, loving Mother, I am your own, keep me and guard me as your property and possession. Amen.

Confirmation (Coming of Age)

As a follow-up to First Communion, parish confirmation programs can organize a formal ceremony, best preceded by a chastity retreat, in which the young people consecrate their purity—in mind, thought, eyes, body, and soul—to the Blessed Virgin Mary. The most splendid way in which this can be carried out is to consecrate the youth on a Marian solemnity, like the solemnity of the Immaculate Conception, in the context of the Holy Sacrifice of the Mass. After the homily, the priest blesses and gives the young people a symbol of the consecration of their purity to Mary. For the girls, it is a chastity ring that bears the image of the Miraculous Medal. For the boys, it is a Saint Benedict cross on a chain. Through these religious items, these young people, especially when tempted, will be reminded of the formal consecration of their purity to Mary. Indeed, this reminder could prove to save many young people from tarnishing their purity. The mere wearing and visibility of the ring or the cross radiates a power of the presence of Mary to preserve them body and soul from impurity and to prevent sin.

Holy Matrimony (Marriage and Family Life)

In the celebration of the vows of Holy Matrimony within the Holy Sacrifice of the Mass, there is the option of consecrating the newly married couple to the Blessed Virgin Mary. There are various forms or options to carry out this humble but very beautiful ceremony. The common occurrence is that before the final blessing in the Mass, the couple processes with a bouquet of flowers to place at the feet of the Blessed Virgin Mary—for example, a statue of Our Lady of Fatima. The couple kneels down in front of the statue and places the flowers before Mary while the *Ave Maria* is being sung. This simple but significant gesture enfolds within it a great depth of meaning. The couple is giving a visible sign that they want to give themselves to Jesus through Mary; they want to consecrate their married life to Jesus through Mary; they want to give their children to Jesus through Mary. In other words, they want to entrust the salvation of their souls and the souls of their children to Jesus through Mary.

Anointing of the Sick and Our Last Hours (Sickness and Death)

Of course, the most important moment in our life is the moment that we die. May the Immaculate Heart of Mary, through her most powerful prayers, obtain for us the grace to receive the last sacraments—confession, Anointing of the Sick, and Viaticum (our last Holy Communion), so as to attain the salvation of our immortal soul! However, may we also receive another special grace from the Immaculate Heart of Mary: that of being surrounded by our loved ones praying the Chaplet of Divine Mercy, as well as the most holy Rosary, in our last and dying moments, and entering thus into the presence of the Blessed Trinity and Mary, our Blessed Mother! What a grace it will be to join with our loved ones, or at least hear our loved ones saying these words, as we breathe forth our soul unto our Creator, our Redeemer, and our Savior: "Holy Mary, Mother of God, pray for us sinners, now and at the hour of our death. Amen!"

By carrying out a consecration at these key moments of life, we set apart and offer to God those moments. For example, if we do a consecration at our wedding, we are asking Mary to make our marriage a gift to God, who will then bless us abundantly.

Whenever we make a Marian consecration, we should be sure to renew it each year, as is the custom. We renew our love for her and our desire to be given over to Jesus through her hands. Let us pray for the grace to consecrate our whole lives, our whole beings, to Jesus through Mary, most especially within the context of the Church and her sacraments.

The Assumption of the Virgin (fresco) / Cardi Cigoli, Ludovico (1559-1613) /
Italian / © Photo: Vincenzo Pirozzi / Bridgeman Images

CHAPTER 22

The Virgin Mary and Spiritual Warfare

Would it surprise you to know that the Bible is bookended by references to an eternal duel between Satan and the Virgin Mary? Let us explain.

In Genesis, right after God confronts Adam and Eve for eating the forbidden fruit, we read what has been called the Protoevangelium, or the "first Gospel." It is the first announcement of the coming of a Savior who would reconcile God's children with Him, and it is directed to the very creature who tempted Eve, and whom this Savior would come to crush. To the serpent, God says: "I will put enmity between you and the woman, and between your seed and her seed; he shall bruise your head, and you shall bruise his heel" (Gn 3:15).

Enmity means "hostility." And the woman in question here is Mary. It is Mary's offspring who will strike at [the] head of our ancient enemy, while Satan will strike at Christ's heel. We can see this as a reference to the Crucifixion, with the heel being a symbol of Christ's humanity, and yet Our Lord would ultimately crush death and Satan with His Resurrection. The "yes" of Eve to a fallen angel is overthrown by the "yes" of Mary to the angel of God. Hence the hostility between Mary and Satan.

If we leap ahead to the last book of the Bible—Revelation—we read in chapter 12 about a battle between a woman and a dragon:

And a great portent appeared in heaven, a woman clothed with the sun, with the moon under her feet, and on her head a crown of twelve stars; she was with child and she cried out in her pangs of birth, in anguish for delivery. And another portent appeared in heaven; behold, a great red dragon, with seven heads and ten horns, and seven diadems upon his heads. His tail swept down a third of the stars of heaven, and cast them to the earth. And the dragon stood before the woman who was about to bear a child, that he might devour her child when she brought it forth; she brought forth a male child, one who is to rule all the nations with a rod of iron, but her child was caught up to God and to his throne, and the woman fled into the wilderness. (Rv 12:1–6)

And just a few verses later, after Michael and the other angels cast the dragon down: "And when the dragon saw that he had been thrown down to the earth, he pursued the woman who had borne the male child. . . . Then the dragon was angry with the woman, and went off to make war on the rest of her offspring, on those who keep the commandments of God and bear testimony to Jesus" (Rv 12:13, 17).

Again, the woman being described here is Mary. She is the woman who brought forth the male child who would "rule all the nations with a rod of iron." And we see the eternal battle again between Mary and Satan, now depicted not as a serpent but as a dragon. He makes war on her offspring, which is clearly us, as we are "those who keep the commandments of God and bear testimony to Jesus." Is there any clearer evidence from Scripture that we are truly Mary's children?

So we can see that, from the beginning to the end of Scripture, there is a constant and mortal battle between good and evil, light and darkness, the devil with his fallen angels and God with His mighty army. And in this battle, the Blessed Virgin Mary has been chosen as one of the Lord's chief allies, friends, and spiritual soldiers. Yes, in one sense, she is a tender mother, soft and beautiful. But be not mistaken, she is also a warrior queen who protects her subjects!

In Guadalajara, Mexico, Our Lady is called *La Generala del Ejercito*—the General and Chief of the army. What a powerful image! In Scripture, we read that she is "terrible as an army with banners" (Sg 6:10).

Let us never forget that our life on earth is constant warfare. As the Bible tells us: "My son, if you come forward to serve the Lord, prepare yourself for temptation" (Sir 2:1). In this battle, in the economy of salvation, Our Lady has an essential role. God has chosen Mary to be Queen in the army of the King, and to labor with the King to conquer the enemy, and that enemy is the devil. We are soldiers in this battle from the crib to the grave!

Perhaps a story from the lives of the saints will help to show this battle being waged within the soul of one man. That man is Blessed Bartolo Longo (1841–1926), but he was not always on the path to sainthood. This young man was brought up in an Italian family with good Catholic roots. However, as is all too common today, as he went off to university, he began to question his faith and became enamored with the promises of the world. To make matters worse, Longo became acquainted with a group of Satanists. Bartolo Longo became so immersed in the devil and this satanic group that he was consecrated as a satanic priest.

A Dominican priest, aware of the plight of Bartolo, decided to pray and fast for this forlorn and lost sheep. Moved by grace, Longo went to the Sacrament of Confession. He seemed to hear a gentle but insistent voice: *"If you want to be saved, pray the Rosary. If you want to be saved, pray and propagate the Rosary."* He would come to know that this was the voice of the Blessed Virgin Mary, Queen of the Rosary. However, hers was not the only voice he heard! Another voice—insidious, malicious, but also insistent—insisted that Bartolo belonged to him. Finally, by a strong act of the will, by corresponding to grace, and through the prayers of she who is known as *full of grace*, Longo decided to denounce his allegiance to the devil and give himself into the hands of Our Lady of the Rosary. He began to pray the Rosary daily and spread news of this powerful prayer to all he encountered.

Because of the prayers, work, and insistence of Blessed Bartolo Longo, eventually a church was established in Naples, Italy with the title Our Lady of the Rosary. Since then, this sanctuary has become one of the most loved and visited Marian sanctuaries in the world.

This man, who was a renegade Catholic, who renounced his Catholic faith so as to become a Satanist; this man who gave his life to the devil, the Father of lies and a murderer from the beginning; this man who was actually consecrated a priest of Satan; this man was converted by the prayers and presence of Our Lady of the Rosary. He was beatified by Pope Saint John Paul II in 1980.

The message is clear. Through the prayers of Mary, and the power of the recitation of the Holy Rosary, the worst of sinners, those who seem to be totally lost, can be converted back to the love of Jesus and the Church and even become great saints! For nothing is impossible with God!

The sacraments are the greatest weapon in spiritual warfare as we battle the devil and his allies, but Our Lady and her Rosary are next in order. Saint Pio of Pietrelcina called the Rosary "the weapon for these times." By "these times," he meant this modern age, when clearly the devil is on the prowl more than ever. Dominicans, as well as Carmelites, wear long rosaries at their sides to imitate knights who wore their swords at their sides. What a powerful image! This can remind us that Our Lady is there to accompany us in all the battles we face if only we would call upon her!

The Marriage of the Virgin (circa 1660-70) / Murillo, Bartolome Esteban /
© Wallace Collection, London, UK / Bridgeman Images

CHAPTER 23

Mary and Saint Joseph

Ornament of the Domestic Life, Loving Spouse of the Mother of God, Foster Father of Jesus, Patron of Families, Patron of the Church, Master of the Interior Life, Patron of Workers, Patron of Purity, Patron of Holy Courtships, Patron of a Holy and Happy Death, Patron of Patience in Tribulations, Terror of Demons!

All of these glorious titles and more are given to the greatest of all saints after the Blessed Virgin Mary—that is, of course, the great Saint Joseph! A serious, fundamental, and comprehensive devotional treatise on the Blessed Virgin Mary would be incomplete if there were not a chapter dedicated to glorious Saint Joseph, the beloved and cherished husband of Mary. Similarly, a life devoted to Mary would be incomplete without a strong devotion to her spouse!

The Holy Family is composed of three persons: Jesus, Mary, and Joseph. Therefore, it is obvious that when talking about Jesus and Mary, good Saint Joseph also occupies an important role and position in the economy of salvation. Yet Joseph is so humble and silent in the Gospels, it is possible for us to forget about him. Let us not make that mistake, for he is a man of heroic virtue, and a man who can pass on his virtues to us.

Some of the most authoritative theologians, as well as Doctors of the Church, such as Saint Frances de Sales and Saint Bernardine of Siena, assert that when God calls an individual to carry out a specific mission, He endows that individual with corresponding and commensurate graces so as to fulfill that mission. It is called "the grace of office." For example, a couple who has received the Sacrament of Holy Matrimony are endowed with the grace to carry out their marriage commitment. That is to say, the grace to be faithful to one another until death parts them, as well as to accept children and raise them as future citizens of the kingdom of God. Also, a man who has been ordained a priest is endowed with grace through the Sacrament of Holy Orders to be a faithful priest—to celebrate worthily and with joy the sacraments, to preach the Word of God with truth, and to work zealously to save souls for the kingdom of God.

In a very true and parallel sense, this grace of office can be applied to Saint Joseph. His mission was most sublime to say the least. Of all the men on earth, Joseph was called by God to carry out with perfect fidelity the role of being the husband of the Blessed Virgin Mary and the earthly father of Jesus, the Son of the living God. How sublime indeed! How ineffable! And with these roles given to Saint Joseph by Almighty God, he was endowed with the most special graces to carry out this double mission to perfection, which indeed he accomplished.

It is true that the marriage between Joseph and Mary was a virginal marriage and commitment. That is to say, both of them, inspired by the Holy Spirit, decided freely to renounce the marital choice of conjugal intimacy. For that reason, the Church has always defended as one of Mary's glorious titles and dogmas her Perpetual Virginity. And it was the most pure and glorious Saint Joseph who defended this most sublime grace and gift.

Yet this lack of conjugal intimacy in no way diminished the utmost sincerity with which they cherished each other. The love that existed between them was both sublime and intimate. They loved each other profoundly in the Holy Spirit. They prayed for each other and they prayed with each other. They were totally united in mind, soul, and spirit—one of the deepest unions that could exist on a human level. Their union was total, complete, undivided, and strong—worthy of the greatest admiration in time and in eternity. Let us briefly highlight some of these areas of undivided unity between Saint Joseph and Mary, his cherished and loving spouse.

Prayer
Both had a most profound prayer life. They prayed individually, they prayed together, and also, they prayed with Jesus, the Son of the living God. Their union in prayer should motivate us to pray all the more and with greater fervor and devotion, especially with our families.

Work
Mary and Joseph worked hard. Joseph worked side by side with Jesus in his carpenter shop. Mary worked diligently as well, attending to all the details of maintaining a household in their little home in Nazareth. However, together they worked chiefly for the honor and glory of God, as a means of being of mutual help to each other, and

> ### Prayer to the Holy Family
>
> Jesus, Mary, and Joseph, I give you my heart and my soul.
> Jesus, Mary, and Joseph, make my heart like unto yours.
> Jesus, Mary, and Joseph, assist me in my last agony.
> Jesus, Mary, and Joseph, I breathe forth my soul unto thee. Amen.

as a model for us to work with diligence, unity, and purpose in our own families so as to build up the kingdom of God.

Family Time

Unfortunately, in our modern culture, we find ourselves being too busy. Yes, as we just noted, we must learn to work hard to support ourselves and our families, but if we are honest, our busyness does not always correspond to our work. There are too many distractions that we let creep in and erode family time. This lifestyle can wreak havoc in our families, and consequently in the world at large. The family is the domestic church, and Pope Saint John Paul II called the family the basic building block of society. The Holy Family teaches us how wrong, divisive, and noxious is this attitude of being too busy for each other.

On a daily basis, we can imagine Mary preparing the dinner meal for the family. We can imagine Saint Joseph arriving home with Jesus after a long, hard, tiring, and yet satisfying day's work and being received warmly and lovingly by Mary. We can imagine the three of them sitting down to a nourishing meal together. We can imagine the simple yet profound and loving conversation that takes place at the dinner table of the Holy Family. They are the best listeners, but they are also the best conversationalists. Why? For the simple reason that Jesus, Mary, and Saint Joseph have a profound love for God, for each other, and for the family—with a full understanding of the importance of the family, which is severely under attack today more than ever before.

Now it is your turn. Try to imagine that you are seated at the dinner table with Jesus, Mary, and Joseph as a welcomed guest. They greet you lovingly and invite you to enter into conversation with them—they ask about your family, your interests, your concerns. Speak to each and every one of them with openness, humility, and love. They will listen to you, help you, and love you. And once you have established this relationship with their family, bring those graces back to your own family.

Litany of Saint Joseph

Lord, have mercy on us.

Christ, have mercy on us.

Lord, have mercy on us.

Christ, hear us.

Christ, graciously hear us.

God the Father of heaven, have mercy on us.

God the Son, Redeemer of the World,
    have mercy on us.

God the Holy Spirit, have mercy on us.

Holy Trinity, one God, have mercy on us.

Holy Mary, pray for us.

Saint Joseph, pray for us.

Renowned offspring of David, pray for us.

Light of Patriarchs, pray for us.

Spouse of the Mother of God, pray for us.

Chaste guardian of the Virgin, pray for us.

Foster father of the Son of God, pray for us.

Diligent protector of Christ, pray for us.

Head of the Holy Family, pray for us.

Joseph most just, pray for us.

Joseph most chaste, pray for us.

Joseph most prudent, pray for us.

Joseph most strong, pray for us.

Joseph most obedient, pray for us.

Joseph most faithful, pray for us.

Mirror of patience, pray for us.

Lover of poverty, pray for us.

Model of artisans, pray for us.

Glory of home life, pray for us.

Guardian of virgins, pray for us.

Pillar of families, pray for us.

Solace of the wretched, pray for us.

Hope of the sick, pray for us.

Patron of the dying, pray for us.

Terror of demons, pray for us.

Protector of Holy Church, pray for us.

Lamb of God, who takes away the sins
    of the world,
        spare us, O Jesus.

Lamb of God, who takes away the sins
    of the world,
        graciously hear us, O Jesus.

Lamb of God, who takes away the sins
    of the world,
        have mercy on us, O Jesus.

He made him the lord of his household
And prince over all his possessions.

Let us pray:

O God, in Your ineffable providence You were pleased to choose Blessed Joseph to be the spouse of Your most holy Mother; grant, we beg You, that we may be worthy to have him for our intercessor in heaven whom on earth we venerate as our Protector: You who live and reign forever and ever.

Saint Joseph, pray for us.

Devotion to Saint Joseph comes in many forms and flavors. There are dozens of traditional Church prayers asking for his intercession. One of the most powerful is the Litany of Saint Joseph, found here and in the back, which we encourage you to pray. Joseph fulfilled the most important mission ever entrusted to a man—to love and protect the two most important people to walk the earth! By remaining close to good Saint Joseph, he will teach us how to enter into a relationship with Jesus and Mary. He will help us to love them as he did, and there is no better life than one spent loving Jesus and Mary!

Saint Joseph, pray for us!

The Holy Family, c.1660-70 / Murillo, Bartolome Esteban (1618-82) / Bridgeman Images

Mary and the Battle for Purity

Spiritual writers assert that we have to defend ourselves against three unrelenting enemies: the devil, the flesh, and the world. The battle ends only when our life comes to an end. How these forces attack us vary based on our own weaknesses and the times in which we live. Now more than ever, temptations wage against the virtue of chastity, or if you like, the virtue of purity.

Our Lady of Fatima revealed a powerful vision of hell on July 13, 1917 to the three shepherd children. With deep sadness, Our Lady stated that most of the souls who go to hell and lose God for all eternity do so because of sins against the virtue of purity. More than one hundred years have passed and the world now offers even more aggressive temptations against this most important virtue. Our purity is constantly assaulted everywhere we look, everywhere we go, from sunup to sundown!

But we know that Jesus wants us to live out this most challenging virtue: "Blessed are the pure of heart, for they will see God" (Mt 5:8). In other words, for us to see God through faith in this life, we must have pure interior vision. The final reward will be to contemplate God forever in heaven through the beatific vision.

A young man destined for great things in the vineyard of the Lord, Anthony Mary Claret, was put to the test. Even in his early years, Anthony had a fervent prayer life, a deep knowledge of God, and clarity of conviction on the importance of striving for holiness and eternal life. However, God allowed young Anthony to be tested. On one occasion, struck with sickness and confined to bed, Anthony was fiercely and insistently attacked by impure thoughts. Being a real soldier of Jesus and Mary, he prayed. Despite his prayers, the temptations did not disappear; rather, they seemed to invade and attack him with even greater violence! It seemed as if all hell was let loose against this young man. As Anthony lay in bed, he opened his eyes only to stare at an army of enemies—evil spirits and devils surrounding him. They wanted to win the victory and tempted Anthony ferociously to give into sin.

When the battle was at its fiercest, Anthony prayed all the more fervently to the Blessed Virgin Mary for help combating this imperious assault. The most pure Virgin and Queen of Heaven and Earth came to his rescue, appearing to him when it seemed as if the battle was lost. The many evil spirits, the evil spirits of impurity, terrified at the presence of the Virgin Mary, fled!

With the devil and his minions vanquished, Anthony was given the very special grace of perfect chastity. He would go on to be ordained a priest and bishop, and he became the founder of the Claretians, who are devoted to spreading

The Assumption of the Virgin (1673) / Cerezo, Mateo / Bridgeman Images

devotion to the Immaculate Heart of Mary. He also became a prolific writer, an eloquent and powerful preacher, a tireless missionary in Spain and even in Cuba, and finally, a great saint, now praising God forever in heaven.

Life is a constant battle. We will have frequent and sometimes powerful temptations. Saint Peter compares the devil to a fierce and roaring lion seeking to devour whomever he can (see 1 Pt 5:8). Therefore, being soldiers of Jesus and Mary, we should know what to do when the attacks descend upon us. We should entrust ourselves to the Blessed Virgin Mary and place all that we have and all that we are in her hands. Pray fervently the prayer that Mary loves most— the Hail Mary, the Angelic Salutation. Mary, most pure and most holy, will rush to your aid and conquer the enemy, as in the case of Saint Anthony Mary Claret and countless other saints who were put to the test. We are all weak, but Jesus and Mary are all-powerful. Let us not rely upon our own strength but in the most powerful intercession of Mary, who is truly the Mother of God, the Mother of the Church, and our loving, pure, and tender mother.

Annunciation (Circa 1767) / Anton Raphael Mengs /
© A. Dagli Orti / © NPL - DeA Picture Library / Bridgeman Images

CHAPTER 24

Mary and the Person of the Holy Spirit

Counselor and Consoler, Paraclete, Interior Master of the Soul, Finger of God, Divine Architect, Sweet Guest of the Soul, Faithful Friend, Gift of Gifts—all of the titles describe in different ways some aspect of the Third Person of the Most Blessed Trinity, the Holy Spirit.

The Blessed Virgin Mary has a profound union with the Triune God—Father, Son, and Holy Spirit. Mary is the daughter of God the Father, the mother of God the Son, and the mystical spouse of the Holy Spirit. Mary's union with the Three Divine Persons is personal, intimate, and profound.

On one occasion, Cardinal Joseph Suenens of Belgium (d. 1996) was asked to celebrate a special outdoor Mass at Duquesne University for the Charismatics—a group known for their love and devotion to the Holy Spirit and His gifts, particularly His charismatic gifts. The outdoor stadium was packed to the gills. All were enthusiastic to participate in the Holy Sacrifice of the Mass. However, there was a serious problem hovering over those present, including Cardinal Suenens: an ominous sky threatened to bring a storm! In a downpour, Mass in the open stadium would have to be cancelled.

Nonetheless, the Mass began and evolved into the Liturgy of the Word with a homily given by the cardinal. One of the most salient points of his homily was related to Mary and the Holy Spirit. The cardinal posed a rhetorical question: "Would you like to know the secret of deep union with the Holy Spirit?" All were listening attentively for the answer. He proceeded: "The secret of deep union with the Holy Spirit is love and devotion to Mary!" As soon as these words were spoken, there came the flash of a white-hot lightning bolt, followed by a clap of thunder! Then, to the utter amazement of all present, the clouds disappeared and a brilliant sun shone down upon the stadium.

The message is as clear as the sun that beamed down on the stadium that day. If we truly desire a deep union with our Triune God, and particularly with the Third Person—the Holy Spirit—we must have true devotion to Mary, we must have a deep and loving relationship with her, who indeed is the daughter of God the Father, the mother of God the Son, and the mystical spouse of the Holy Spirit.

Due to God's loving Divine Providence, from the very moment Mary entered into the world in the womb of her mother Saint Anne, during the whole of her life while on earth, until her last moments before being assumed into heaven, Mary was endowed, permeated, and imbued with the Person of the Holy Spirit. However, there were three primary moments of intimate union that Mary experienced with this Sweet Guest of the Soul—the Holy Spirit of God.

First: The Immaculate Conception

From the first moment of her existence on earth, the Holy Spirit took full and total possession of Mary. In what way? We call it the Immaculate Conception. At the very moment that Mary was conceived in the womb of Saint Anne, her earthly mother, the Holy Spirit was powerfully at work in her little body and soul. Indeed, it was the glorious workings of the Holy Spirit that preserved Mary from the stain of original sin, and therefore, all the effects of original sin. As the English poet Wordsworth so accurately penned: "Mary is our tainted nature's solitary boast." By honoring Mary's Immaculate Conception, we receive signal graces to fight the good fight and run the good race in our battles against the pernicious presence and reality of sin in our lives. May Our Lady and her Mystical Spouse, the Holy Spirit, help us to triumph over all forms of sin in our mortal bodies in preparation for our eternal life!

Second: The Virginal Conception (Lk 1:26–38)

In the history of the world and in the economy of salvation, the moment in which the Virginal Conception of the Son of God in Mary's womb took place transformed humanity and its destiny. The Virginal Conception is a result of the message of the Archangel Gabriel to the Blessed Virgin Mary in which God invited Mary to become the Mother of God. Giving her full and total consent, Mary said: "Behold, I am the handmaid of the Lord; let it be done to me according to your word" (Lk 1:38). At that moment, Mary was overshadowed by the Holy Spirit and conceived Jesus in her most pure womb. "And the Word became flesh and dwelt among us" (Jn 1:14). Therefore, both Mary's Virginal Conception and the Incarnation of the Son of God were accomplished by the power and workings of the Holy Spirit. Our Lady and her deep union with the Holy Spirit can attain for us all great purity of mind, memory, understanding, and affections of body and soul.

Third: Pentecost (Acts 2)

The word *Pentecost* means "fifty"; this means the feast refers to the fifty days after the Resurrection of Our Lord and Savior Jesus Christ. That first Pentecost effected a powerful transformation in the apostles. However, that transformation was preceded by a novena—nine days and nine nights in which the apostles, united with Mary, the Mother of God, were praying and fasting in silence. It was only after the novena that the Holy Spirit came down upon Mary and the apostles with a powerful wind, a shaking of the room where they were praying, and tongues of fire that settled over their heads. As a result, these twelve apostles who were fearful, confused, and lacking in faith just a few days prior were transformed into valiant soldiers of Jesus and Mary! All of the apostles, with the exception of Saint John the Evangelist, received the glorious crown of martyrdom—that is to say, they shed their blood in imitation of their Master, who shed His Precious Blood for them and for us on the cross. Indeed, it was the Holy Spirit who descended in power, wind, and fire. However, it must be noted that it was the Blessed Virgin Mary whose prayers and presence facilitated the coming of the Holy Spirit. If we desire in our lives to experience a powerful infusion and outpouring of the Holy Spirit, then we should turn to Mary and beg for her prayers and intercession!

These three events show the intimate connection Mary has with her Mystical Spouse, which is only deeper now as she reigns in heaven as Queen. Therefore, in our devotion to the Blessed Virgin Mary, let us never neglect to turn to her so that she might attain for us this special union with the Holy Spirit. Let us pray frequently: "Come Holy Spirit, come to us through the Heart of Mary."

Come, Holy Spirit, fill the hearts of Your faithful and enkindle in them the fire of Your love.

V. Send forth Your Spirit and they shall be created.
R. *And You shall renew the face of the earth.*

Let us pray: O God, Who did instruct the hearts of the faithful by the light of the Holy Spirit, grant us in the same Spirit to be truly wise, and ever to rejoice in His consolations. Through Christ Our Lord. Amen.

The Virgin of the Host (1866) / Ingres, Jean Auguste Dominique /
Bridgeman Images

Mary and the Most Holy Eucharist

In *Sacrosanctum Concilium*—the Constitution on the Sacred Liturgy, a Vatican II document—we read that the Mass is the source and summit of our life. In other words, the very high point, pinnacle, apex, zenith of our earthly life becomes a reality with the celebration of Holy Mass.

At the moment of the consecration, when the priest pronounces the words, "Take and eat, this is my Body; take and drink, this is my Blood; do this in memory of me," Jesus truly becomes present on the altar in His Body, Blood, Soul, and Divinity.

In various ways, both the Holy Sacrifice of the Mass and the celebration of the Holy Eucharist can be related and connected to the Blessed Virgin Mary. Let us present some ways for our reflection, prayer, and meditation.

Mary's Fiat and Our Holy Communion

Pope Saint John Paul II offers us a brilliant, mystical Eucharistic insight on the relationship between the Annunciation and our worthy reception of the Holy Eucharist. He notes that when the Blessed Virgin Mary gave her consent to the Archangel Gabriel with the words, "Behold, I am the handmaid of the Lord; be it done to me according to your word" (Lk 1:38), she was in that moment overshadowed by the Holy Spirit, receiving Jesus into her womb and into the very depths of her most pure and Immaculate Heart. Pope John Paul II explains that when we approach the altar to receive Holy Communion and respond by saying "Amen," it is similar to the "yes" of Mary—her *fiat*—to the archangel Gabriel. Both her "yes" and our "amen" result in the reception of Jesus into our innermost being—into Mary's womb and, likewise, into our very depths as well. If we really have an ardent desire to receive Jesus with greater purity of heart, greater fervor, and greater love, then we should make the effort and strive to receive Holy Communion through the presence and intercession of Mary in the moment we receive our Eucharistic Lord. As Mary undoubtedly received Jesus with lively faith, profound humility, and burning love, so she can attain for us more efficacious communions that will help us live out the Pauline expression "It is no longer I who live, but Christ who lives in me" (Gal 2:20).

The Visitation and the Effects of Holy Communion

As a follow-up to the mystery of the Annunciation and Mary receiving Jesus through her *fiat*, we have the mystery of the Visitation. What is the lesson that Mary teaches us in this gospel episode that relates to the Holy Sacrifice of the Mass and Holy Communion? Simply this: Mary teaches us that receiving Jesus into our hearts should be a powerful motivation for all of us not to keep Jesus to ourselves in a selfish way. On the contrary, the reception of Jesus in Holy Communion should result in an explosion of fraternal charity and service in our heart, in the sense that we cannot keep Jesus to ourselves but feel the irresistible motivation to bring Him to others with our words and our deeds. Upon receiving Jesus at the Annunciation, Mary went *in haste* to bring Jesus to her cousin Elizabeth, who was with child, Saint John the Baptist, in her womb. May we also go *in haste* to bring the love of Jesus whom we have just received to others!

The Visitation and Mary as Patron of Eucharistic Processions—Corpus Christi

The Blessed Virgin Mary, after conceiving Jesus within her womb, traveled approximately eighty miles to visit her cousin Elizabeth in the town of Ain Karem. It was located in the hill country, so Mary had to climb an ascending terrain. However, it is worthy of note that during this long journey of the Blessed Virgin Mary, which obviously took several days, *she carried Jesus within her*. Thus, in a very real sense, Mary was a living tabernacle, a living monstrance, a living sanctuary! Still more, it can be said that the Blessed Virgin Mary was also a living and moving Corpus Christi! Or if you like, Mary in her very being, with Jesus alive in her womb, was a living Eucharistic procession! Immediately after receiving Jesus in Holy Communion, we too are a moving Corpus Christi, we too are a living Eucharistic procession! Thus, Mary teaches us to receive Jesus in Holy Communion with lively faith, profound humility, and burning love that carries over into our daily lives and daily encounters! Moreover, Mary was constantly communing or conversing with Jesus, who lived within her. Thus, Mary teaches us to continue with faith, love, and devotion, visiting with, talking to, and

> O Sacrament most holy, O Sacrament divine,
>
> all praise and all thanksgiving, be every moment Thine!

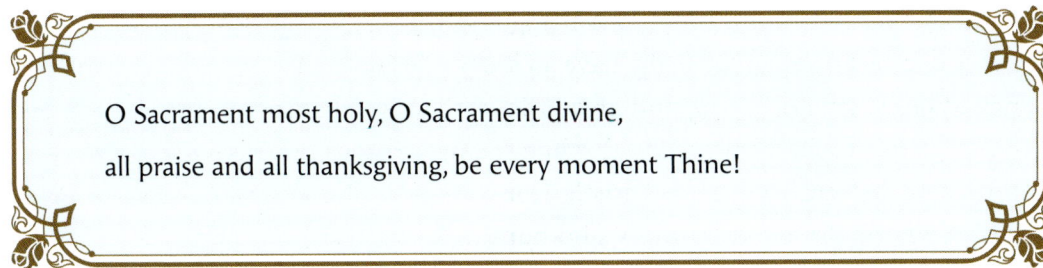

adoring Jesus who is truly present in us after receiving Holy Communion, who is truly present in the Blessed Sacrament, who is truly present in the tabernacle, who is truly present in the monstrance! "O come let us adore Him!"

Mary Greets Elizabeth

But it does not end there. Arriving at the home of Elizabeth and Zachariah, Mary greets Elizabeth, most likely with the word *Shalom* (peace). As soon as Mary speaks, the baby in Elizabeth's womb, John the Baptist, leaps with joy, all through the word of Mary and the silent presence of Jesus in the womb of Mary! Like John the Baptist, through Mary's intercession, may our encounters with Jesus in Holy Communion be moments of great joy, moments of deep conversion, moments of growing friendship with Jesus, our Eucharistic Lord! And may we bring this joy to others!

There are so many lessons for us here in this brief span of days that connect the Annunciation and the Visitation—splendid lessons for all of us to meditate upon and try to put into practice in our daily lives. May Mary's "yes" to receiving Jesus into her womb and her Immaculate Heart motivate us to receive Jesus with greater love, fervor, and frequency in Holy Communion! May Mary's love for Jesus expressed in her love for neighbor, motivate us to bring forth the fruits of our Holy Communions in loving service of our neighbor! May Our Lady as the living tabernacle of the Incarnate Jesus draw us like a magnet to the tabernacle to visit the Eucharistic Jesus, talk to the Eucharistic Jesus, entrust our cares to the Eucharistic Jesus, and love the Eucharistic Jesus with all our heart, mind, soul, and strength so that when we go out into the world and encounter others, they leap with joy like John the Baptist because we carry Jesus in our hearts!

The Assumption of the Virgin by Michel Sittow (Master Michiel) (c. 1469-1525), Oil On Panel, c. 1500,
National Gallery of Art, Washington / © Stefano Bianchetti / Bridgeman Images

CHAPTER 26

Mary and the Angels

As we have seen thus far, there are many honorific titles attributed to the Blessed Virgin Mary. She is the Daughter of God the Father, the Mother of God the Son, and the Mystical Spouse of God the Holy Spirit. In Marian litanies, we know her as the Mystical Rose, the Tower of Ivory, the House of God, the Ark of the Covenant, the Cedar of Lebanon, and the Queen of Virgins, Confessors, Martyrs, and Saints. However, the topic of our present chapter involves her title as Mary, Queen of Angels!

There are different levels of perfection in the ladder of God's creation. We see this by our own intuition, knowing a rock is something less than a plant, and yet an animal as something more than a plant. Then we, human beings, who were created in the image and likeness of God, rise above the other animals in dignity.

But exalted even above the creation of the human person, man and woman, was the creation of the angels, pure heavenly spirits. God actually created them even before the creation of the natural universe, including the human person.

Myriad upon myriads of angels were created, each of them reflecting God's glory in their own way. They have an intellect and a will, like us, but possess a superior knowledge and vision of God. Thanks to the Angelic Doctor, Saint Thomas Aquinas, the angels have been divided into choirs, some more brilliant and perfect than others of lower rank:

1. The Guardian Angels
2. The Archangels
3. The Principalities

4. The Powers
5. The Virtues
6. The Dominations
7. The Thrones
8. The Cherubim
9. The Seraphim

If an angel were to appear to us—even just our guardian angel, the lowest rank—as has happened often in the lives of the saints, our natural reaction would be to fall to our knees in rapt veneration of the beauty, the majesty, and the splendor of the angelic being. And yet, the Blessed Virgin Mary far surpasses the beauty, majesty, and splendor of the angels, such that when the angels approach her, it is they who are overcome by her presence, as they reverence her as their heavenly Queen.

But how does the loving bond between Mary and the angels affect us when both parties are so far beyond us in holiness and splendor? To answer this question, let us meditate on the event of the Annunciation, when the Archangel Gabriel appeared to Mary with the good news that she was to become the Mother of God. This is the only instance in which we have scriptural documentation of Mary's interaction with the angels, represented by Gabriel.

Read carefully and meditate on this key passage:

In the sixth month the angel Gabriel was sent from God to a city of Galilee named Nazareth, to a virgin betrothed to a man whose name was Joseph, of the house of David; and the virgin's name was Mary. And he came to her and said, "Hail, full of grace, the Lord is with you!" But she was greatly troubled at the saying, and considered in her mind what sort of greeting this might be.

And the angel said to her, "Do not be afraid, Mary, for you have found favor with God. And behold, you will conceive in your womb and bear a son, and you shall call his name Jesus. He will be great, and will be called the Son of the Most High; and the Lord God will give to him the throne of his father David, and he will reign over the house of Jacob forever; and of his kingdom there will be no end."

And Mary said to the angel, "How can this be, since I have no husband?"

And the angel said to her, "The Holy Spirit will come upon you, and the power of the Most High will overshadow you; therefore the child to be born will be called holy, the Son of God. And behold, your kinswoman Elizabeth in her old age has also conceived a son; and this is the sixth month with her who was called barren. For with God nothing will be impossible."

And Mary said, "Behold, I am the handmaid of the Lord; let it be to me according to your word." And the angel departed from her. (Lk 1:26–38)

This sublime encounter between Mary and the Archangel Gabriel radically transformed the history of the world. If we study this interaction, we discover that both Mary and Gabriel are teaching us many important lessons about the spiritual life:

Hail, Full of Grace

The words of the Archangel Gabriel are "Hail, full of grace." This of course begins the well-known Hail Mary prayer. In fact, the Hail Mary is also called "The Angelic Salutation"—meaning, the greeting of the angel. Therefore, every time we pray the Hail Mary, first and foremost we honor Mary, full of grace, and secondarily, we honor the Archangel Gabriel.

Hail, a Royal Greeting

Furthermore, we see that the Angel greeted Mary with the salutation of "Hail," which is a greeting for royalty. This shows us with what esteem the angels hold Mary, and so we should as well. We may ask for the angels' assistance in learning how to treat Mary as our Queen.

The Archangel Gabriel and the Virginal Conception

The conversation between Mary and Gabriel continues. The archangel reveals that Mary will conceive a child through the overshadowing and power of the Holy Spirit. We call this Mary's Virginal Conception. We must honor this great mystery of the faith whenever we can and ask that Mary and Gabriel give us the grace to pursue angelic purity in our own personal lives.

The Miracle and Sign of another Child with a Mission

The archangel encourages Mary by highlighting another miracle: Mary's aged cousin, Elizabeth, is pregnant with a child. Yes, Gabriel reveals the person of John the Baptist, who is to be born of an elderly and sterile woman. "For nothing is impossible for God." The presence of the angels, under the command of Mary, can also perform stupendous miracles in our own lives if only we have the faith to believe.

The Name above All Names: Jesus!

What a sublime task and mission the heavenly Father entrusts to the Archangel Gabriel—to announce to the Blessed Virgin Mary the actual name that she will give (along with Saint Joseph) to the God Child. The name which is a name above all other names is that of Jesus! Mary and the Archangel Gabriel can help us to praise the Holy Name of Jesus—in our words and in our lives—if we ask for their help.

Mary's Silence before Her Consent to the Angel Gabriel

Of course, Mary, the great contemplative, would have pondered seriously this most sublime message of the Incarnation in silence. The angels, and Mary, the Queen of the Angels, both teach us the importance of a life of contemplation, of silence, of prayer and reflection, before we act.

The Annunciation, detail of St. Gabriel the Archangel (1501) by Pinturicchio

Mary's Generous Response to the Archangel Gabriel

Mary responds to the Archangel Gabriel with her *fiat*, her generous and total affirmative response: "Behold, I am the handmaid of the Lord; be it done to me according to your will." In imitation of Mary, we too are called and challenged to be more docile, open, and generous in our response to God. By meditating on this interaction between Mary and Gabriel, we mysteriously learn to accept this spirit of trust in God.

And the Word Became Flesh and Dwelt Among Us

The result of Mary's "yes" to God was the Incarnation of the Word. In that moment, Mary conceived by the power of the Holy Spirit. Instrumental in this sublime moment in the history of salvation was the presence of the Archangel Gabriel. With the assistance of Mary and the Archangel Gabriel we can receive Jesus into our hearts, minds, and souls in Holy Communion. Let us beg Mary, the Queen of the Angels, to send these heavenly messengers to help us to receive Jesus in Holy Communion with greater recollection, faith, fervor, devotion, and love.

The Archangel Gabriel: Modern Patron of Communication

During his pontificate, Pope Saint Paul VI proclaimed the Archangel Gabriel as the modern patron of communication. The reason behind this proclamation? Quite simply because Gabriel announced to Mary and the world at large the most important message possible: that Jesus would come as the Savior of the whole human race through the *fiat* of Mary. Our Lady, the Queen of Angels, with the help and assistance of the Archangel Gabriel, can help us to use our words, our language, and our conversation as a powerful means to communicate the Gospel—the Good News of salvation.

The Annunciation/Incarnation Passage

While we must make a daily habit of reading Sacred Scripture, meditating on this passage in particular in Luke's Gospel is of primary importance. The most common interpretation or title for this passage is that of the Annunciation, but it is also when the Incarnation took place. The Annunciation refers to the verbal announcement to Mary that she would be the Mother of Jesus, whereas the Incarnation refers to the result of Mary's consent and the taking of flesh by Jesus in her most pure womb. This moment began the life of Jesus on earth, which would split time and history in two. By meditating on the mystery of the Incarnation, the other mysteries of the faith begin to gain clarity in our minds and hearts. If we ask them to, Mary and Gabriel, and the rest of the angels, will nurture our meditation of this event and of the rest of the scriptures, enlightening us to God's life-giving truths.

Though we are a different form of God's creation, we share a common Queen with the angels. By uniting ourselves to them under the mantle of the Blessed Virgin Mary, they are all the more ready to come to our assistance when we need it, fighting our spiritual battles that take place beyond the reach of our eyes. We know this, because we know Our Lady will send them to us, and loving her as they do, they will obey her call.

Let us humbly beg the Archangel Gabriel, and all the angels in heaven, to help us come to know Mary, love Mary, and entrust our lives to Mary so that one day we will be her loving sons and daughters forever in heaven.

Prayer to Mary, Mistress of the Angels

O Exalted Queen of Heaven, Sovereign Mistress of the Angels, thou who from the beginning hast received from God the power and the mission to crush the head of Satan, we humbly beseech thee to send down thy holy angels, that under thy command and by thy power, they may pursue the evil spirits, encounter them on every side, resist their bold attacks and drive them hence into the abyss of hell.

"Who is like unto God?" "Holy Angels and Archangels, defend us and protect us!" "O kind and tender Mother, thou shalt ever remain our love and our hope." Amen.

O MARIE CONQUE SANS PÉCHÉ PRIEZ POUR NOUS QUI AVONS RECOURS A VOUS

Apparition of the Virgin to St. Catherine Laboure / Le Cerf, (fl.1835) /
French / © Archives Charmet / Bridgeman Images

CHAPTER 27

Marian Saints

The saints are God's best friends, but they are also *our* friends, men and women who have left us an illuminating path to follow on our journey to heaven. The saints can help us in a variety of ways. First, they can pray for us and attain for us signal graces so that we can grow in grace, persevere in a state of grace, and die in a state of grace. Second, the saints are models for us to emulate. All of us need models after whom we can pattern our lives; the saints are those models. As we study their lives and their works, we can grow to be like them. Third, we are never truly alone because even though we do not see them with our eyes, the saints, like the angels, are present with us. If you like, the saints are our faithful friends, always at our side ready to intercede for us, to assist us, and to help us on our pilgrimage to heaven.

One of the hallmarks of the saints is their strong love and devotion to Mary. While every saint loved the Blessed Virgin Mary, there are some whom we might label as "Marian saints" because their life and work in a special way propagated devotion to the Mother of God. No list like this is exhaustive, and we will set aside some saints who are discussed in other chapters of this text, such as those tied to Marian apparitions (Saint Bernadette, Saint Catherine Laboure, the children of Fatima, etc.), as well as what we might call the "biblical saints" who loved Mary (John, Elizabeth, Joseph, etc.). Nonetheless, the following saints are special jewels in the Blessed Virgin's crown, shining for all to see. It is this crown she wears as the Queen of the Saints!

Saint Cyril of Alexandria (376–444)

Thanks be to God for this great saint of the early Church, Cyril of Alexandria, who gave us the Marian dogmatic proclamation in the year AD 431 at the Council of Ephesus that Mary is the *Theotokos*—the God-bearer. Indeed, this great Marian saint and defender of Mary's Divine Maternity should rouse us to look with confidence into the eyes of Mary and tenderly call her mother!

Santo Domingo de Guzmán (circa 1685) by Claudio Coello

Saint Dominic (1170–1221)

Dominic Guzman was a Spanish saint and Catholic priest and founder of the Dominican Order. During the course of his life, the Albigensian heresy was spreading across Europe. This heretical teaching, which maintained that all material creation was evil, was tearing many souls away from the Catholic faith. Tradition tells us that Mary appeared to Dominic and told him to defeat this awful heresy through the power of her Rosary. Saint Dominic did just this, preaching about the power of praying the Rosary to defeat the heretics. To this day, the Rosary is a central piece of Dominican life.

Saint John of the Cross (1545–1591) and Saint Teresa of Avila (1515–1582)

These two Carmelite saints had a great devotion to Our Lady, but most especially Our Lady of Mount Carmel and the scapular. The typical depiction of Our Lady of Mount Carmel is that she is dressed in brown and wearing a long brown scapular over her dress, in the front and the back. The Carmelite saints should encourage all of us to have an ardent desire to wear the scapular of Our Lady of Mount Carmel as the exterior sign of our consecration to Mary. We should kiss the scapular frequently as a sign of our love for Mary and promote others to wear the scapular as a sign of their consecration to Mary.

Saint Louis de Montfort (1673–1716)

Of all the ways we can reach heaven, Saint Louis de Montfort offers us the key: true devotion to Mary! This was the title of his early eighteenth-century work *True Devotion to Mary*. As he predicted, saying devils would come to take his work away, the book was lost for many years, only to be rediscovered through the hands of Providence in 1842. This work is the primary source for spreading and explaining Marian Consecration. Many lives have been transformed by this book, including that of Pope Saint John Paul II, who said it was the "decisive turning point" of his life. Millions of copies have been sold all across the world in dozens of languages. It is a must-read for all children of Mary!

Saint Alphonsus Liguori

Saint Alphonsus Liguori (1696–1787)

A towering giant of a saint, Saint Alphonsus had an overflowing love for and devotion to Mary. So strong was his devotion to her that he penned and published one of the greatest literary masterpieces on the Blessed Virgin Mary in the history of the Church, titled *The Glories of Mary*. In addition to this Marian masterpiece that all lovers of Mary should read with devotion, Alphonsus founded a new congregation, the Congregation of the Most Holy Redeemer, known as the Redemptorists. The Marian title and patroness for the Redemptorists is Our Lady of Perpetual Help—a title very dear not only to Catholics in America but in the Philippines as well.

Saint John Bosco (1815–1888)

Following on the heels of Saint Alphonsus, we encounter the great saint of the nineteenth century, Saint John Bosco. A man of extraordinary gifts and talents, John Bosco had a filial and loving devotion to Mary. It was under the title Our Lady Help of Christians that Bosco would frequently have recourse to her. One of the most majestic churches in Italy can be found in the northern city of Turin, the Basilica of Our Lady Help of Christians. It was built by John Bosco and now contains his remains. He didn't have the money to pay for it when the contractor began the work, but Bosco assured him Our Lady would provide the money needed. And she did! Our Lady is always ready and willing to help us, if we simply call out to her!

Saint Maximilian Kolbe (1894–1941)

This modern saint died in Auschwitz, the German concentration camp of World War II. When a prisoner in the camp escaped, ten men were selected at random to die. Maximilian sacrificially volunteered his life to save the life of a man with a family. The ten were starved to death in an underground bunker. Maximilian survived the longest and received a lethal injection of carbolic acid to hasten his death. During his life, he had a fiery devotion to the Blessed Virgin Mary, forming the Militia of the Immaculata, a spiritual "army," a valiant group of soldiers under the leadership of Mary. He loved the Miraculous Medal and would distribute it far and wide with the purpose of converting souls through Mary. He called the medals his "spiritual bullets." His missionary efforts under the mantle of Mary extended from Europe to Japan.

Saint Teresa of Calcutta (1910–1997) and Pope Saint John Paul II (1920–2005)

Like Saint Maximilian Kolbe, Mother Teresa of Calcutta had the practice of distributing the Miraculous Medal—she actually gave one to me the day after my ordination to the priesthood, as well as to my family, when the Missionaries of Charity invited us to visit them. Mother Teresa knelt before me, a newly ordained priest, kissed my hands, and then asked for my priestly blessing. Only the day before, Pope John Paul II had placed his hands upon my head and ordained me a priest forever! Then as a gift, the saintly pope gave me a rosary, symbolic of my life as a priest and member of the religious order, the Oblates of the Virgin Mary, as well as symbolic of my call to become an apostle propagating Mary and the Rosary. Both Pope Saint John Paul II and Saint Teresa of Calcutta had a very special love for Mary and the Rosary.

For his part, Pope John Paul II took for his motto *totus tuus* (meaning *totally yours* Mary), and had an *M* for Mary placed on his papal coat of arms, below the arm of the cross, to symbolize Mary standing at the foot of the cross. He also gave us the great gift of the Luminous Mysteries of the Rosary and constantly implored his spiritual children to pray the Rosary daily. Finally, Pope John Paul II is also closely tied to Our Lady of Fatima through his attempted assassination attempt on May 13, 1981 (the anniversary of the first apparition at Fatima) and his subsequent efforts to consecrate the world to the Immaculate Heart of Mary. When he recovered from the attempt on his life, he journeyed to Fatima to place the bullet in her crown, thanking her for her intercession and for saving his life.

Mother Teresa also had a special love for the Rosary. We can see many pictures of her holding a rosary in her hands. It is said that, while walking with her nuns, when one of them asked what the distance was from one place to the next, Mother Teresa would respond by saying the number of Rosaries that could be recited! She also had a heart tied closely to Our Lady of Sorrows, having suffered from the dark night of the soul for most of her adult life.

The Saints Speak about Mary

Having met a few Marian saints, let us now close out this chapter by meditating on some of the words of these saints and others about our Blessed Mother.

"If the horror of sin terrifies you and the voice of conscience overwhelms you, if the fear of judgment, the depths of sadness, and the abyss of despair assail you, think of Mary. In dangers, troubles and sin think of Mary and call upon her."
—Saint Bernard

"God has decreed that the whole of Redemption should be accomplished through Mary, with Mary, and in Mary. Just as nothing was created without Christ, so nothing has been re-created without the Blessed Virgin."
—Saint Peter Damian

"What greater prodigy could the world behold than a woman become the Mother of God and a God clothed in human flesh? Mary, by her humility, became the Mother of the Creator. The Creator, in His goodness, became the Son of His own creature!"
—Saint Alphonsus Maria Liguori

"The Fathers of the Church recognized the tremendous praise heaped on Mary in Scriptures. She is singled out as having a King for her father (the noble David) and the King of kings and Lord of lords for her Son, whose reign will never end."
—Saint Peter Canisius

"Those who want to prevent their heart from being pervaded by the evils of earth should entrust it to the Blessed Virgin, our Lady and our Mother. They will then regain it in heaven, freed from all evils."
—Saint Francis de Sales

"We are all children of Eve according to the flesh, and children of the Blessed Virgin according to the spirit. For all of us, Mary has the love of a mother and the courage of a defender. All find room in her. Sinners find pardon through her prayers, and the righteous are preserved in grace."
—Saint John of Avila

"Open your heart to faith, O Blessed Virgin Mary, your lips to praise, your womb to the Creator. See, the Desired of All Nations is at your door, knocking to enter. Arise in faith, hasten in devotion, open in praise and thanksgiving."
—Saint Bernard

"Entrust your cause to her who is the Mother of mercy, and zealously offer her day by day most special marks of reverence. Endeavor to maintain within body and soul the spotlessness of her purity and walk in her footsteps, humbly and gently like her."
—Saint Bonaventure

"At the moment when Mary presents her Son to the Magi, she not only performs a personal action as Mother, but also acts as the figure of the Church. As the mother of all peoples, the Church, in the person of Mary, initiates her work of evangelization."
— Pope Saint John Paul II

"Happy are those to whom the Holy Spirit reveals the Secret of Mary in order that they may come to know her. Happy are those to whom He opens the 'Enclosed Garden' and to whom He gives access to the 'Sealed Fountain' that they may drink of the living waters of grace."
— Saint Louis de Montfort

"Seek refuge in Mary because she is the city of refuge. We know that Moses set up three cities of refuge for anyone who inadvertently killed his neighbor. Now the Lord has established a refuge of Mercy, Mary, even for those who deliberately commit evil. Mary provides refuge and strength for the sinner."
— Saint Anthony of Padua

"The Eternal Father delights in regarding the Heart of the Blessed Virgin Mary as the masterpiece of His hands. The Son delights in it as the Heart of His Mother, the source from which He received the Blood that redeemed us. The Holy Spirit dwells in Mary as in a temple."
— Saint John Marie Vianney, the Cure of Ars

"Let Mary never be far from your lips or heart. With her support, you will never fall. Beneath her protection, you will never fear. Under her guidance, you will never tire. And with her help, you will reach your heavenly goal."
— Saint Bernard

"True devotion to Mary is disinterested. True clients of Mary serve her not because they seek earthly gain, nor even corporal or spiritual well-being, but because she deserves to be served—and God alone in her. . . . True devotion to Mary is constant. It strengthens us in good and makes us courageous in opposing the world, the flesh, and the devil. Those devoted to Mary live by the faith of Jesus and Mary, not the sentiments of nature. . . . True devotion to Mary is holy. It leads us to avoid sin and to imitate the virtues of Mary: her deep humility, lively faith, ready obedience, continuous prayer, universal mortification, divine purity, ardent charity, heroic patience, angelic sweetness, and heavenly wisdom. . . . True devotion to Mary is tender. It is full of confidence in Mary, like a child's confidence in its mother. This ensures that we will run to Mary in all our needs. . . . True devotion to Mary is internal, starting from the spirit and the heart. It flows from the esteem we bear toward Mary, the sublime idea we have of her greatness, and the love we feel for her."
— Saint Louis de Montfort

Statue of the Virgin Mary in St Bavo's Cathedral of Ghent.
Photo by Javier Navero / Shutterstock

CHAPTER 28

Marian Feasts

Pope Saint Paul VI wrote a short, clear, and inspiring document on the role and place of the Blessed Virgin Mary in the context of the Church's liturgical year. The name of this document that we encourage for your reading and prayerful meditation is *Marialis Cultus*—meaning the "Cult given to Mary." Underneath the name of the document, the saintly pope wrote, "For the right ordering and development of devotion to the Blessed Virgin Mary." This Mariological apostolic exhortation was published February 2, 1974.

Mary is not separate from the Church, or even parallel to the Church, but is a most preeminent member of the Church. The Vatican II document *Lumen Gentium*, chapter 8, states that Mary is the first disciple of Christ. And indeed, she is the Mother of the Church as well!

Therefore, it is fitting that the Church would honor her at various times throughout the year. Not all of them are holy days of obligation (though some are); still, we encourage you to attend Mass on these special days and receive Holy Communion to honor Mary, your mother, and Mother of the Church.

In this list, we will follow the Church year, beginning with the Church New Year, which starts with the season of Advent and ends with the solemnity of Christ the King—the end of the Church liturgical cycle.

December 8—Solemnity of the Immaculate Conception

The Church celebrates with intense joy Mary's privilege of the Immaculate Conception. Mary was conceived in the womb of her mother, Saint Anne, and preserved from the stain of original sin from the very moment of her conception. Mary under her title of the Immaculate Conception is patroness of the United States of America.

December 12—Our Lady of Guadalupe

With great joy, especially in the Mexican and Latin American cultures, the Church celebrates the Feast Day of Our Lady of Guadalupe, who appeared in 1531 to Saint Juan Diego, encouraging him, and all of us, to trust in her motherly love. Through the visions of Our Lady of Guadalupe, millions were brought into her Son's Church.

December 25—Solemnity of Christmas

The Solemnity of Christmas is the celebration of the most important birthday in the history of humanity—the birthday of Jesus. However, we cannot separate Our Lord's birthday from the person whom God used to bring Jesus into this world—the Blessed Virgin Mary. We contemplate the Infant Child Jesus in the arms of Mary.

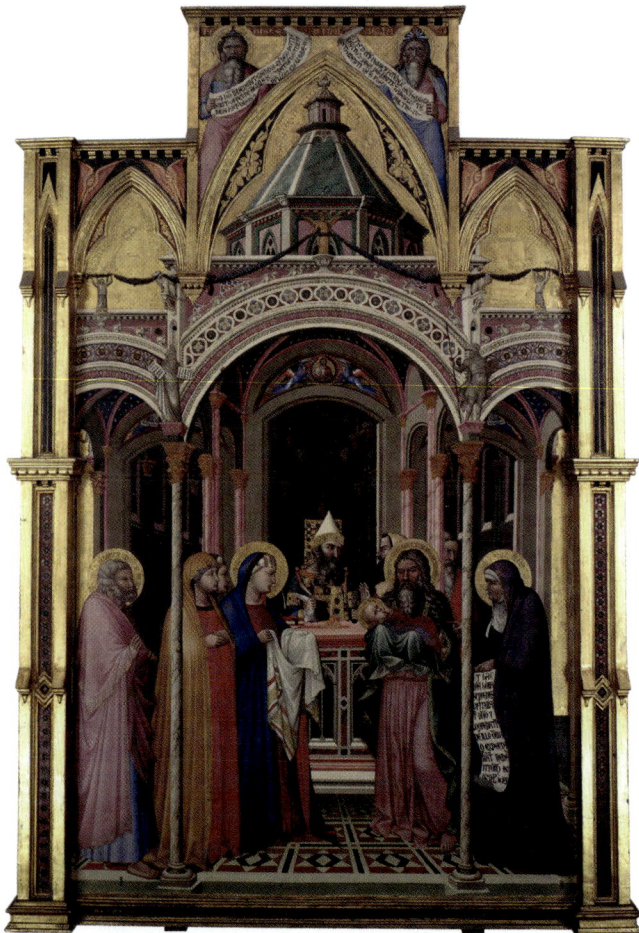

Presentation of Jesus in the Temple (1342) by Ambrogio Lorenzetti

January 1—Solemnity of Mary, the Holy Mother of God

A little less than a week after Christmas, we enter into a New Year with the Solemnity of Mary, the Holy Mother of God. What an extraordinary way to start off the New Year— placing ourselves in the arms of Mary, who is the Mother of God, the Mother of the Church, and our own dear and loving Mother.

February 2—The Presentation of Jesus in the Temple

Forty days after Christmas, the Child Jesus was presented in the Temple of Jerusalem. The prophet Simeon, who had been waiting many years for the Messiah, saw Jesus in the arms of Mary and recognized Jesus as the Light to all the nations. Then the elderly holy man predicted a sorrow that would pierce the heart of His Mother. "(and a sword will pierce through your own soul also), that thoughts out of many hearts may be revealed" (Lk 2:35). In the Hispanic culture, this is a day in which many come to Church and present their little statues of the Child Jesus to be blessed. Often Hispanics will bring their newly born babe to be presented in the Temple after thirty days of birth.

February 11—Our Lady of Lourdes

In 1858, Our Lady appeared eighteen times to a poor, sickly, little peasant girl named Bernadette Soubirous. She finally revealed her name to Bernadette and the world at large, lifting her eyes to heaven and proclaiming: "I am the Immaculate Conception." This was proclaimed as a dogma only four years earlier in 1854 by Pope Pius IX. Our Lady of Lourdes also revealed to Bernadette (now Saint Bernadette!) the location of a spring of water that brought forth miraculous healings. Millions still today flock to the shrine where this spring of water is located.

March 25—Solemnity of the Annunciation

The Solemnity of the Annunciation is often celebrated in the context of Lent. It is of profound importance because it recalls the moment when the Blessed Virgin Mary freely and willingly consented to being the Mother of God. For Mary's "yes," we offer her infinite gratitude. Thank you, Mother Mary! Jesus came into the world through Mary, and Jesus wants us to come to Him through Mary. Let us never forget this!

May 13—Our Lady of Fatima

May is the month of Mary. However, in a very special way on May 13, the Church honors Our Lady of Fatima, who appeared six times to three little shepherd children: Lucia, Francisco, and Jacinta. Every time she appeared, Mary said to pray the Rosary for world peace and for the family. For that reason, Our Lady of Fatima is also known as Our Lady of the Rosary.

May 31—The Visitation of Mary to Saint Elizabeth

On this wonderful feast, we recall the great charity of Mary who moved in haste to help her elderly cousin Elizabeth, serving her needs as she prepares to give birth to Saint John the Baptist. May we imitate Mary's charity in our own lives!

June 4—Immaculate Heart of Mary

In June, after the Solemnity of the Most Sacred Heart of Jesus, which falls on Friday, the following day the Church celebrates the Feast of the Immaculate Heart of Mary. These two hearts are always beating in unison. These hearts love us intensely. We can always find refuge in these two hearts.

July 16—Our Lady of Mount Carmel

Every year in the middle of July, the Church celebrates the Feast of Our Lady of Mount Carmel. Among the many important notes is the importance of wearing the brown scapular of Our Lady of Mount Carmel that she gave to Saint Simon Stock. It is the exterior sign of our belonging to Mary. We are in Mary's family, and this is the sign for the world to see.

The Death and the Assumption of the Virgin / Coxcie, Michiel (1499-1592) / Photo © Fine Art Images / Bridgeman Images

August 15—Solemnity of the Assumption of the Blessed Virgin Mary into Heaven

In the middle of August, the Church celebrates another Marian Solemnity—the Assumption of Mary into heaven, body and soul. This is the fourth Glorious Mystery and the last Marian dogma proclaimed by Pope Pius XII on November 1, 1950.

August 22—The Crowning of Mary, Queen of Heaven and Earth

A week after Mary's entrance into heaven, we celebrate her crowning as Queen of Heaven. What a glorious day! This is the last mystery of the most Holy Rosary—the fifth Glorious Mystery. Perhaps if we are fortunate enough to get to heaven, we can ask why it took the angels and saints a week to prepare for this ceremony!

September 8—The Nativity of Mary

This day falls exactly nine months after the Immaculate Conception; thus, it honors the birth of Mary. What a superb birthday gift you might offer to Mary, to go to Mass and receive Holy Communion.

September 12—The Holy Name of Mary

For the Oblates of the Virgin Mary (this humble author's order), the Holy Name of Mary is their titular feast day. What a wonderful day in which Saints Anne and Joachim gave the beautiful name of Mary to this child who would become the Mother of God!

September 15—Our Lady of Sorrows

The day before, on September 14, the Church celebrates the Feast of the Exaltation of the Holy Cross. Therefore, most appropriately, the following day, the Church celebrates Our Lady of Sorrows. Jesus suffered most intensely for our salvation; however, there at the foot of the cross stood Mary, Our Lady of Sorrows (*Stabat Mater*) suffering most intensely in her Sorrowful and Immaculate Heart what Jesus suffered in His body. We invite all to form the habit of meditating on and contemplating the Seven Sorrows of Mary, most especially on this Feast.

October 7—Our Lady of the Rosary

Commemorating and giving thanks to Our Lady for her powerful intercession in the victory of the Battle of Lepanto, the Church celebrates specifically the Feast of Our Lady of the Rosary. We indeed would be remiss if we did not mention the fact that the whole of the month of October is dedicated to honoring Our Lady of the Rosary.

November 21—The Presentation of the Child Mary in the Temple

This day the Church honors Mary who—according to ancient tradition—was presented in the Temple as a small child by her parents. As such, Mary would be prepared for her sublime mission as the Mother of God.

As a closing remark, we would like to point out indeed how closely Our Lady is related to the Church with respect to approved Marian apparitions. How interesting it really is that in Mexico City (1531), in Lourdes (1858), and in Fatima (1917), in all of these approved Marian apparitions, Our Lady always asked that a Church be built. Why, you might ask? The response is very simple: so that Jesus will be brought to us through His Church and the Sacraments. The greatest of all the Sacraments is the Holy Eucharist.

In conclusion, Mary, who always strives to bring us to Jesus, is present in the liturgical calendar every year. Let us try to remember the presence of Our Lady, present in the Mystical Body of Christ throughout the liturgical year. Let us strive to participate on these special days in Holy Mass, fully, actively, and consciously. This will give great joy to the Hearts of Jesus and Mary!

Virgin of Guadalupe with the four apparitions (circa 1777) by Juan de Sáenz

CHAPTER 29

Our Lady of Guadalupe

The country of Mexico and the region of Latin America just below it is one of the most Catholic areas in the world. But that was not always so. It took a visit from Our Lady to a humble peasant to change the people there from a violent, pagan culture into lovers of the Catholic faith.

The Story of Guadalupe[1]

In the early sixteenth century, Spanish conquistadors, led by Hernan Cortes, arrived on the shores of what is now Mexico and stumbled into a violent culture. This of course was the Aztec Empire, remembered today for the horrific practice of offering human sacrifice to appease the wrath of their pagan deities. While it is true that the Aztecs were a people of great ingenuity and developed an impressive civilization that dominated the area, it is difficult to get past their practice of ripping out the hearts of virgins, children, slaves, and others (while they were still alive) atop their pyramid-like temples dedicated to grotesque gods.

Armed conflict ensued when the Spanish forces arrived. But in time, missionaries arrived and began the process of attempting to Christianize the region. They erected

---

[1] Parts of this review of the story of Our Lady of Guadalupe originally appeared in the *Queen of Heaven* (TAN Books, 2017) by Brian Kennelly and Rick Rotondi. Though some minor changes were made, it is presented here for those who are unfamiliar with the story of Juan Diego. If you already know the story, feel free to skip ahead to the next subheading.

Indians and Spaniards, detail from Miracle of virgin of Guadalupe / 17th-century /
G. Dagli Orti /© NPL - DeA Picture Library / Bridgeman Images

churches where temples once stood, and built schools and hospitals. But the pagan practices of the Aztecs were hard to uproot, and unfortunately, not all of the Spanish treated the natives in a Christian manner. The distrust and tension between the two cultures ran deep.

Such was the situation when Bishop Juan de Zumarraga pled to the Mother of God for help in bringing the two cultures together. He asked her to send him Castilian roses, then unknown in Mexico, as a sign that she had heard his plea. The good bishop would receive his roses and more!

On December 9, 1531, the feast of the Immaculate Conception, a peasant named Juan Diego was walking to Mass, passing by a hill called Tepeyac. Juan Diego had been received into the Church six years prior along with his wife and uncle, some of the small number of Aztecs to accept the Church of Jesus Christ. As he journeyed to the church, he was surprised to hear beautiful music filling the air. He then saw a glowing cloud, lit up by the dazzling lights of a rainbow. When the music stopped, a voice called out his name.

Juan Diego.

He followed the voice, climbing over boulders toward the summit of the hill, and found himself face-to-face with a beautiful lady. She told Juan Diego that she was the Virgin Mary and that she wanted a shrine to be built in this spot where she could show her love and compassion to his people. It was no coincidence that this spot on Tepeyac had been the site of a pagan shrine dedicated to the mother goddess Tonantzin. Our Lady was showing that she was the Mother of the one, true God.

Juan Diego went at once to tell the bishop, but Zumarraga was skeptical and sent him away. Juan Diego was devastated, and upon seeing Our Lady a second time, he begged her to choose a nobler messenger. She merely smiled and said, "I have chosen you."

Juan Diego returned to the bishop but again was met with skepticism. Bishop Zumarraga said that he would only believe Juan Diego if the lady gave him a sign. When Juan Diego told Our Lady this, she promised to deliver the requested sign the following day.

But when the next day arrived, Juan Diego found his uncle sick with a strong fever. He did not keep his appointment with Our Lady, staying instead at the bedside of his uncle, who would soon take a turn for the worse, sending Juan Diego out to find a priest to offer him Last Rites. On the way,

Painting of Juan Diego by Miguel Cabrera

he took a different route to avoid running into Our Lady again, ashamed that he had stood her up. But she placed herself in his new path and greeted him not with anger but with love: "Listen and let it penetrate your heart, my dear little son. Do not be troubled or weighted down with grief. Do not fear any illness or vexation, anxiety or pain. Am I not here who am your mother?"

She assured Juan Diego that his uncle was cured of his fever. Then she sent him to Tepeyac. At its summit, he found the sign Our Lady had promised the bishop: a beautiful garden of flowers growing in the frozen soil, including Castilian roses!

Juan Diego gathered up the flowers and returned to Our Lady. She arranged them in a beautiful bouquet, placed them in his *tilma* (a cloak-like garment worn over the torso), and told him not to reveal them until he stood before the bishop.

When Juan Diego returned to the bishop, he opened his cloak, and the beautiful Castilian roses dropped to the floor. The bishop fell to his knees as well. He had received the very sign he had asked Our Lady for!

Yet the roses were only half the miracle, for on the cloak there was an image imprinted upon it of a young, mestiza woman, beautiful and gentle—an image that would become known as Our Lady of Guadalupe.

The Miraculous Image

The image that Bishop Zumarraga saw that day can still be seen today, almost five hundred years later, in the shrine that would eventually be built in modern day Mexico City. It is this image of Our Lady that brought peace to the region and resulted in the baptism of millions.

The Aztec people had struggled to let go of their own religious rituals and practices. But in the miraculous image, they saw layers of meaning that spoke to them. They saw, for example, that the lady in the image wore her hair straight down—a sign of virginity. Yet she was clearly pregnant, and the black belt around her waist was an Aztec symbol of maternity. In other words, she was both a virgin and a mother. And since there was a small angelic child carrying her, they saw her as a queen, for it was so in their culture that rulers were held aloft.

It was this mother, this virgin, this queen, who had appeared at Tepeyac, the site of an old mother goddess shrine. They would come to know her too as the woman of Revelation 12, clothed with the sun and with the moon under her feet, clearly a heavenly figure, dressed in a star-scattered robe.

And yet, despite her clear royal status, her eyes were cast down, and her hands were folded in prayer, a humble posture that indicated there was one higher than her. She clearly did not bear the same harsh and cruel appearance of their other gods and goddesses but was tender and dear. She would not demand their lives in the form of

The old Guadalupe Basilica, known as the "Templo Expiatorio a Cristo Rey" (1923)

bloody sacrifice. Instead, she was coming to bring them something, or rather, *someone*. She was coming to lead them to her Son who rested in her swollen womb.

Within days of Juan Diego gathering the roses in his tilma, thousands were flocking to the site of the apparition. The bishop would eventually erect a small chapel there, and two cultures that had once been at war now knelt together in prayer.

News of the miraculous image spread far and wide. Artists painted replicas, and people carried the story with them wherever they went. They were captivated by the humility of the Lady of Tepeyac, and were in awe of her power, manifested in several miracles, including the miracle of the roses, of the tilma, and miracles of healing that came from those who drew near it.

She was clearly more powerful than their Aztec gods, and yet she pointed beyond herself to someone else, a God who would not demand their blood in the form of human sacrifice but would instead pour out His own blood for them.

The Aztecs who had been slow to convert were won over. Estimates vary, but as many as nine million Aztecs entered the Church within twenty years of Mary's appearance to Juan Diego. It is said that one priest baptized over one million people with his own hands. Never before in history, nor since, had there been such a mass conversion to the Faith. This is made all the more striking when one considers that the Protestant Reformation was ripping the Faith apart in Europe at this time, with millions leaving the Church. The devil was busy, but so was Our Lady!

The image itself has been proven to be miraculous for several reasons. The first is the sheer fact of how long the garment—the tilma—has remained intact. Its rough cactus fibers should have decayed within a few decades, but it still remains almost five centuries later. Still more, the vibrant colors have not faded. Modern scientists have also pointed out that the rough texture of the fabric does not lend itself to such an intricately painted image. Studies have found no evidence of brush strokes, or of a priming treatment, or paint. Clearly, it was not imprinted by human hands.

In addition to surviving the sheer passing of time, the tilma has also survived a flood, a bomb detonated by a terrorist, and nitric acid accidentally spilled on it by a clumsy shrine worker.

Why "Guadalupe"?

A common and reasonable question usually is asked: Why is this lady known as Our Lady of Guadalupe? It seems an odd title for the mestizo woman on the tilma. Guadalupe was not an Aztec word but a Spanish one; indeed, Guadalupe was the site of a Marian shrine in Spain. Why would Our Lady reveal herself under this title when appearing as a native woman in the New World?

The most likely answer is that she did not. Guadalupe was probably a misunderstanding by Bishop Zumarraga's interpreter of the name she gave herself in the Aztec language. It was merely a happy accident that the word *Guadalupe* would resonate with the Spanish. But the name which Our Lady gave herself was likely something that sounded like Guadalupe to Spanish ears but meant something different to the Aztecs.

What name could she have given? One Aztec phrase that could have been misconstrued by a Spanish interpreter is *Coatlaxopeuh*; another is *Tequantlaxopeuh*. These names were clearly chosen by Providence, as they mean "She who crushes the serpent" and "who saves us from the Devourer." Our Lady had come to save an entire nation from the grip of the evil one!

Our Lady of Guadalupe's Treasure Box

Now, let us accentuate and highlight the extraordinary fruits that have blossomed and flourished as a result of Our Lady of Guadalupe coming to visit us. In truth, it is impossible to number these! But let us narrow them down to ten lessons from this most influential apparition.

Mary's Tender and Loving Motherhood

To Saint Juan Diego, and to each and every one of us, Mary calls herself Mother. Saint Thérèse of Lisieux stated: "Mary is Queen, but more than Queen, Mary is Mother." Saint Augustine, with flaring eloquence asserts: "Put all the love of all the mothers of all times and places together, the love of Mary for each and every one of us is much greater." In Guadalupe, she confirms this, saying to Juan Diego and to all of us, "Am I not here who am your mother?"

Mary Heals!

The great dilemma of Juan Diego as he hurried along heading to Mexico City to fetch a priest was the health of his elderly uncle, Juan Bernardine. Mary appears to Juan Diego and reassures him not to worry about his uncle, and she heals him immediately. This shows us we can turn to Mary in our illnesses, as well as the illnesses and infirmities of our loved ones, and entrust these sicknesses to her. Among the many titles given to Mary is "Health of the sick."

Mary Tells Us Not to Worry

Our Lady of Guadalupe told Juan Diego not to worry, that he was in the crossing of her arms, in her shadow, and in the opening of her garment. How many of us have worries, fears, doubts, and anxieties? Mary wants us to entrust our cares to her maternal protection. As we pray in the Memorare: "Never was it known that anyone who fled to your protection, implored your help, or sought your intercession was left unaided." Right now, let us cast our cares, worries, fears and anxieties into the Heart of Mary. She will never forget us!

Mary and the Church

Then there is the ecclesial aspect of the appearances of Our Lady of Guadalupe. With great insistence and determination, Our Lady commanded Juan Diego to inform the Bishop Juan Zumarraga that she wanted a Church built where she had appeared. This shows us that she wanted to work through the Magisterium of the Church, to respect the hierarchy of her Son's Church. Mary loves the Catholic Church and she encourages all of us to love her Son's Church as well and to submit humbly to the Church's authority. She also wants us to pray for the Church and to be precious, living stones in the structure of the Church.

Mary, Holy Mass, and Holy Communion

Furthermore, Mary as Mother of the Church desires most ardently that we attend Mass frequently and participate in the Holy Mass fully, actively, and consciously. By this is meant to be well-prepared to receive the Sacred Body and Blood of her Son, Jesus, in Holy Communion. Mary always leads us to Jesus.

Mary and Confession

In the present Basilica of Our Lady of Guadalupe, many Masses are celebrated every day. Still more, during the course of the day, from the opening of the basilica until its close in the evening, there are confessors attending to lines of pilgrim people, reconciling their souls and their lives to God through a Sacramental Confession. Therefore, each day we see why Our Lady wanted the basilica built—to bring millions to her Son through the sacraments!

Mary and Conversion of Souls to Christ

In the history of the world, never has there been recorded such a massive conversion to the Catholic faith as from the apparitions of Our Lady of Guadalupe. As mentioned in the opening comments, it is calculated that in the short span of thirty years, millions of people in Mexico were converted to the Catholic faith! It is now the country with the highest number of Spanish-speaking Catholics in the world! Thanks to Jesus who sent His loving Mother to Mexico in 1531!

Our Lady of Guadalupe and the Pro-Life Movement

Of critical importance in the modern world is the presence, power, and purpose of Our Lady of Guadalupe as an icon against the greatest moral evil of our times: abortion. The black ribbon around her waist points to the fact of her pregnancy. She is carrying the baby Jesus in her womb. The Pro-Life movement has adopted Our Lady of Guadalupe as their patron against the onslaught and murder of innocent babies.

Our Lady as Missionary, Evangelist, and Star of Evangelization (Pope Saint John Paul II)

One of the most frequently visited pilgrimages for Pope John Paul II was Mexico and the Basilica of Our Lady of Guadalupe. This great pontiff had in mind the massive conversion of Mexico in the mid-1500s and the present need for evangelization. Our Lady was proclaimed as the patroness of the Americas and the New Star of Evangelization. May Our Lady of Guadalupe motivate all of us to leave our comfort zone and do our part to drop the nets into the deep (*Duc et altum*) and haul in an abundant catch of fish, an abundant harvest of souls. "The harvest is rich but the laborers are few" (Mt 9:37).

Our Lady Cares for All, but Especially for the Poor, Elderly, and Abandoned of Society

Our Lady of Guadalupe showed tender care for the elderly and ill Juan Bernardino. She desired that the basilica be built, first for the Sacraments and to house the

Eucharistic Presence of her Son in the tabernacle and, second, so that all (not just a select few) could come to her with their problems and she would be there to help them in all in their needs. Mary is the Universal Mother, but she has a very special love for the poor, the elderly, the sick, the marginalized, the abandoned, the downcast, and those who seem to have lost all hope. She is that shining star in the midst of the dark clouds, storms, and tempests in life. Indeed, Our Lady of Guadalupe, as in the prayer the Hail Holy Queen, is "our life, our sweetness, and our hope!"

In conclusion, our humble little literary exposition is simply an invitation for all of us to get to know, love, pray to, and entrust our lives, fears, and cares to Our Lady under the title of Our Lady of Guadalupe. Read about Our Lady of Guadalupe. Make a pilgrimage, if possible, to her basilica in Mexico. Purchase a beautiful image of Our Lady of Guadalupe and enthrone it in your home. Invite many, starting with your family, to pray the Rosary in front of Our Lady of Guadalupe. Never forget the words that she addressed to Saint Juan Diego, as well as to you and to me: "My little one, do not worry. I have you in the very crossing of my arms," that is to say: you are hidden in the very depths of my Immaculate Heart. Let us find our sure refuge in two places: the Most Sacred Heart of Jesus and the Immaculate Heart of the Blessed Virgin Mary.

Our Lady of Guadalupe, pray for us!

Prayer to Our Lady of Guadalupe

Our Lady of Guadalupe, Mystical Rose, intercede for Holy Church, protect the sovereign pontiff, help all those who invoke you in their necessities; and since you are the ever Virgin Mary and Mother of the True God, obtain for us from your most holy Son the grace of keeping our faith, sweet hope in the midst of the bitterness of life, burning charity, and the precious gift of final perseverance. Amen.

The rock cave at Massabielle with the statue of the Virgin Mary.
Photo by Semmick Photo / Shutterstock

CHAPTER 30

Our Lady of Lourdes

France is a land made holy by saints. Joan of Arc, Vincent de Paul, Margaret Mary Alacoque, Francis de Sales, John Vianney, King Louis IV, Catherine Laboure, Louis de Montfort, and Thérèse of Lisieux, to name just a few, are all like jewels in the Church's crown!

It is likely for this reason that the devil set his sights on France late in the eighteenth century, inciting a revolution that sought to tear this "Eldest Daughter of the Church" apart. But in the aftermath of this revolution, the Mother of God would visit a humble peasant girl named Bernadette, a future jewel in the crown of the Church herself, to deliver a message of hope, and offer miraculous healings to her children.

The Story of Lourdes[1]

The village of Lourdes sits at the foothills of the Pyrenees Mountains in southern France. In the mid-nineteenth century, it was a simple mill town, full of peasants and ordinary people. The Soubirous family was no different, perhaps the poorest of all of Lourdes. They lived in a place called Rue du Bourg up against the rock of the local castle that overlooked the village. It was nicknamed "the dungeon." They lived a

---

[1] Parts of this review of the story of Our Lady of Lourdes originally appeared in the *Queen of Heaven* (TAN Books, 2017) by Brian Kennelly and Rick Rotondi. Though some minor changes were made, it is presented here for those who are unfamiliar with the story of Saint Bernadette. If you already know the story, feel free to skip ahead to the next subheading.

Bernadette Soubirous (circa 1858)

hard life and often struggled to find work. Nonetheless, they were very devout and gathered each night around their crucifix to pray as a family.

Bernadette was the first of nine children, born in 1844. She was a tiny, sickly child, suffering from severe asthma, and was uneducated. But she was also a very pious child.

The Church in France at this time was under attack. The so-called Enlightenment, led by writers like Voltaire, Diderot, and Jean Jacque Rousseau, had attacked the Church for decades, mocking religious faith and pushing skepticism. The spirit of the movement could best be summarized in a line from one of Diderot's famous works: "Man will never be free until the last king is strangled with the entrails of the last priest."

This spirit of hostility toward the Crown and the Church preceded what would be called the French Revolution, which began in 1789. The French National Assembly eroded King Louis XVI's power before turning to the Church. It abolished Church tithes and seized Church properties. Things were even grimmer when, in 1793, the Reign of Terror began. In a period of just fifteen months, forty thousand people were executed, including many clergy. Along the Nantes River, hundreds of priests were tied to rocks and tossed into the deep to drown, and the heroic Carmelite nuns of Compiegne were beheaded at the guillotine. The government also launched a campaign of "dechristianization," outlawing public worship and removing all visible signs of Christianity. Churches were closed and turned into warehouses or stables or converted into "temples of reason." They even formulated a new calendar centered around the French Republic instead of the birth of Christ. Altars were desecrated, outrageous sacrileges were committed against the Blessed Sacrament, and in Notre Dame Cathedral in Paris, a prostitute was hailed as the goddess of reason and placed upon the high altar for mock veneration. The effects of this persecution would last long after those in power were gone, extending into the life of Bernadette Soubirous.

Thursday, February 11, 1858 was a dreary and bitterly cold day. Fourteen-year-old Bernadette, her sister, and a friend headed down to a rocky crag at the foot of the mountains known as Massabielle to gather firewood. It was a lowly place, often called the pigsty because a local swineherd would use it as a watering hole.

Bernadette became briefly separated from the others and, while alone, suddenly felt a gust of wind and then saw a beautiful woman wearing a flowering, white robe with a blue sash around her waist. She was afraid and reached into her pocket to grab her rosary. But she was comforted when she saw this woman had a rosary of her own, following along silently with Bernadette's prayers. A moment later, the lady was gone.

Bernadette told her sister and friend about it, and soon the whole town knew. Bernadette's parents became worried and didn't want her to return to Massabielle. But Bernadette felt compelled to return and argued the woman couldn't be dangerous since she had a rosary.

She would return on Sunday, February 14 and see the lady again. This time, about twenty other people came with her. They saw nothing, but they did witness Bernadette experiencing a kind of ecstasy. Bernadette asked if she was from God and then sprinkled holy water below her feet. The lady smiled, which Bernadette took as a sign she was from heaven. Bernadette remained in such ecstasy that a family friend had to carry her home.

During the third apparition, again there were others with Bernadette, but again no one saw or heard anything except her. It was on this third visit that the lady spoke for the first time. She asked Bernadette to return each day for a fortnight. She also spoke words that hinted at future suffering, followed by a crown of glory: "I do not promise to make you happy in this life, but in the next."

Bernadette journeyed to Massabielle each day for the next two weeks as the lady had asked. More crowds followed, including journalists and doctors hoping to prove that the little girl was delusional. Yet all who were there knew she was seeing *something*; people spoke of a presence they could feel there. Our Lady spoke repeatedly to Bernadette of the importance of prayer and penance to save poor sinners.

On February 25, the day of the ninth apparition, the lady told Bernadette she should drink at the "fountain," pointing to a little puddle under a rock. Bernadette obeyed, scooping up the muddy water, digging with her hands to find some fresh water. This would have proven to be an odd sight to those watching, perhaps supporting claims she had lost her mind—little did they know she was just a little girl obeying her mother. What began as a trickle of muddy water became a spring that still flows to this day, a spring that, in time, would offer miraculous physical healings, the very first of which occurred days later when a local woman regained the use of her paralyzed arm after bathing in the water.

The apparitions would continue until, at the end of February, the lady asked Bernadette for a chapel to be built in the spot where she had appeared. Bernadette relayed this request to the local clergy but was sent away. When she persisted, a priest asked for the lady's name. Up to this point, Bernadette had not claimed it was Mary.

She had asked for her name, but the lady had not revealed it.

Finally, toward the end of March, on the feast of the Annunciation, Bernadette asked the lady her name again, and this time got a reply: "I am the Immaculate Conception."

Bernadette had no idea what this meant but ran to tell the priest, repeating the phrase over and over again to keep from forgetting it. This simple, uneducated girl would have had no idea that just four years earlier, in 1854, Pope Pius IX had infallibly declared the dogma of Mary's Immaculate Conception. It was as if Mary was confirming the authority of her Son's Church by confirming the dogma.

The revelation of this name by the lady, combined with the miraculous spring of water, gave credibility to Bernadette's story. The clergy in the area could not deny the miraculous healings, and they knew Bernadette would have never heard of the "Immaculate Conception," so how could she have made it up? Thus, the chapel that the lady asked for would be built, eventually becoming a pilgrimage shrine that millions visit each year.

After the apparitions, Bernadette years later joined the Sisters of Charity in Nevers, France, where she lived out the remainder of her hidden life in a convent. When asked about the apparitions, Bernadette once said, "The Virgin used me as a broom to remove the dust. When the work is done, the broom is put behind the door again."

Two of Bernadette's greatest virtues were her humility and her silent suffering, both physical suffering from chronic ill-health and mental anguish from the ill treatment she endured because of the apparitions. She was declared blessed on June 14, 1921 by Pope Pius XI and was canonized by Pius XI on December 8, 1933, the feast of the Immaculate Conception.

Her body remains incorrupt and has been placed in a gold reliquary in the Chapel of Saint Bernadette at the motherhouse in Nevers.

Lessons from Lourdes

It would do us well to now highlight some of the messages and lessons we can take away from this miraculous story, for there are pearls of infinite value and precious diamonds of wealth that flow from this Church-approved Marian apparition.

First and foremost, let us understand that we should found our Catholic faith upon biblical truths and the dogmatic truths revealed by the Church. The "public revelation" we read in the Scriptures and the deposit of faith we receive from the tradition of the Church are what we must believe as Catholics. Private revelation like those granted to Bernadette need not be believed to be a member of the Roman Catholic Church.

Nonetheless, approved Marian apparitions can foster, bolster, and fortify our faith and love for Holy Mother Church, for the Blessed Trinity, and for Our Heavenly Mother. Indeed, many popes, scholars, saints, and ordinary pilgrims have traveled to Lourdes and received many blessings—including moral, emotional, spiritual, and quite often physical healings.

Therefore, let us dive into the deep riches and treasures found in the messages and teachings proclaimed by Our Lady of Lourdes and her messenger—Saint Bernadette.

Our Lady Loves and Cares for Children

Two of the most celebrated approved Marian apparitions are Fatima and Lourdes. In both of these apparitions, Our Lady chose to appear not to scholars or intellectuals, or the rich, powerful, and prestigious. Rather, she chose to appear to simple children. Jesus himself reiterated this basic theme. "Let the little children come to me" (Mt 19:14). "Unless you become like little children you will not enter the kingdom of heaven" (Mt 18:3). Our Lady wants us to bring the children to her tender and loving Immaculate Heart!

Our Lady Affirms the Teaching of the Magisterium

At Fatima, Our Lady revealed herself to the children—Lucia, Francisco, and Jacinta—as Our Lady of the Rosary. In Mexico, she asked Juan Diego, "Am I not your mother?" But to Bernadette, this beautiful lady revealed her name by saying, "I am the Immaculate Conception." Only four years earlier, in 1854, Pope Pius IX had proclaimed dogmatically the dogma of the Immaculate Conception. Therefore, true and authentic devotion to Mary will always align us with the authentic teaching of the

Prayer to Our Lady of Lourdes

O Ever Immaculate Virgin, Mother of Mercy, Health of the Sick, Refuge of Sinners, Comfortress of the Afflicted, you know my wants, my troubles, my sufferings. Look upon me with mercy. When you appeared in the grotto of Lourdes, you made it a privileged sanctuary where you dispense your favors, and where many sufferers have obtained the cure of their infirmities, both spiritual and corporeal. I come, therefore, with unbounded confidence to implore your maternal intercession. My loving Mother, obtain my request (here mention request). I will try to imitate your virtues so that I may one day share your company and bless you in eternity. Amen.

The Words of St. Bernadette

"Everything is nothing to me, but Jesus— neither things nor persons, ideas nor emotions, honor nor sufferings; only Jesus is my honor, delight, heart and soul."

"I must die to myself continually and accept trials without complaining. I work, suffer, and I love with no other witness than His heart. Anyone who is not prepared to suffer for the Beloved and to do His will in all things is not worthy of the sweet name of Friend, for here below, Love without suffering does not exist."

"When my emotions are strong, I remember the words of Our Lord: 'It is I, do not be afraid.' Immediately I appreciate and thank Our Lord for this grace of rejections and humiliations from my Superior and Sisters. It is the love of this Good Master who would remove the roots from this tree of pride. The more little I become, the more I grow in the Heart of Jesus."

"O Jesus and Mary, let my entire consolation in this world be to love you and to suffer for sinners."

"My weapons, I decided, would be prayer and sacrifice, which I would hold on to till my last breath. Then only would the weapon of sacrifice fall from my hand, but the weapon of prayer would follow me to Heaven."

Magisterium of the Church. For that reason, the Second Vatican Council proclaimed Mary as the Mother of the Church. And let us also realize that Our Lady, in her perfect humility, waited for her Son's Church to declare her as the Immaculate Conception!

Our Lady Asked for a Church to Be Built

As in the apparitions in Fatima and in Mexico, Our Lady of Lourdes desired that a Church be built. Why? The reason is crystal clear: Mary desires our conversion, our sanctification, and the eternal salvation of our immortal souls. Two of the most important supports for our salvation are frequent reception of the Sacraments of Confession and the Holy Eucharist. Once a Church is built, Masses will be celebrated frequently and priests will be available to reconcile souls to God through the Sacrament of Confession.

Our Lady of Lourdes and the Miraculous Spring of Water

As we read, Our Lady told Bernadette to dig in the ground to discover water. In front of curious onlookers, Bernadette obeyed by digging into the ground. Many thought she was crazy! But little by little, water began to seep forth from where the little girl had dug. Consequently, a miraculous spring of water has flowed forth even to this day. Through the intercession of Mary, many of the sick who have washed and bathed themselves with this water have been miraculously healed. Jesus worked His first public miracle at the Wedding Feast of Cana through the intercession of Mary by turning water into wine. Still to this day, God works miracles through the powerful intercession of Mary most holy. We must not base our belief and faith in God solely in miracles, but they are still a gift from Him that can support our belief and faith, and they are given to us often through the hands of Mary!

Our Lady Loves the Sick

The miraculous cures that take place at Lourdes are carried out among the terminally ill, the sick, the suffering, the forlorn, and abandoned of the world. Our Lady of Lourdes teaches us to pray for the sick, help the sick, support the sick, and love the sick, because in the sick and suffering, we discover the face of the suffering Jesus. At Lourdes, she beckons the sick to come to her for comfort. Following her example, let us also invite the sick to come before us to receive love and care.

The Salvific Value of Suffering

Not only is the concept of suffering part of the message of Our Lady of Lourdes, but so is the idea that human suffering united to the suffering Hearts of Jesus and Mary has infinite value. If we can give our sufferings to Jesus through the Sorrowful and Immaculate Heart of Mary, and place it on the altar in the Mass, then this suffering can serve to repair for a multitude of sins, as well as touch and convert the hearts of many hardened sinners. Lourdes is a place where human suffering comes to be offered to God as a means for their own sanctification, as well as that of others.

Prayer and Sacrifice

The message of Our Lady of Lourdes and Our Lady of Fatima have a common thread: offer prayer and penances (sacrifices) for sinners! Our Lady points out that many souls can be saved from eternal loss if generous persons offer fervent prayers and generous sacrifices for the salvation of souls. Remember, even one soul is worth more than the whole created universe!

Eucharistic Processions at Dusk

Our Lady of Lourdes desired that Jesus be honored by processions. To this very day, at dusk, there are outdoor Eucharistic Processions at the shrine of Lourdes. The Eucharistic Face of Jesus present in the monstrance is honored and worshipped in the plaza. It is interesting to note that most of the healings at Lourdes occur during these Eucharistic Processions. Mary leads us to Jesus, and Jesus, who is truly the Divine Physician, heals us. May Mary's prayers bring us healing! May the Eucharistic Lord heal our bodies, minds, and hearts!

Our Lady of Lourdes, pray for us!

The stattie of Our Lady of Fatima / Mondadori Portfolio / Archivio Claudia Beretta / Claudia Beretta / Bridgeman Images

Our Lady of Fatima

Throughout the ages, Mary has appeared many times to devout souls delivering messages that concerned the salvation of her children. Arguably no other Marian apparition was more dramatic and left more of an impact on the Church and the world than the story of Our Lady of Fatima. It is impossible to unpack all the treasures of this story in one chapter, but we shall try! Let us begin with what actually transpired.

The Story of Fatima[1]

Fatima is a small village town in a hilly region of central Portugal on the edge of the Serra de Aire Mountains. There would be no reason for anyone to know or care about Fatima if it were not for the astonishing events that transpired there over the course of 1916 and 1917.

The story begins with three simple shepherd children: Lucia dos Santos and her two cousins, Francisco and Jacinta Marto. In the spring of 1916, when Lucia was nine, Francisco eight, and Jacinta six, an angel appeared to them on a secluded hillside where they were tending their flocks. He told them not to be afraid and revealed himself as the "Angel of Peace." He taught them a new prayer and asked that they

---

[1] This review of the story of Our Lady of Fatima originally appeared in *Inside the Light* (TAN Books, 2019) by Sister Angela Coelho. Though some minor changes were made, it is presented here for those who are unfamiliar with the story of Fatima. If you already know the story, feel free to skip ahead to the next subheading.

Lúcia Santos, Francisco and Jacinta Marto (1917)

pray it with him, assuring them that the "hearts of Jesus and Mary" were listening to their prayers.

This angel also appeared later that summer. At that time, he once again encouraged the children to pray. In addition, he asked them to make sacrifices to save sinners. The angel asked the little shepherds to offer up penances and sacrifices to console Jesus and Mary for the innumerable sins committed against the Sacred Heart of Jesus and the Immaculate Heart of Mary. In the fall of that year, the angel would appear a third time, when he gave the children Holy Communion.

They did not tell anyone about these supernatural visits, but they had a profound impact on the children and prepared them for what would happen the following year.

On May 13, 1917, while Lucia, Francisco, and Jacinta were out tending flocks and playing games in a secluded area called the Cova da Iria, they noticed what seemed like a sudden storm and flash of lightning. The two girls saw a woman "more brilliant than the sun" resting over a small tree, but at first, Francisco saw nothing; only once he started praying the Rosary were his eyes opened. This woman would eventually reveal herself to be the Mother of God, but she specifically called herself "Our Lady of the Rosary" (and is also commonly referred to today as Our Lady of Fatima). But on this first visit, she did not give her name. She simply said she was from heaven and asked that the children return to this same spot five more times on the same day and time in each of the following months.

Lucia warned her cousins not to say anything about what they'd seen, but little Jacinta, unable to contain her excitement, immediately told her mother, and the news quickly spread around the town. Some people believed the children while others scoffed. Lucia's mother fell into this latter group, considering her daughter a liar. This would become a great source of pain for Lucia.

Nonetheless, the children obeyed the lady and returned to the Cova da Iria on June 13, when she appeared to them again. A small group of people came with them but could see nothing. Lucia asked Our Lady if she would take her, Francisco, and Jacinta to heaven. Mary replied that she would take Francisco and Jacinta very soon but that Lucia would remain behind. Our Lady told Lucia that God wanted to establish devotion to the Immaculate Heart and that Lucia would be an instrument to make this happen. During this visit, the Blessed Mother also asked the children to pray the Rosary every day.

The following month—July 13—was perhaps the most dramatic visit, when Our Lady revealed the famous three-part "secret" of Fatima. After telling the children again to pray the Rosary and make sacrifices for sinners, she promised to tell them who she was in October, when she said she would perform a miracle for all to see, to help verify the shepherds' stories. She then showed the children a violent image of hell and told them that many souls were being lost not only because of their own immorality but because there was no one to pray and make sacrifices for them. To save them, she told the children to pray and offer sacrifices, encouraging them to develop a compassionate heart for sinners. Finally, she said that God wanted to establish devotion to her Immaculate Heart. This was the first part.

In the second part of the secret, she said that World War I, raging across Europe at the time, would end but that a worse war would break out if people did not stop offending God. Our Lady said that she would return at a later date to ask for the consecration of Russia to her Immaculate Heart and for the Communion of Reparation on the first Saturdays. If her requests were heeded, she prophesied that there would be peace, but if not, Russia would spread her errors throughout the world.

Finally, in the third part of the secret, Our Lady showed them yet another vision that predicted the suffering of the Church and the persecution of the "bishop dressed in white," the Holy Father, who, in the vision, was shot by legions of soldiers with bullets and arrows.

News that the children had been told a "secret" spread around town, and the local authorities demanded that its contents be revealed. Things reached such a fever pitch that the administrator of the town actually imprisoned them, keeping them from meeting Our Lady on August 13. He even threatened them with death if they did not reveal the secret. But the children stood firm and would not betray Our Lady's trust.

Eventually, after they were released, Mary appeared to them again, this time on the nineteenth of the month. She once again asked them to pray the Rosary and said there would still be a miracle in October, but it would not be as extraordinary as it would have been if the local authorities had not imprisoned the children and threatened them with death.

With each visit, the number of people accompanying the children to the site of the apparitions grew, and in September, there were so many people that the children struggled to reach the Cova da Iria. Our Lady appeared again and told them God was pleased with their sacrifices. She also said that the following month, when the promised miracle would occur, Our Lord would come, and that she would appear as Our Lady of Sorrows and Our Lady of Mount Carmel. She foretold that Saint Joseph would also appear with the Child Jesus to bless the world.

Finally, October 13 came. More than seventy thousand people showed up to see the miracle, including many non-believers, some of whom worked for news and media outlets hoping to debunk the children's story and embarrass those who believed.

The weather was dire all morning and the fields were soaked in rain and mud. When Our Lady appeared, she finally told the children her name, identifying herself as Our Lady of the Rosary. She told the children she wanted a chapel built in her honor in the place where she had appeared. She pleaded with them on behalf of humanity to stop offending God, who was already gravely offended by the world's sins. She then ascended, and as promised, Our Lady of Carmel and Our Lady of Dolores appeared, as well as Saint Joseph and the Child Jesus, who blessed the world.

The sun then grew brighter and began to spin and emit vivid colors before dropping to the earth. The thousands present screamed in terror. People cried out for mercy, thinking it was the end of the world. Yet a moment later, the sun resumed its normal position. When the uproar calmed down, all who were there noticed that the ground had dried and people's clothes were no longer muddy and wet. This event, which came to be known as the miracle of the sun, was seen by people for miles around. As a result of this miracle, many non-believers came to believe and converted to Christianity.

After this, the children struggled to live a normal life, often being swarmed by crowds. For Francisco and Jacinta, however, this life in the limelight would not last long. Our Lady had promised to take them to heaven soon, and indeed, both of them were stricken by the Spanish flu epidemic of 1918. Francisco died on April 4, 1919. Meanwhile, Jacinta was moved to a hospital several miles away. But she told the doctors and her family that she was going to die and that their efforts to save her would be futile. Her prophecy was fulfilled when she died on February 20, 1920 in Lisbon.

Lucia was grief-stricken not just because she had lost her cousins but because she had also lost the only two people in the world with whom she had shared the apparitions of Fatima. Many people continued to seek out Lucia, some coming from far away to see her. The local bishop recommended that she leave for Porto, where she could avoid the crowds and attend a special school. She did not want to leave Fatima, but when she visited the Cova da Iria on June 15, 1921, Our Lady appeared to Lucia for a seventh time and assured her it was God's will for her to go to Porto.

Our Lady of Fatima. Photo by Steven Wielenberg / Shutterstock

After several years spent studying in Porto, Lucia entered the Institute of the Sisters of St. Dorothy as a postulant in a convent in Pontevedra, Spain, on October 24, 1925. Just a few months later on December 10, Our Lady fulfilled her promise of coming again—appearing to Lucia in the Dorothean convent. On this visit, Mary explained the specific requirements for the Communion of Reparation on first Saturdays. In another visit in Tui, four years later in 1929, Our Lady appeared alongside a visible presence of the Most Holy Trinity and asked for the consecration of Russia to her Immaculate Heart.

Though Lucia had taken her final vows in 1934 to become a Dorothean sister, she was later released from these vows so she could become a Carmelite sister in 1948. During this period, Our Lady's prediction of a worse worldwide conflict came to pass with the outbreak of World War II. Lucia felt the pain of this war most acutely, feeling a strong personal responsibility to pray for peace. She spent the rest of her life trying to spread devotion to the Immaculate Heart of Mary and imploring people to pray the Rosary and embrace a spirituality of reparation. Under holy obedience, she was directed to record all that had happened to her and all that Our Lady had told her, which we find today in several different books (though the contents of the secret were only released to the pope and special members of the Magisterium for some time, not being released to the general public until much later).

Over the years, Lucia also met with several popes, urging them to consecrate Russia to Our Lady according to what she had specified. Though several popes tried to make this consecration, confusion and unforeseen circumstances prevented it from taking place. One specific area of confusion concerned the consecration being made in union with the bishops around the world, which failed to happen on several occasions. This all took place amidst the backdrop of the Cold War, when the atheistic Soviet Union began a systematic takeover of Eastern Europe and became embroiled in a nuclear arms race with the United States.

Saint John Paul II, one of the popes most devoted to the Blessed Mother, and who had grown up under Soviet oppression in Poland, would play a significant role in the Fatima story. On May 13, 1981, on the anniversary of Our Lady's first apparition to the children, he was shot in Saint Peter's Square by Mehemet Ali Agca, a Turkish man with unclear motives. John Paul credited Our Lady of Fatima with saving his life. While recovering, he read Lucia's words about the secret, specifically about the "bishop dressed in white" being shot. This obviously resonated with him, and he became determined to fulfill Our Lady's request to consecrate Russia to her Immaculate

Pope John Paul II at the Sanctuary of Fatima / Mondadori Portfolio / Archivio Grzegorz Galazka / Grzegorz Galazka / Bridgeman Images

Heart. Though it took several tries, he was able to accomplish this on March 25, 1984, in front of 250,000 people in Rome. Lucia gave credence to this attempt by assuring everyone that heaven had finally accepted the consecration.

In the years that followed, Communist Russia began to collapse, symbolically illustrated by the dramatic fall of the Berlin Wall in 1989. Though many factors no doubt contributed to this outcome, believers pointed to the consecration as a divine aid in defeating the Soviet Union, which had been the globe's leading atheistic world power.

Lucia herself saw the turn of the millennium, dying on February 13, 2005, at the age of ninety-seven. Her cause for canonization is still ongoing at the time of this writing, but her cousins, Jacinta and Francisco, were canonized on May 13, 2017, the hundredth anniversary of Our Lady's first apparition at the Cova de Iria. Today, millions seek their intercession and practice a strong devotion to Our Lady of Fatima.

Now that we are all familiar with the events of Fatima, let us unpack the story's meaning!

Five Warnings from Our Lady of Fatima

In our chronicle of the story of Fatima, we did not give much detail about Our Lady's actual words and messages to the children. Let us dive more deeply into what she said, then, because she came like a prophet warning us of the dangers of sin.

It must be said that Our Lady did not come to add anything new to the Gospel; rather, Our Lady came to bring us back to the essentials of the Gospel message, to bring us to the Heart of Our Lord and Savior Jesus Christ. Her message is perennial, just as important now as it was one hundred years ago.

As the good Mother that she is, Our Lady came to warn us of certain perils or dangers that could place in jeopardy that which is most important—the eternal salvation of our immortal souls. Here we would like to list and explain five of the most salient warnings that Our Heavenly Mother invites us to think about, meditate upon, and incorporate into our lives.

The Brevity of Life

On one of her visits, Our Lady told the children: "If men would only meditate upon eternity, then they would change their lives immediately." The short, ephemeral, and transitory character of human life can be seen clearly in two of the children visionaries—Saint Jacinta Marto and her brother, Saint Francisco Marto. Both of them contracted a serious illness not long after Our Lady's six apparitions and passed from this life to the next. In her words, Our Lady is clearly warning all of us that our life is short, uncertain, and precarious. We know neither the day nor the hour when the Lord will call us to render an account of our lives. Ask yourself this all-important question: if you were to die this very day, would you be ready?

The Evil of Sin

Our Lady pointed out that sin is what hurts Jesus most. In the Fatima message, contemplating the Sacred Heart of Jesus and especially the Immaculate Heart of Mary surrounded and pierced by sharp thorns manifests powerfully what sin actually does—it pierces the loving Hearts of Jesus and Mary! Sin is not simply breaking a law; it is hurting the ones you love and who love you—Jesus and Mary!

The Reality of Hell

Mary is a tender and loving Mother; she is, as we pray in the Hail Holy Queen, our life, our sweetness, and our hope. Still, Our Lady of Fatima does not shy away from revealing to the three children, and to the world at large, a graphic vision of hell. Seeing and hearing the utter suffering and despair of the damned souls moved the children to the very depths of their souls with an insatiable desire to pray fervently, to suffer willingly, as well as to offer frequent and difficult sacrifices to save poor sinners from precipitating into the fiery pit of hell. Even though this is an unpleasant topic, something many today deny or forget, Our Lady challenges us to meditate often on God's Infinite Mercy, but also His justice which is manifested by hell and those who choose this reality by dying unrepentant in the state of mortal sin.

Sins against Purity

Continuing on the topic of lost souls, with great sadness of heart, Our Lady revealed that the primary reason for the loss of souls to the eternal chastisement of hell is due to sins against the virtue of holy purity. Our Lady revealed that many marriages were not pleasing to God, lacking purity and true love. She also lamented the many immodest fashions that would enter into the world and be very displeasing to God. It is difficult to deny in recent times the rampant diffusion of immodesty in dress, fashion, movies, television programs, commercials, ads, billboards, the internet, and much more. In the midst of the storms of impurity that seek to inundate the world, we must seek out a sure refuge and haven in the Immaculate Heart of Mary.

Warning to Priests

In one of the later visions received by Lucia, Our Lady spoke about priests, conveying two important messages: (1) priests should strive to be pure; and (2) priests should dedicate their time and effort to that which refers to God and the salvation of souls, and not to extraneous matters. This being said, let us turn to Our Lady, Mother of the High Priest, Our Lord and Savior Jesus Christ, and beg for vocations to the priesthood. Let us turn to Mary to pray for priests, for bishops, for the Holy Father, and for the Catholic Church and all its shepherds and leaders.

With the story of Fatima stretching for decades and containing such miraculous events, we do not want to lose the primary message Our Lady delivered to the three children. That important message can be boiled down to this simple statement: *souls are going to hell because there is no one to pray and offer sacrifices for them.* To save poor sinners, including ourselves, we must pray and make sacrifices daily for the salvation of souls. In this way we will be on the path to salvation and bring others with us.

Our Lady of Fatima particularly asked that they pray the Rosary. She implored the children to pray the Rosary every day, and by extension, she asks us to do this as well. The children obeyed this command.

The children also made many sacrifices throughout their day to save poor sinners. Following the vision of hell that they received, they mourned the souls lost to hell and desired to save souls from going there, especially little Jacinta. She wanted to offer everything she could to save souls. She gave up the sweet grapes of Portugal that she loved and her favorite activity, which was dancing. Like Francisco and Lucia, she wore a cord around her waist that chafed her skin, often gave her lunch to poor children they met on their way to shepherd their sheep, and at times would refrain from drinking cold water on hot days in the fields. Once when she complained of a terrible headache, Francisco reminded her to offer it up for poor sinners, and this she did immediately. She also offered her intense sufferings in her last illness to save poor sinners.

Pope John Paul II presided over the beatifications of Francisco and Jacinta on May 13, 2000 at the Basilica of Our Lady of the Rosary in Fatima. This saintly pope called Francisco "a little mystic." Francisco was especially drawn to a life of contemplative prayer. He loved to kneel before the Blessed Sacrament and keep "the Hidden Jesus" company. What a beautiful image for us when we adore or receive Jesus truly present in the Eucharist! John Paul II called Jacinta "a little victim soul" willing and ready to sacrifice and offer all she possibly could to Jesus through the Immaculate Heart of Mary for the conversion and salvation of poor sinners.

When the sufferings of these three shepherd children were offered to God, in union with Christ's suffering and sacrifice on the cross, through the hands of the Immaculate Heart of Mary, they became powerful saving acts for others. Love is all about sacrifice—we make sacrifices for those we love. But like the children of Fatima, can we love and offer sacrifices for those we don't even know? That is what Christ asks of us in the Gospel. "Whatever you do for the least of these, you do for me" (Mt 25:40).

Our Lady assured the children, we can offer up everything, with the exception of our sins, to God through the Immaculate Heart of Mary as a sacrifice to save souls, especially poor sinners most in need of God's Infinite Mercy and forgiveness. Saint Paul expressed it in these words: "Whether you eat or drink, do all for the honor and glory of God" (1 Cor 10:31).

If we really love Jesus and Our Lady, then we should love what they love most. Let us beg for the grace, like the children of Fatima, that we will be willing to offer prayers and sacrifices to the Immaculate Heart of Mary for the conversion of sinners and salvation of souls. Saint Thomas Aquinas, the Angelic Doctor, states that one soul is worth more than the whole created universe. Let us work with Our Lady of Fatima for an abundant harvest of souls for the kingdom of God!

Consoling the Immaculate Heart of Mary

We further discern in the visions of Fatima that the Hearts of both Jesus and Mary are sad. Our Lady is saddened by the loss of her children to the eternal fires of hell. Jesus is saddened by the loss of those souls He so painfully suffered and died for. Moreover, both Jesus and Mary are deeply saddened by the sins committed against the Immaculate Heart of Mary.

If our earthly mothers are sad, we try to cheer them up, or show them compassion. This we must also do with Our Heavenly Mother. Mary tells us right from her very lips, telling the children, and by extension us, how to console her: "Sacrifice yourself for sinners and say many times, especially when you make some sacrifice: 'O Jesus, it is for Thy love for the conversion of sinners and in reparation for the sins committed against the Immaculate Heart of Mary.'"

Through the story of Fatima, we learn that there are five sins against Mary's Immaculate Heart. These were revealed many years later to Sister Lucia when she was living in the convent as a nun. The words were actually spoken by Jesus, who ardently desires that acts of prayer and reparation be made so that those who have so grievously offended Mary, His Mother, will beg pardon for these grave sins and thereby receive His mercy.

Let us take each of these offenses and consider what we can do to offer worthy acts of reparation (to make amends) to the Hearts of Mary and Jesus.

Blasphemies against the Immaculate Conception

The Immaculate Conception, as we have noted, is one of the four Marian dogmas of the Church, proclaiming that Mary was preserved from sin when she was conceived in the womb of her mother. Yet there are those who mock, deride, and make fun of this most profound, sublime, and holy gift that God endowed upon Mary. To make up for these outrages, we suggest praising God and thanking Him for having endowed Mary with this most sublime gift. Reflecting on Mary's Immaculate Conception, purity, and virginity helps us understand the mysteries of Christ's redemptive plan for humanity. Furthermore, we must celebrate and participate with great joy and gratitude in the Solemnity of the Immaculate Conception on December 8. Offer your

Holy Communion on that day especially in reparation for all the sins and blasphemes against the Immaculate Conception. Finally, pray this prayer as often as you can: "O Mary, conceived without sin, pray for us who have recourse to thee." These words are inscribed on the front of the Miraculous Medal, and so wearing this medal is another way you can make reparation for offenses against the Immaculate Conception and console the Heart of Mary.

Blasphemies against Mary's Perpetual Virginity

Another one of the Church's Marian dogmas, the Perpetual Virginity of Mary, is also denied and mocked by many people. How can we repair for the sins against the Perpetual Virginity of Mary? To start, we can be ready and willing to explain to all the meaning of this wonderful privilege given to Mary from God Himself. We must defend our Mother by defending the Church's teachings. Still more, in imitation of the sublime purity of Mary, let us all strive to live lives of great modesty in the way we dress, walk, speak, and act. This is a great means to repair for sins against the Perpetual Virginity of Mary.

Blasphemies against Mary's Divine Maternity

This is the greatest of all of Mary's privileges—her Divine Maternity! Mary is truly the Mother of God. Once again, we invite all to make due reparation for the sins and blasphemes against Mary, this time against the Divine Maternity of the Blessed Virgin Mary, by celebrating with preparation, attention, devotion, and joy the liturgical solemnity of Mary's Divine Maternity on January 1. We can also give special gratitude to her on Christmas, for we cannot separate the birth of Jesus from Mary's Divine Motherhood. On these two glorious feasts, strive to make fervent Holy Communions and offer them in reparation for all the sins against Mary as Mother of God. We can also pray the Hail Mary often with the purpose of reparation for the sins of the world, but most especially for the sins against Mary as Mother of God, for in this prayer, we proclaim her as "Holy Mary, Mother of God."

Blasphemies against Children

All those who try to sow in the hearts of children a coldness, indifference, rejection, or even hatred toward their Immaculate Mother Mary grieve her terribly. The words of Jesus expressing His tender love for children resonate in our hearts: "Let the little children come to me, and do not hinder them, for the kingdom of heaven belongs to such as these" (Mt 19:14). This scandal of blasphemes against children lacerates the Hearts of Jesus and Mary, especially when adults, particularly those in authority, speak negatively, sarcastically, and derisively as they demean, mock, and make fun of the person of the Blessed Virgin Mary. How much Mary really loves all, but children in a special way, and how much Mary desires their purity, innocence, and the salvation of their immortal souls. It is not by chance that Our Lady of Fatima appeared to three simple shepherd children—Lucia, Francisco, and Jacinta! We must offer due reparation to the Sorrowful and Immaculate Heart of Mary for sins committed against children. Let us baptize them as soon as possible, making them sons and daughters of God. Let us name them after Mary and the saints. Let us teach them about Mary, catechize them in the Marian dogmas, and help them grow to love her by praying the Rosary, giving them the Miraculous Medal, and hanging images of her in our homes. Let us consecrate them to her so she can make them pure offerings to her Son. Mary truly loves our children, let them know and love her in return!

Scandal and Blasphemies against Images of Mary

In recent times, there has been a series of blasphemes against images of the Blessed Virgin Mary. Statues have been graffitied or destroyed. Paintings and pictures have been ruined. Possibly even worse, there have been movies and programs that have mocked and blasphemed the Blessed Virgin Mary. How this wounds deeply the Immaculate Heart of Mary and the Sacred Heart of Jesus! It is true that the devil both hates and has a mortal fear of the Blessed Virgin Mary and will do all in his power to blaspheme her, often using human agents or instruments. Let us offer due reparation by displaying beautiful images of Mary in our homes and by consecrating our homes to Jesus through her. You can actually have a priest come to "enthrone" your home. He can even help consecrate and enthrone your whole family! We should also encourage and support the beautification of our Churches with sacred images of Our Lady, and we should pass out to anyone we meet holy cards of her. Many are won over to God's kingdom through beauty; what better way to draw them in than with images of the most beautiful woman to have ever lived!

We hope and pray that all will have a greater love, respect, devotion, and limitless trust in the power, presence, and prayers of the Immaculate Heart of Mary in our daily lives. Therefore, let us do all in our power to show our great love and tenderness towards Our Heavenly Mother by offering due reparation for the many sins committed against her great honor and singular role in our eternal salvation!

The First Saturdays Devotion

No chapter on Our Lady of Fatima would be complete if we did not talk about the First Saturdays Devotion. Traditionally, Saturday has been a day devoted to the Blessed Virgin Mary. Tradition tells us that we think of Mary on Saturday because it is the day that followed her Son's death. Christ was killed on Good Friday and rose on

Easter Sunday. On the day between, Our Lady mourned. It is believed by some that Jesus appeared to her and her alone on this Saturday, even though Sacred Scripture does not bless us with this story.

The dedication of Saturday to Mary became even more prevalent after the apparitions at Fatima. This is because of what Our Lady told Lucia on December 10, 1925, several years after the initial apparitions. On this day, Mary appeared to Lucia at her convent in Pontevedra, Spain. By Our Lady's side, on a luminous cloud, was the Child Jesus, and her Heart could be seen. Mary told Lucia: "Look, my daughter, at my Heart encircled by these thorns with which men pierce it at every moment by their blasphemies and ingratitude. You, at least, strive to console me, and so I announce: I promise to assist at the hour of death with the grace necessary for salvation all those who, with the intention of making reparation to me, will, on the first Saturday of five consecutive months, go to confession, receive Holy Communion, say five decades of the beads, and keep me company for fifteen minutes while meditating on the fifteen mysteries of the Rosary."

Let us expand on each of these requests briefly so that we can fully understand what Our Lady is asking of us.

Sacramental Confession of Reparation

Mary, Queen of Mercy, wants all of us to have recourse to the Sacrament of Confession. Therefore, try to examine your conscience thoroughly, and if necessary, have a spiritual guide or director. Beg for the grace of sincere, total, and heartfelt sorrow for your sins. Also, have a firm purpose of amendment, in which you try to avoid all occasions of sin, that is to say, persons, places, things, or circumstances that might lead you into sin. Confess your sins to the priest who represents Christ. You are obliged to confess the number and kind of mortal sins. Then, do not neglect to carry out the penance that the priest imposes on you. This confession can be made a week before the first Saturday, or a week after. Finally, one very important specification: the confession must be a "confession of reparation," that is, a confession made with the intention of reparation for all sins, your sins as well as all the sins that have pierced the Immaculate Heart of Mary.

Holy Communion of Reparation

Our Lady desires ardently that we attend Mass, but she also desires most especially that we receive Holy Communion—the Body, Blood, Soul, and Divinity of Jesus her Son. During these five Saturdays, we must approach the altar with the intention of receiving Communion as a sign of reparation, just as we made a confession of reparation. The Communion received on five consecutive first Saturdays of the month should be received with the desire to offer reparation for all the sins against the Immaculate Heart of Mary.

The Recitation of the Most Holy Rosary

Another condition required to attain the enormous blessings of the promise associated with the First Saturdays Devotion is the recitation of the most holy Rosary. In every one of the six apparitions at Fatima to the children, Our Lady insisted on the praying of the Rosary. In practicing the First Saturday Devotion of Fatima, Mary desires that the Rosary be offered in reparation for sins against her Immaculate Heart. Our Lady wants us to go deeper and deeper in our union with her Immaculate Heart and the Sacred Heart of Jesus. This is done through prayer!

Meditation on the Mysteries of the Rosary

The final requirement for the First Saturdays Devotion is that of spending at least fifteen minutes meditating upon the mysteries, or at least one of the mysteries, of the most Holy Rosary. Even though not expressed explicitly, one of the primary reasons for this quiet meditation of at least fifteen minutes is for us to go deeper in the profound meaning of these mysteries. Pope Saint John XXIII said that the Rosary is a summary of the Gospel itself. Indeed, if we truly want to know Jesus and Mary and love them, and be willing to imitate and follow them, it is necessary to spend time thinking about their lives and actions. This is done most efficaciously by meditating on the mysteries of the most holy Rosary. We can obviously do this while praying the Rosary, but also on our own, or while reading the scriptural passages associated with each mystery.

If we carry out this practice, we will not only console Our Mother when she is sad but we will also be the beneficiary of extraordinary graces. Look at her words again: "I promise to assist at the hour of death with the graces necessary for salvation." This means that at the most important moment of our earthly existence, the very moment that we die and pass from this life to the next to be judged by Jesus, Our Lady will be present to us and she will attain for us the grace of all graces, the grace of final perseverance! This means that she will attain for our hearts sincere sorrow for our sins, true repentance, and great love of God. Thereby we will attain the purpose of our life—the eternal salvation of our immortal soul!

Hopefully we can see now why the apparition of Our Lady of Fatima was such an impactful event in the life of the Church and the world. To be sure, other Marian apparitions had a profound effect on many souls, but no other apparition had such far-reaching implications for the salvation of the world, or involved such dramatic geopolitical elements, with the fall of Communism and the nuclear arms race. The miracle of the sun was also the most witnessed and the most dramatic of miraculous events associated with Marian apparitions. For these reasons, and for giving us the powerful First Saturday Devotion and for the spreading of the most holy Rosary, Our Lady of Fatima has assumed a primary place in the life of the Church.

Fatima Prayers

From the story of Fatima, the Church was gifted many new prayers, which were conveyed to the children by the Angel of Peace and by Our Lady.

Pardon Prayer

My God, I believe, I adore, I hope, and I love Thee! I ask pardon for those who do not believe, do not adore, do not hope, and do not love Thee.

The Angel's Prayer

Most Holy Trinity, Father, Son, and Holy Ghost, I adore Thee profoundly. I offer Thee the Most Precious Body, Blood, Soul and Divinity of Jesus Christ, present in all the tabernacles of the world, in reparation for all the outrages, sacrileges, and indifferences by which He Himself is offended. And through the infinite merits of His Most Sacred Heart and the Immaculate Heart of Mary, I beg of Thee the conversion of poor sinners.

Blessed Sacrament Prayer

Most Holy Trinity, I adore Thee! My God, my God, I love Thee in the Most Blessed Sacrament!

O My Jesus

To be prayed after the Glory Be following each decade of the Rosary.
O my Jesus, forgive us our sins, save us from the fires of hell; lead all souls to heaven, especially those in most need of Thy mercy.

Sacrifice Prayer

To pray while making a sacrificial act.
O Jesus, I offer this for love of Thee, for the conversion of sinners, and in reparation for the sins committed against the Immaculate Heart of Mary.

Lesser-Known Marian Apparitions

Arguably the three most famous Marian apparitions took place in Guadalupe, Lourdes, and Fatima. But the Church has approved just over a dozen others as worthy of belief.

Our Lady of Good Help

This apparition has the distinction of being the only one approved in the United States. Mary appeared to Adele Brise, an immigrant from Belgium, three times over the course of 1859 in Champion, Wisconsin. She called herself the "Queen of Heaven" and encouraged Adele to use the *Catechism* to teach the children in the area about the Catholic faith. In October of that year, a massive wildfire scorched the area. Adele organized a procession to beg the Virgin Mother for her protection. The chapel where she and the others were was spared from the flames, while the area around it was completely destroyed. Over a million acres were torched, making it the worst fire disaster in United States history.

Our Lady of Akita Japan

Our Lady of Akita

In 1973, Sister Agnes Katsuko Sasagawa was visited by the Mother of God in the remote area of Yuzawadai, outside Akita, Japan. Unlike other apparitions, where the seers saw a vision, Sister Agnes heard messages through a wooden statue of Our Lady. The statue also wept tears dozens of times, several of which were broadcast on Japanese TV. Further credibility was given to the events when Sister Agnes experienced a miraculous healing of her hearing impairment. Our Lady spoke to her of the importance of prayer, especially the Rosary, and prophesized persecution and heresy within the Church.

Our Lady of La Salette

In September of 1846, Our Lady appeared in the hill country of La Salette, France to two simple shepherd children named Melanie and Maximin. Unlike most apparitions, she appeared only once and was seated, bent over, and weeping into her hands. Our Lady revealed that she cried for the sins committed by mankind against God, and she implored the children to pray and offer sacrifices for sinners.

Statue of Our Lady of La Salette and the two children

Our Lady of Knock

In the Irish village of Knock, County Mayo, the Virgin Mary appeared in 1879 near a humble church. But she was not alone this time. Appearing alongside her was an altar with a cross hanging above it, and upon the altar rested the Paschal Lamb. Mary was also flanked by Saint John the Evangelist and Saint Joseph. Over a dozen people witnessed the vision, though no words were spoken or messages given. It was a wet night with a storm coming through, yet the area where Mary and the two saints stood remained completely dry. The shrine located there today receives pilgrims from all over the world, some of which report miraculous healings.

Our Lady of Kibeho

The apparitions that took place in southwestern Rwanda are the only Church approved apparitions on the continent of Africa. Mary appeared to several adolescents in the 1980s at a secondary school for girls. She revealed to them an apocalyptic vision of their country descending into violence, which many believed was a prediction of the 1994 Rwandan genocide. Our Lady called herself *Nyina wa Jambo*, the "Mother of the Word," and asked the children to pray to prevent the violent war.

Procession of Candles at the Sanctuary of Our Lady of Fatima, Portugal.
Photo by Ricardo Perna / Shutterstock

CHAPTER 32

Mary's Universal Presence in the World

There is no woman in the history of the world who has a more powerful presence than the most holy, loved, and venerated Blessed Virgin Mary. No woman who ever lived can even come close to wielding the same influence as God's Masterpiece of Creation. Mary has left her indelible seal on all of humanity, and it will persevere until the end of time and extend into eternity.

Therefore, let us highlight the many ways that Mary has engraved her mark upon the world.

We humbly invite all who are willing to open their eyes to the wonderful world that envelops us and to become more cognizant and aware of Mary's far-reaching, powerful, and sanctifying influence.

Honoring the Name of Mary

Parents have the moral obligation to choose a name for their child. The *Catechism of the Catholic Church* stresses the importance of choosing a name that bears a Christian meaning. Thanks be to God that in the history of the world, over the last two millennia, huge numbers of parents have willfully chosen to name their child after Mary. These include many derivative names of Mary, such as Maria, Mara, and Maryanne, but also other names that are simply tied to Mary in a poetic sense, like Fatima, Rose, Carmen, and many others. Parents who have chosen to bless their child with a Marian name bring her blessing down upon them!

Cities, towns, countries, streets, and landmarks also bear the name of Mary, or some other name that is connected to her. Think of the state of Maryland, or the capital of Paraguay, *Asuncion* ("Assumption"), or the province of Argentina, *Rosario* ("Rosary"), or the beautiful town of Carmel in California, after Our Lady of Mount Carmel. Chile has a city with the name *Concepcion*, as in the Immaculate Conception. Obviously, we are just scraping the surface of the almost universal geographical presence of Mary throughout the entire world, and this says nothing of the tens of thousands of churches around the world that bear her name, which is where we shall turn next.

Architecture

It is likely that there is a church named after Mary in nearly every country in the world. Obviously, there are too many to highlight, so let us just mention a few.

The most famous is arguably the Cathedral of Notre Dame (Our Lady) in Paris. Sadly, this glorious structure was devastated by a fire in 2019, but the process to restore it is currently underway. Millions of pilgrims have traveled to Paris to see Notre Dame and place their lives in the hands of their Mother. Meanwhile, in Rome, the oldest basilica built and dedicated to the Blessed Virgin Mary is Santa Maria Maggiore (Saint Mary Major). Before traveling on important apostolic missions, popes will kneel in front of an image of Mary in this basilica and beg for special graces and blessings. Mary indeed does bless them!

In the United States, the Basilica of the Immaculate Conception rises high into the sky in Washington, DC. It is one of the largest churches in the world and is dedicated to Our Lady. The main sanctuary is surrounded by dozens of side chapels honoring Mary's different titles around the world, and even more can be found in the crypt.

In addition to churches and cathedrals, there are dozens of major Marian shrines around the world, many of which were erected in honor of her apparitions, those times she came back to draw us back to God. At three of the most prominent, in Lourdes, Guadalupe, and Fatima, a combined twenty million pilgrims visit each year to pay homage to the Mother of God!

And finally, let us not forget all the hidden monasteries and convents sprinkled in the quiet corners of the world where humble religious Brothers and Sisters bring glory to God and His Mother through their prayerful, contemplative life.

Literature

It is almost impossible to mention the universal presence and significance of Mary in the realm of literature, specifically that of poetry. In *The Divine Comedy*, Dante depicts Mary in counter-position to the capital sin of sloth, manifested in how she

Notre Dame de Paris cathedral, France. Photo by Viacheslav Lopatin / Shutterstock

moved in haste to visit her cousin Elizabeth after the Annunciation. Then, as his literary poem nears its majestic conclusion, Dante ascends with Saint Bernard to the sublime and mystical heights of heaven, where Mary is depicted as the Mystical Rose, beyond which the Holy Trinity—Father, Son, and Holy Spirit—is encountered in the Beatific Vision!

Another touching Marian poem was written by the Mellifluous Doctor, Saint Bernard, entitled *Stella Maris—Mary, the Star of the Sea*. In the midst of life's trials, storms, and tempests, like sailors tossed and turned by the tumultuous waves, we must lift our gaze to Mary. She is the Star of the Sea that will lead us safely and surely to the port of salvation—Heaven .

The presence of Mary abounds not only in an abundance of poetic excellence but also in prose. One book we have already mentioned in this text is *True Devotion to Mary* by Saint Louis de Montfort, which has sold millions of copies around the world. But arguably the greatest Marian text is *The Glories of Mary* by Saint Alphonsus Maria Liguori. This spiritual masterpiece is a Marian compendium of biblical passages, as well as sayings from the Fathers and Doctors of the Church and other saints, writers, and poets expressing their love and confidence in Mary, in her infinite mercy towards all of humanity. This classic also explains in great detail every word from the beautiful Hail Holy Queen prayer. Like *True Devotion*, it has sold millions of copies all over the world.

Music

Saint Augustine has correctly commented, "He who sings, prays twice!" Music is an integral part of the life of humanity and can indeed enrich our emotional, moral, and spiritual life.

Countless Marian songs and hymns have been composed over the past two millennia and in a wide variety of languages. What cannot be fully expressed in prose can be better expressed in poetry, and at times even better in song! It is beyond the realm of possibility to name and express all the Marian hymns, but with great simplicity and humility we will list a mere few: "The Hail Holy Queen," "Salve Regina," "Immaculate Mary," "Sing of Mary," "Ave, Ave Maria" (to Our Lady of Fatima), "Regina Caeli" (Easter season hymn), and of course "Ave Maria." These are gems among the precious jewels in the traditional Catholic musical heritage. By song and chant, we joyfully lift our hearts, minds, and souls to pay tribute and homage to our heavenly queen and loving mother.

Art

Throughout the course of human history—ancient times, the Middle Ages, the Renaissance, and into these modern times—never has there been a woman depicted in art more often than the Virgin Mary, most notably in iconography, in the Eastern Church as well as in the Latin, but also in other forms, capturing her beauty, her elegance, her purity, her allure. One of the most famous and beloved is the *Pieta* sculpted by Michelangelo and found today in a side apse in Saint Peter's Basilica in Rome. He and other artists often spent long hours in prayer and fasting before embarking on their work to honor the Blessed Mother.

Madonna and Child Enthroned (circa 1250-1275)

Another noteworthy artist is the renowned Dominican Blessed Fra Angelico, with many magnificent depictions from the lives of Jesus and Mary, the most famous of which is arguably the *Annunciation of Cortona*, a panel-painting altarpiece once housed in the Church of Gesù in Cortona (Italy) but now found at the Museo Diocesano in Cortona.

Movies

The mediums of art have changed over the years, and in our time, movies have become the dominant form. Too many movies celebrate sinful themes, but there have been some that promote virtue, and even some that honor the Blessed Mother.

The Song of Bernadette is a movie about the apparitions at Lourdes, released in 1943, and there have been several movies made about the apparitions at Fatima. A movie released in 2015 titled *Full of Grace* depicts the later years of Mary's life after Jesus's ascension into heaven. And in 1958, the famous rosary-priest, Venerable Father Patrick Peyton, along with Family Theatre in Hollywood, and with the support of many excellent Catholic actors, helped compose a film on the fifteen mysteries of the Rosary. Father Peyton offers for our viewing the life of Jesus and Mary from the crib to the cross, and to the empty tomb. In our love for the Blessed Virgin Mary and the most holy Rosary, this movie is a must watch. Viewing this cinematic masterpiece will enhance our love for praying the most holy Rosary. Remember the immortal saying of Venerable Patrick Peyton: "The family that prays together stays together."

In this brief overview, we can perceive the profound and universal influence that the Blessed Virgin Mary has on all of humanity in all times and all places. In honoring Mary, we are honoring her Son, Jesus Christ. More than that, we are honoring the Blessed Trinity, for Mary is the daughter of God the Father, the mother of God the Son, and the mystical spouse of the Holy Spirit. Finally, let us beg for the unique grace to perceive Mary present behind the scenes and always at work with the purpose of glorifying God in all times, in all places, and in all circumstances, for it is she who says, "My soul magnifies the Lord and my spirit rejoices in God my Savior" (Lk 1:46–47).

The Coronation of the Virgin, c.1591-92 / Greco, El (Domenico
Theotocopuli) (1541-1614) / Greek / Photo © Bridgeman Images

Conclusion

We hope that as a result of our humble work highlighting various aspects of Marian devotion, your knowledge, love, devotion, and trust in Mary will soar high as the eagle soars. We hope and pray that Mary, your gentle, loving, and all-powerful Mother, will have a central place in your life and in your heart with Jesus, your Lord and Savior. May you wake up each day and consecrate yourself to Jesus through Mary. May you walk and talk to Mary throughout your day as your friend, guide, companion, and Mother—your life, your sweetness, and your hope. In your joys, may you rejoice with Mary, and in your sorrows, may you weep with Mary. In your moments of trial and temptation, may you seek refuge in Mary.

And of greatest importance, we pray that Our Lady will be present to you at all times, but most especially in the hour of your death. May it be through the powerful intercession of Mary that you die in a state of grace so that upon dying, you will open your eyes and be welcomed into the eternal and loving embrace of Jesus, the Son of Mary, who will be your Lord, God, King, Friend, and Lover for all eternity! Through Mary, may the end of your life be a happy and victorious ending!

The Virgin in Prayer, after Giovanni Battista Salvi da Sassoferrato

Marian Prayers

My Mother, My Confidence!

O Mary Immaculate, the precious name of Mother of Confidence,
with which we honor thee,
fills our hearts to overflowing with the sweetest consolation
and moves us to hope for every blessing from thee.

If such a title has been given to thee,
it is a sure sign that no one has recourse to thee in vain.

Accept, therefore, with a mother's love, our devout homage,
as we earnestly beseech thee to be gracious unto us in our every need.

Above all do we pray thee to make us live in constant union
with thee and thy Divine Son, Jesus.

With thee as our guide, we are certain that we shall ever walk in the right way, in such wise that it will be our happy lot to hear thee say on the last day of our life those words of comfort: "Come then, my good and faithful servant; enter thou into the joy of my Lord." Amen.

My Mother, my Confidence!

Hail Holy Queen

Hail Holy Queen, Mother of mercy, our life, our sweetness,
and our hope!

To thee do we cry, poor banished children of Eve.

To thee do we send up our signs, mourning and weeping in this
valley of tears.

Turn then, most gracious advocate, thine eyes of mercy toward us.

And after this our exile, show unto us the blessed Fruit of thy womb, Jesus.

O clement, O loving, O sweet Virgin Mary.

> V. Pray for us, O holy Mother of God,
> R. *That we may be made worthy of the promises of Christ.*

Mary, Queen of Heaven and Earth, pray for us!

Prayer to Mary, the New Eve

Dear Mother Mary, you are the true Mother of the Living. Help me to know and love you and Jesus more and more each day. Mary, Mother of the Living, help me to avoid the near occasions of sin, keep me away from the forbidden fruits in my life. In moments of temptation, come to my aid and crush with your heel the ugly head of the serpent, the devil. Amen.

Prayer to Mary, the New Ark of the Covenant

Dearest Mary, mother of Jesus and my mother, I thank you for saying "yes" to God and bringing Jesus to be with us always, even until the end of time. Help me to be more aware of your presence in my life. Help me to be more aware of Jesus's real presence in my soul in Holy Communion. Help me to be more aware of Jesus's real presence in the tabernacle. Jesus, Mary, and Joseph, I love you! Amen.

The Magnificat

My soul proclaims the greatness of the Lord;
My spirit rejoices in God my Savior;
For He has looked with favor on His lowly servant.
From this day all generations will call me blessed;
For the Almighty has done great things for me, and holy is His Name.
He has mercy on those who fear Him in every generation.
He has shown the strength of His arm;
He has scattered the proud in their conceit.
He has cast down the mighty from their thrones,
and has lifted up the lowly.
He has filled the hungry with good things,

and the rich He has sent away empty.
He has come to the help of His servant Israel;
for He has remembered His promise of mercy,
the promise He made to our fathers,
to Abraham and his children forever. (Lk 1:46–55)

Sub Tuum Praesidium

We fly to thy protection,
O Holy Mother of God;
Despise not our petitions
in our necessities,
but deliver us always
from all dangers,
O Glorious and Blessed Virgin.
Amen.

The Angelus

V: The Angel of the Lord declared unto Mary,
R: *And she conceived by the power of the Holy Spirit.*

Hail Mary, full of grace,
the Lord is with thee.
Blessed art thou among women,
and blessed is the fruit of thy womb, Jesus.
Holy Mary, Mother of God,
pray for us sinners,
now and at the hour of our death. Amen.

V. Behold the handmaid of the Lord.
R. *Be it done unto to me according to thy word.*
(*Repeat the Hail Mary*)

V. And the Word was made flesh,
R. *And dwelt among us.*
(*Repeat the Hail Mary*)

V. Pray for us O Holy Mother of God,
R. *That we may be made worthy of the promises of Christ.*

Pour forth we beseech thee, O Lord, thy grace into our hearts, that we to whom the Incarnation of Christ thy son was made known by the message of an angel, may by His Passion and cross, be brought to the glory of His resurrection. Through the same Christ Our Lord. Amen.

The Regina Caeli

V. Queen of Heaven, rejoice, alleluia.
R. *For He whom you did merit to bear, alleluia.*

V. Has risen, as He said, alleluia.
R. *Pray for us to God, alleluia.*

V. Rejoice, and be glad, O Virgin Mary, alleluia.
R. *For the Lord is truly risen, alleluia.*

Let us pray:

O God, who gave joy to the world through the Resurrection of Thy Son, Our Lord Jesus Christ, grant we beseech Thee, that through the intercession of the Virgin Mary, His Mother, we may obtain the joys of everlasting life. Through the same Christ Our Lord. Amen.

The Litany of the Blessed Virgin Mary of Loreto

Lord, have mercy.
Christ, have mercy.
Lord, have mercy.
Christ, hear us.
Christ, graciously hear us.
God, the Father of Heaven, have mercy on us.
God the Son, Redeemer of the World, have mercy on us.
God the Holy Spirit, have mercy on us.
Holy Trinity, One God, have mercy on us.
Holy Mary, pray for us.
Holy Mother of God, pray for us.
Holy Virgin of Virgins, pray for us.
Mother of Christ, pray for us.
Mother of Divine Grace, pray for us.
Mother most Pure, pray for us.
Mother most Chaste, pray for us.
Mother Inviolate, pray for us.
Mother Undefiled, pray for us.
Mother most Amiable, pray for us.
Mother most Admirable, pray for us.
Mother of Good Counsel, pray for us.
Mother of our Creator, pray for us.
Mother of our Savior, pray for us.
Virgin most Prudent, pray for us.
Virgin most Venerable, pray for us.

Virgin most Renowned, pray for us.
Virgin most Powerful, pray for us.
Virgin most Merciful, pray for us.
Virgin most Faithful, pray for us.
Mirror of Justice, pray for us.
Seat of Wisdom, pray for us.
Cause of our Joy, pray for us.
Spiritual Vessel, pray for us.
Vessel of Honor, pray for us.
Singular Vessel of Devotion, pray for us.
Mystical Rose, pray for us.
Tower of David, pray for us.
Tower of Ivory, pray for us.
House of Gold, pray for us.
Ark of the Covenant, pray for us.
Gate of Heaven, pray for us.
Morning Star, pray for us.
Health of the Sick, pray for us.
Refuge of Sinners, pray for us.
Comforter of the Afflicted, pray for us.
Help of Christians, pray for us.
Queen of Angels, pray for us.
Queen of Patriarchs, pray for us.
Queen of Prophets, pray for us.
Queen of Apostles, pray for us.
Queen of Martyrs, pray for us.
Queen of Confessors, pray for us.
Queen of Virgins, pray for us.
Queen of all Saints, pray for us.
Queen conceived without Original Sin,
    pray for us.
Queen assumed into Heaven, pray for us.
Queen of the most Holy Rosary, pray for us.
Queen of the Family, pray for us.
Queen of Peace, pray for us.

Lamb of God, Who takes away the sins
    of the world,
        spare us, O Lord!

Lamb of God, Who takes away the sins
    of the world,
        graciously hear us, O Lord!
Lamb of God, Who takes away the sins
    of the world,
        have mercy on us.

V. Pray for us, O Holy Mother of God.
R. *That we may be made worthy of the
    promises of Christ.*

Grant, we beg you, O Lord God, that we your servants may enjoy lasting health of mind and body, and by the glorious intercession of the Blessed Mary ever Virgin, be delivered from present sorrow and enter into the joy of eternal happiness. Through Christ Our Lord. Amen.

Prayer to Our Lady of Mount Carmel

O most beautiful flower of Mount Carmel, Fruitful Vine, Splendor of Heaven, Blessed Mother of the Son of God, Immaculate Virgin, assist me in this necessity. *(Mention your petition.)* O Star of the Sea, help me and show me in this that thou art my Mother.

O holy Mary, Mother of God, Queen of Heaven and earth, I humbly beseech thee, from the bottom of my heart, to succor me in this necessity; there are none that can withstand thy power. Oh, show me in this that thou art my Mother!

O Mary, conceived without sin, pray for us who have recourse to thee. *(three times)*

Sweet Mother, I place this cause in thy hands. *(three times)*

(It is suggested to offer three times the Our Father, Hail Mary and Glory Be in thanksgiving.)

Memorare

Remember, O most gracious Virgin Mary, that never was it known, that anyone who fled to your protection, implored your help, or sought your intercession was left unaided. Inspired with this confidence, I fly to thee, O Virgin of virgins, my Mother; to thee do I come, before thee I stand, sinful and sorrowful. O Mother of the Word Incarnate, despise not my petitions, but in thy mercy hear and answer me. Amen.

Prayer to the Holy Family

Jesus, Mary, and Joseph, I give you my heart and my soul.
Jesus, Mary, and Joseph, make my heart like unto yours.
Jesus, Mary, and Joseph, assist me in my last agony.
Jesus, Mary, and Joseph, I breathe forth my soul unto thee. Amen.

Prayer to Mary, Mistress of the Angels

O Exalted Queen of Heaven, Sovereign Mistress of the Angels, thou who from the beginning hast received from God the power and the mission to crush the head of Satan, we humbly beseech thee to send down thy holy angels, that under thy command and by thy power, they may pursue the evil spirits, encounter them on every side, resist their bold attacks and drive them hence into the abyss of hell.

"Who is like unto God?" "Holy Angels and Archangels, defend us and protect us!"
"O kind and tender Mother, thou shalt ever remain our love and our hope." Amen.

Prayer to Our Lady of Guadalupe

Our Lady of Guadalupe, Mystical Rose, intercede for Holy Church, protect the sovereign pontiff, help all those who invoke you in their necessities; and since you are the ever Virgin Mary and Mother of the True God, obtain for us from your most holy Son the grace of keeping our faith, sweet hope in the midst of the bitterness of life, burning charity, and the precious gift of final perseverance. Amen.

Prayer to Our Lady of Lourdes

O Ever Immaculate Virgin, Mother of Mercy, Health of the Sick, Refuge of Sinners, Comfortress of the Afflicted, you know my wants, my troubles, my sufferings. Look upon me with mercy. When you appeared in the grotto of Lourdes, you made it a privileged sanctuary where you dispense your favors, and where many sufferers have obtained the cure of their infirmities, both spiritual and corporeal. I come, therefore, with unbounded confidence to implore your maternal intercession. My loving Mother, obtain my request (here mention request). I will try to imitate your virtues so that I may one day share your company and bless you in eternity. Amen.

The Fatima Prayers

Pardon Prayer

My God, I believe, I adore, I hope, and I love Thee! I ask pardon for those who do not believe, do not adore, do not hope, and do not love Thee.

The Angel's Prayer

Most Holy Trinity, Father, Son, and Holy Ghost, I adore Thee profoundly. I offer Thee the Most Precious Body, Blood, Soul and Divinity of Jesus Christ, present in all the tabernacles of the world, in reparation for all the outrages, sacrileges, and indifferences by which He Himself is offended. And through the infinite merits of His Most Sacred Heart and the Immaculate Heart of Mary, I beg of Thee the conversion of poor sinners.

Blessed Sacrament Prayer

Most Holy Trinity, I adore Thee! My God, my God, I love Thee in the
Most Blessed Sacrament!

O My Jesus

(*To be prayed after the Glory Be following each decade of the Rosary.*)
O my Jesus, forgive us our sins, save us from the fires of hell; lead all souls to heaven, especially those in most need of Thy mercy.

Sacrifice Prayer

(*To pray while making a sacrificial act.*)
O Jesus, I offer this for love of Thee, for the conversion of sinners, and in reparation for the sins committed against the Immaculate Heart of Mary.

The Seven Sorrows Devotion

The First Sorrow: The Prophecy of Simeon

I grieve for thee, O Mary most sorrowful, in the affliction of thy tender heart at the prophecy of the holy and aged Simeon. Dear Mother, by thy heart so afflicted, obtain for me the virtue of humility and the gift of the holy fear of God.

Hail Mary, full of grace, . . .

The Second Sorrow: The Flight into Egypt

I grieve for thee, O Mary most sorrowful, in the anguish of thy most affectionate heart during the flight into Egypt and thy sojourn there. Dear Mother, by thy heart so troubled, obtain for me the virtue of generosity, especially toward the poor, and the gift of piety.

Hail Mary, full of grace, . . .

The Third Sorrow: The Loss of the Child Jesus in the Temple

I grieve for thee, O Mary most sorrowful, in those anxieties which tried thy troubled heart at the loss of thy dear Jesus. Dear Mother, by thy heart so full of anguish, obtain for me the virtue of chastity and the gift of knowledge.

Hail Mary, full of grace, . . .

The Fourth Sorrow: Mary Meets Jesus on the Way to Calvary

I grieve for thee, O Mary most sorrowful, in the consternation of thy heart at meeting Jesus as He carried His cross. Dear Mother, by thy heart so troubled, obtain for me the virtue of patience and the gift of fortitude.

Hail Mary, full of grace, . . .

The Fifth Sorrow: Jesus Dies on the Cross

I grieve for thee, O Mary most sorrowful, in the martyrdom which thy generous heart endured in standing near Jesus in His agony. Dear Mother, by thy afflicted heart, obtain for me the virtue of temperance and the gift of counsel.

Hail Mary, full of grace, . . .

Sixth Sorrow: Mary Receives the Dead Body of Jesus into Her Arms

I grieve for thee, O Mary most sorrowful, in the wounding of thy compassionate heart, when the side of Jesus was struck by the lance and His heart was pierced before His body was removed from the cross. Dear Mother, by thy heart thus transfixed, obtain for me the virtue of fraternal charity and the gift of understanding.

Hail Mary, full of grace, . . .

The Seventh Sorrow: Jesus Is Placed in the Tomb

I grieve for thee, O Mary most sorrowful, for the pangs that wrenched thy most loving heart at the burial of Jesus. Dear Mother, by thy heart sunk in the bitterness of desolation, obtain for me the virtue of diligence and the gift of wisdom.

Hail Mary, full of grace, . . .

V. Pray for us, O Virgin most sorrowful,

R. *That we may be made worthy of the promises of Christ.*

Let us pray:

Let intercession be made for us, we beseech Thee, O Lord Jesus Christ, now and at the hour of our death, before the throne of Thy mercy, by the Blessed Virgin Mary, Thy Mother, whose most holy soul was pierced by a sword of sorrow in the hour of Thy bitter Passion. Through Thee, O Jesus Christ, Savior of the world, who with the Father and the Holy Ghost lives and reigns world without end. Amen.

Prayer to Our Mother of Sorrows for a Happy Death

O Mother of Sorrows, by the anguish and love with which thou didst stand by the Cross of Jesus, stand by me in my last agony. To thy maternal heart I commend the last three hours of my life. Offer these hours to the Eternal Father in union with the agony of our dearest Lord. Offer frequently to the Eternal Father, in atonement for my sins, the Precious Blood of Jesus, mingled with thy tears on Calvary, to obtain for me the grace to receive Holy Communion with most perfect love and contrition before my death, and to breathe forth my soul in the actual presence of Jesus.

Dearest Mother, when the moment of my death has come, present me as thy child to Jesus; say to
Him on my behalf: "Son, forgive him, for he knew not what he did. Receive him this day into Thy kingdom." Amen.

Prayer to Our Lady, Undoer of Knots

Mary, Undoer of Knots, pray for me. Virgin Mary, Mother of fair love, Mother who never refuses to come to the aid of a child in need, Mother whose hands never cease to serve your beloved children because they are moved by the divine love and immense mercy that exist in your heart, cast your compassionate eyes upon me and see the snarl of knots that exists in my life. You know very well how desperate I am, my pain, and how I am bound by these knots. Mary, Mother to whom God entrusted the undoing of the knots in the lives of his children, I entrust into your hands the ribbon of my life. No one, not even the evil one himself, can take it away from your precious care. In your hands there is no knot that cannot be undone. Powerful Mother, by your grace and intercessory power with Your Son and My Liberator, Jesus, take into your hands today this knot. [Mention your request here] I beg you to undo it for the glory of God, once for all. You are my hope. O my Lady, you are the only consolation God gives me, the fortification of my feeble strength, the enrichment of my destitution, and, with Christ, the freedom from my chains. Hear my plea. Keep me, guide me, protect me, o safe refuge! Amen.

Stabat Mater

At the Cross her station keeping,
stood the mournful Mother weeping,
close to her Son to the last.

Through her heart, His sorrow sharing,
all His bitter anguish bearing,
now at length the sword has passed.

O how sad and sore distressed
was that Mother, highly blest,
of the sole-begotten One.

Christ above in torment hangs,
she beneath beholds the pangs
of her dying glorious Son.

Is there one who would not weep,
whelmed in miseries so deep,
Christ's dear Mother to behold?

Can the human heart refrain
from partaking in her pain,
in that Mother's pain untold?

Bruis'd, derided, curs'd, defiled,
she beheld her tender child
all with bloody scourges rent.

For the love of His own nation,
saw Him hang in desolation,
till His spirit forth He sent.

O thou Mother! Fount of love!
Touch my spirit from above,
make my heart with thine accord.

Make me feel as thou hast felt;
make my soul to glow and melt
with the love of Christ my Lord.

Holy Mother! Pierce me through,
in my heart each wound renew
of my Savior crucified.

Let me share with thee His pain,
who for all my sins was slain,
who for me in torments died.

Let me mingle tears with thee,
mourning Him who mourned for me,
all the days that I may live.

By the Cross with thee to stay,
there with thee to weep and pray,
is all I ask of thee to give.

Virgin of all virgins blest!
Listen to my fond request,
let me share thy grief divine.

Let me, to my latest breath,
in my body bear the death
of that dying Son of thine.

Wounded with His every wound,
steep my soul till it hath swooned,
in His very Blood away.

Be to me, O Virgin, nigh,
lest in flames I burn and die,
in His awful Judgment Day.

Christ, when Thou shalt call me hence,
be Thy Mother my defense,
be Thy Cross my victory.

While my body here decays,
may my soul Thy goodness praise,
safe in Paradise with Thee.

Daily Offering to the Blessed Virgin Mary

My Queen and my Mother, to you I offer myself without any reserve; and to give you a mark of my devotion, I consecrate to you during this day my eyes, my ears, my mouth, my heart, and my whole person. Since I belong to you, O my good Mother, preserve and defend me as your property and possession. Amen.

Remember, O Virgin Mother

Remember, O Virgin Mother of God, when thou shalt stand before the face of the Lord, to speak favorable things in our behalf, that He may turn away His indignation from us.

Rejoice, O Virgin Mary

Rejoice, O Virgin Mary, for thou alone hast destroyed all heresies in the whole world.

O Heart Most Pure

O Heart most pure of the Blessed Virgin Mary, obtain for me from Jesus
a pure and humble heart.

How to Pray the Rosary

1. Make the Sign of the Cross and say The Apostles' Creed.
2. Say the Our Father.
3. Say 3 Hail Marys.
4. Say the Glory Be to the Father.
5. Announce the First Mystery; then say the Our Father.
6. Say 10 Hail Marys.
7. Say the Glory Be to the Father.
8. Say the O My Jesus.
9. Announce the Second Mystery; then say the Our Father, 10 Hail Marys, Glory Be and O My Jesus.
10. Announce the Third Mystery; then say the Our Father, 10 Hail Marys, Glory Be and O My Jesus.
11. Announce the Fourth Mystery; then say the Our Father, 10 Hail Marys, Glory Be and O My Jesus.
12. Announce the Fifth Mystery; then say the Our Father, 10 Hail Marys, Glory Be and O My Jesus.
13. Conclude by saying the Hail, Holy Queen.
14. Follow with Prayer after the Rosary, if desired.

The 54-Day Rosary Novena

The 54-Day Rosary Novena consists of a Rosary (5-decade) prayed every day for 54 consecutive days. The Novena is based on the traditional 15 Mysteries of the Rosary. On the first 27 days of the Novena, the Rosary is prayed in Petition. On the remaining 27 days, the Rosary is prayed in Thanksgiving, whether or not one has received an answer to his Petition. In praying this novena, a person cycles through the Joyful, Sorrowful and Glorious Mysteries over and over. To keep track, a person can mark out the letters J, S, G, J, S, G, etc. on 54 consecutive days of a calendar, then check off the appropriate letter after praying the Rosary on that day.

The Rosary in Latin

Symbolum Apostolorum

The Apostles' Creed

Credo in Deum Patrem omnipotentem, Creatorem caeli et terrae; et in Jesum Christum, Filium eius unicum, Dominum nostrum, qui conceptus est de Spiritu Sancto, natus ex MariaVirgine, passus sub Pontio Pilato, crucifixus,mortuus, et sepultus: descendit ad infernos, tertia die resurrexit a mortuis, ascendit ad caelos, sedet ad dexteram Dei Patris omnipotentis, inde venturus est judicare vivos et mortuos. Credo in Spiritum Sanctum, sanctam Ecclesiam catholicam, sanctorum communionem, remissionem peccatorum, carnis resurrectionem et vitam aeternam. Amen.

Pater Noster

Our Father

Pater noster, qui es in caelis, sanctificetur nomen tuum. Adveniat regnum tuum. Fiat voluntas tua sicut in caelo et in terra. Panem nostrum quotidianum da nobis hodie; et dimitte nobis debita nostra, sicut et nos dimittimus debitoribus nostris. Et ne nos inducas in tentationem. Sed libera nos a malo. Amen.

Ave Maria

Hail Mary

Ave Maria, gratia plena: Dominus tecum: benedicta tu in mulieribus, et benedictus fructus ventris tui, Jesus. Sancta Maria, Mater Dei, ora pro nobis peccatoribus, nunc et in hora mortis nostrae. Amen.

Gloria Patri

Glory Be

Gloria Patri, et Filio, et Spiritui Sancto. Sicut erat in principio, et nunc et semper, et in saecula saeculorum. Amen.

O Mi Jesu

O My Jesus

O mi Jesu, dimitte nobis debita nostra, salva nos ab igne inferni, perduc in caelum omnes animas, praesertim eas, quae misericordiae tuae maxime indigent.

Salve Regina

Hail Holy Queen

Salve Regina! Mater Misericordiae, vita, dulcedo, et spes nostra, salve! Ad te clamamus, exsules filii Evae. Ad te suspiramus, gementes et flentes in hac lacrimarum valle. Eia ergo, advocate nostra, illos tuos misericordes oculos ad nos converte. Et Jesum, benedictum fructum ventris tui, nobis post hoc exsilium ostende. O clemens, O pia, O dulcis Virgo Maria!

> V. Ora pro nobis, sancta Dei Genitrix,
> R. *Ut digni efficiamur promissionibus Christi.*

Novena to Our Lady of Good Remedy

O Queen of Heaven and earth, most holy Virgin, we venerate thee. Thou art the beloved daughter of the Most High God, the chosen Mother of the Incarnate Word, the Immaculate Spouse of the Holy Spirit, the Sacred Vessel of the Most Holy Trinity. O Mother of the Divine Redeemer, who under the title of Our Lady of Good Remedy comes to the aid of all who call upon thee, extend thy maternal protection to us. We depend on thee, dear Mother, as helpless and needy children depend on a tender and caring mother.

> Hail Mary . . .

O Lady of Good Remedy, source of unfailing help, grant that we may draw from thy treasury of graces in our time of need. Touch the hearts of sinners, that they may seek reconciliation and forgiveness. Bring comfort to the afflicted and the lonely; help the poor and the hopeless; aid the sick and the suffering. May they be healed in body and strengthened in spirit to endure their sufferings with patient resignation and Christian fortitude.

> Hail Mary . . .

Dear Lady of Good Remedy, source of unfailing help, thy compassionate heart knows a remedy for every affliction and misery we encounter in life. Help me with thy prayers and intercession to find a remedy for my problems and needs, especially for (Indicate your special intentions here). On my part, O loving Mother, I pledge myself to a more intensely Christian lifestyle, to a more careful observance of the laws of God, to be more conscientious in fulfilling the obligations of my state in life, and to strive to be a source of healing in this broken world of ours.

Dear Lady of Good Remedy, be ever present to me, and through thy intercession, may I enjoy health of body and peace of mind, and grow stronger in the faith and in the love of thy Son, Jesus.

Hail Mary . . .

V. Pray for us, O holy Mother of Good Remedy,
R. *That we may deepen our dedication to thy Son, and make the world alive with His Spirit.*

Salutation to Mary

A copy of this prayer was found in a book belonging to St. Margaret Mary after her death. This salutation was zealously propagated by Father Paul of Moll, O.S.B. (Belgium), 1824-1896. He said: "This salutation is so beautiful! Recite it daily. From her throne in Heaven the Blessed Virgin will bless you, and you must make the Sign of the Cross. Yes! Yes! If only you could see— Our Lady blesses you. I know it!" "Offered for the conversion of a sinner it would be impossible not to be granted."

Hail Mary, Daughter of God the Father!
Hail Mary, Mother of God the Son!
Hail Mary, Spouse of God the Holy Ghost!
Hail Mary, Temple of the Most Blessed Trinity!
Hail Mary, Pure Lily of the Effulgent Trinity!
Hail Mary, Celestial Rose of the ineffable Love of God!
Hail Mary, Virgin pure and humble, of whom the King of Heaven willed to be born
     and with thy milk to be nourished!
Hail Mary, Virgin of Virgins!
Hail Mary, Queen of Martyrs, whose soul a sword transfixed!
Hail Mary, Lady most blessed, unto whom all power in Heaven and earth is given!
Hail Mary, My Queen and my Mother, My Life, my Sweetness and my Hope!
Hail Mary, Mother most amiable!
Hail Mary, Mother most admirable!
Hail Mary, Mother of Divine Love!
Hail Mary, IMMACULATE, conceived without sin!
Hail Mary, Full of grace, the Lord is with thee!
Blessed art thou among women, and blessed is the Fruit of thy womb, JESUS!
Blessed be thy spouse, St. Joseph.
Blessed be thy father, St. Joachim.
Blessed be thy mother, St. Anne.
Blessed be thy guardian, St. John.
Blessed be thy holy angel, St. Gabriel.
Glory be to God the Father, who chose thee.

Glory be to God the Son, who loved thee.

Glory be to God the Holy Ghost, who espoused thee.

O Glorious Virgin Mary, may all men love and praise thee.

Holy Mary, Mother of God, pray for us and bless us, now,

and at death, in the Name of JESUS, thy Divine Son! Amen.

Thirty Days' Prayer to the Blessed Virgin

Ever glorious and blessed Mary, Queen of Virgins, Mother of Mercy, hope and comfort of dejected and desolate souls! Through that sword of sorrow which pierced thy tender heart whilst thine only Son, Christ Jesus Our Lord, suffered death and ignominy on the Cross; through that filial tenderness and pure love He had for thee, grieving at thy grief, whilst from His cross He commended thee to the care and protection of His beloved disciple St. John; take pity, I beseech thee, on my poverty and necessities; have compassion on my anxieties and cares; assist and comfort me in all my infirmities and miseries, of whatsoever kind.

Thou art the Mother of Mercies, the sweet Consolatrix and only refuge of the needy and the orphan, of the desolate and afflicted. Cast, therefore, an eye of pity on a miserable, forlorn child of Eve, and hear my prayer. For since, in just punishment of my sins, I find myself encompassed by a multitude of evils and oppressed with much anguish of spirit, whither can I fly for more secure shelter, O amiable Mother of my Lord and Saviour Jesus Christ, than under the wings of thy maternal protection? Attend, therefore, I beseech thee, with an ear of pity and compassion, to my humble and earnest request.

I ask it through the bowels of mercy of thy dear Son; through that love and condescension wherewith He embraced our nature when, in compliance with the Divine Will, thou gavest thy consent, and whom, after the expiration of nine months, thou didst bring forth from the chaste enclosure of thy womb to visit this world and bless it with His presence.

I ask it through that anguish of mind wherewith thy beloved Son, our dear Saviour, was overwhelmed on Mount Olivet when He besought His Eternal Father to remove from Him, if possible, the bitter chalice of His future Passion. I ask it through the threefold repetition of His prayers in the Garden, from whence afterwards, with dolorous steps and mournful tears, thou didst accompany Him to the doleful theatre of His death and sufferings. I ask it through the welts and sores of His virginal flesh occasioned by the cords and whips wherewith He was bound and scourged when stripped of His seamless garment, for which His executioners afterwards cast lots. I ask it through the scoffs and ignominies by which He was insulted; the false accusations and unjust sentence by which He was condemned to death, and which He bore with heavenly patience. I ask it through His bitter tears and bloody sweat, His silence and resignation, His sadness and grief of heart. I ask it through the blood which trickled from His royal and sacred Head when struck with the scepter of a reed and pierced with His crown of thorns.

I ask it through the excruciating torments He suffered when His hands and feet were fastened with gross nails to the tree of the Cross. I ask it through His vehement thirst and bitter potion of vinegar and gall. I ask it through His dereliction on the Cross when He exclaimed: "My God! My God! Why hast Thou forsaken me?" I ask it through His mercy extended to the Good Thief, and through His commending His precious soul and spirit into the hands of His Eternal Father before He expired, saying: "It is consummated." I ask it through the blood mixed with water which issued from His sacred side when pierced with a lance, and whence a flood of grace and mercy has flowed to us.

I ask it through His immaculate life, bitter Passion and ignominious death on the Cross, at which nature itself was thrown into convulsions by the bursting of rocks, rending of the veil of the Temple, the earthquake, and darkness of the sun and moon. I ask it through His descent into hell, where He comforted the Saints of the Old Law with His presence and led captivity captive.

I ask it through His glorious victory over death, when He arose again to life on the third day; and through the joy which His appearance for 40 days after gave thee, His Blessed Mother, His Apostles, and the rest of His disciples, when in thine and their presence He miraculously ascended into Heaven. I ask it through the grace of the Holy Ghost infused into the hearts of His disciples when He descended upon them in the form of fiery tongues, and by which they were inspired with zeal for the conversion of the world when they went forth to preach the Gospel.

I ask it through the awful appearance of thy Son at the last dreadful day, when He shall come to judge the living and the dead, and the world by fire. I ask it through the compassion He bore thee in this life, and the ineffable joy thou didst feel at thine Assumption into Heaven, where thou art eternally absorbed in the sweet contemplation of His divine perfections. O glorious and ever blessed Virgin! Comfort the heart of thy supplicant, by obtaining for me *(here mention or reflect on your lawful request, under the reservation of its being agreeable to the will of God, who sees whether it will contribute toward your spiritual good).*

And as I am persuaded that my Divine Saviour doth honor thee as His beloved Mother, to whom He refuses nothing, because thou askest nothing contrary to His honor, so let me speedily experience the efficacy of thy powerful intercession, according to the tenderness of thy maternal affection and His filial loving heart, who mercifully granteth the requests and complieth with the desires of those that love and fear Him. Wherefore, O most blessed Virgin, besides the object of my present petition, and whatever else I may stand in need of, obtain for me also of thy dear Son, Our Lord and our God, a lively faith, firm hope, perfect charity, true contrition of heart, unfeigned tears of compunction, sincere confession, worthy satisfaction, abstinence from sin, love of God and my neighbor, contempt of the world, patience to suffer affronts and ignominies, nay, even, if necessary, an opprobrious death itself, for love of thy Son, our Saviour Jesus Christ.

Obtain likewise for me, O sacred Mother of God, perseverance in good works, performance of good resolutions, mortification of self will, a pious conversation through life, and, at my last moments, strong and sincere repentance, accompanied by such a lively and attentive presence of mind as may enable me to receive the Last Sacraments of the Church worthily and die in thy friendship and favor.

Lastly, obtain through thy Son, I beseech thee, for the souls of my parents, brethren, relatives and benefactors, both living and dead, life everlasting, from the only Giver of every good and perfect gift, the Lord God Almighty: to whom be all power, now and forever. Amen.

Miraculous Medal Prayer

O Mary, conceived without sin, pray for us who have recourse to thee.

Act of Reparation to the Immaculate Heart of Mary

O Most Holy Virgin Mother, we listen with grief to the complaints of your Immaculate Heart surrounded with the thorns placed therein at every moment by the blasphemies and ingratitude of ungrateful humanity. We are moved by the ardent desire of loving you as Our Mother and of promoting a true devotion to your Immaculate Heart.

We therefore kneel before you to manifest the sorrow we feel for the grievances that people cause you, and to atone by our prayers and sacrifices for the offenses with which they return your love. Obtain for them and for us the pardon of so many sins. Hasten the conversion of sinners that they may love Jesus and cease to offend the Lord, already so much offended. Turn your eyes of mercy toward us, that we may love God with all our heart on earth and enjoy Him forever in heaven. Amen.

Novena to Our Lady of Hope

In the Name of the Father, and of the Son, and of the Holy Spirit.

I am the mother of fair love, and of fear, and of knowledge, and of holy hope. In me is all grace of the way and of the truth; in me is all hope of life and of virtue. Come to me all that desire me and be filled with my fruits (Sir 24:24–26).

O Blessed Virgin Mary, Mother of Grace, Hope of the world.
Hear us, your children, who cry to you.

Let Us Pray

O God, who by the marvelous protection of the Blessed Virgin Mary has strengthened us firmly in hope, grant we beseech You, that by persevering in prayer at her admonition, we may obtain the favors we devoutly implore. Through Christ Our Lord. Amen.

Prayer to Our Lady of Hope

O Mary, my Mother, I kneel before you with heavy heart. The burden of my sins oppresses me. The knowledge of my weakness discourages me. I am beset by fears and temptations of every sort. Yet I am so attached to the things of this world that instead of longing for Heaven I am filled with dread at the thought of death.

O Mother of Mercy, have pity on me in my distress. You are all-powerful with your Divine Son. He can refuse no request of your Immaculate Heart. Show yourself a true Mother to me by being my advocate before His throne. O Refuge of Sinners and Hope of the Hopeless, to whom shall I turn if not you?

Obtain for me, then, O Mother of Hope, the grace of true sorrow for my sins, the gift of perfect resignation to God's Holy Will, and the courage to take up my cross and follow Jesus. Beg of His Sacred Heart the special favor that I ask in this novena.

(*Make your request*)

But above all I pray, O dearest Mother, that through your most powerful intercession my heart may be filled with Holy Hope, so that in life's darkest hour I may never fail to trust in God my Savior, but by walking in the way of His commandments I may merit to be united with Him, and with you in the eternal joys of Heaven. Amen.

Mary, our Hope, have pity on us.

Hope of the Hopeless, pray for us.

Conclude with three Hail Marys.

A Consecration to Mary

Hail Mary...

My Queen, my Mother! I give myself entirely to you, and to show my devotion to you, I consecrate to you this day my eyes, my ears, my mouth, my heart, my whole being without reserve. Since, loving Mother, I am your own, keep me and guard me as your property and possession. Amen.

IMAGE CREDITS

P. vi: The Heart of Mary, by Leopold Kupelwieser (1796–1862), Author: Diana Ringo, Source: https://commons.wikimedia.org/wiki/File:Immaculate_Heart_of_Mary.jpg, License: (CC BY-SA 4.0) https://creativecommons.org/licenses/by-sa/4.0/deed.en.

P. 4: Madonna with child, by Il Sassoferrato, Author: NikonZ7II, Source: https://commons.wikimedia.org/wiki/File:Madonna_with_child_by_Il_Sassoferrato.jpg, License: (CC BY-SA 4.0) https://creativecommons.org/licenses/by-sa/4.0/deed.en.

P. 72: Fresco of the Seven Sorrows of the Blessed Virgin, by Tempesta and Circignani, Santo Stefano Rotondo, Rome, Author: Alekjds, Source: https://commons.wikimedia.org/wiki/File:Seven_Sorrows_S_Stefano_Rotondo_Roma.JPG, License: (CC BY-SA 4.0) https://creativecommons.org/licenses/by-sa/4.0/deed.en.

P. 76: Immaculate Heart of Mary, Saint Mary of Perpetual Help Church (Defiance, Ohio), Author: Nheyob, Source: https://commons.wikimedia.org/wiki/File:Saint_Mary_of_Perpetual_Help_Church_(Defiance,_Ohio)_-_stained-glass,_Immaculate_Heart_of_Mary.jpg, License: (CC BY-SA 4.0) https://creativecommons.org/licenses/by-sa/4.0/deed.en.

P. 106: Our Lady of the Holy Rosary, by Simone Cantarini (1612–1648), Author: Mattes, Source: https://commons.wikimedia.org/wiki/File:2017-03_Brescia_Mattes_Pana_(111).JPG, License: (CC BY-SA 4.0) https://creativecommons.org/licenses/by-sa/4.0/deed.en.

P. 126: Holy Family Catholic Church (North Baltimore, Ohio) - stained glass, Miraculous Medal 1, Author: Nheyob, Source: https://commons.wikimedia.org/wiki/File:Holy_Family_Catholic_Church_(North_Baltimore,_Ohio)_-_stained_glass,_Miraculous_Medal_1.jpg, License: (CC BY-SA 3.0) https://creativecommons.org/licenses/by-sa/3.0/deed.en.

P. 126: Holy Family Catholic Church (North Baltimore, Ohio) - stained glass, Miraculous Medal 2, (slightly altered angle of image from the original) Author: Nheyob, Source: https://commons.wikimedia.org/wiki/File:Holy_Family_Catholic_Church_(North_Baltimore,_Ohio)_-_stained_glass,_Miraculous_Medal_2.jpg, License: (CC BY-SA 3.0) https://creativecommons.org/licenses/by-sa/3.0/deed.en.

P. 129, 131: Medal of the Immaculate Conception (aka Miraculous Medal), Author: Xhienne, Source: https://commons.wikimedia.org/wiki/File:Miraculous_medal.jpg, License: (CC BY-SA 3.0) https://creativecommons.org/licenses/by-sa/3.0/deed.en.

P. 130: The chapel of Our Lady of the Miraculous Medal in Paris, Author: Peter Potrowl, Source: https://commons.wikimedia.org/wiki/File:Paris_-_Chapelle_Notre-Dame_de_la_M%C3%A9daille_Miraculeuse_-_10.jpg, License: (CC BY-SA 4.0) https://creativecommons.org/licenses/by-sa/4.0/deed.en.

P. 154: 19th century novena painting from France, Author: Léo Mabmacien, Source: https://commons.wikimedia.org/wiki/File:A_neuvaine_immaculee_conception,_novena,_Christian_devotionalism_in_France.jpg, License: (CC BY-SA 2.0) https://creativecommons.org/licenses/by-sa/2.0/deed.en.

P. 158: Statues in Saint Peter's Basilica. Saint Louis de Montfort. Founder Statue by Giacomo Parisini, 1948, Author: Jordiferrer, Source: https://commons.wikimedia.org/wiki/File:2016_-_Statues_in_Saint_Peter's_Basilica_06.jpg, License: (CC BY-SA 4.0) https://creativecommons.org/licenses/by-sa/4.0/deed.en.

P. 191: Alfonso Maria de Liguori, Author: Unknown, Source: https://commons.wikimedia.org/wiki/File:Liguori.jpg, License: (CC BY-SA 3.0) https://creativecommons.org/licenses/by-sa/3.0/deed.en.

P. 192: Mother Teresa of Calcutta, Author: Manfredo Ferrari, Source: https://commons.wikimedia.org/wiki/File:Mutter_Teresa_von_Kalkutta.jpg, License: (CC BY-SA 4.0) https://creativecommons.org/licenses/by-sa/4.0/deed.en.

P. 193: Portrait by Zbigniew Kotyłła, Author: Zkoty1953, https://commons.wikimedia.org/wiki/File:San_Giovanni_Paolo_II.jpg, License: (CC BY-SA 3.0) https://creativecommons.org/licenses/by-sa/3.0/deed.en.

P. 193: Coat of Arms of Pope John Paul II, Author: Magul, Source: https://commons.wikimedia.org/wiki/File:San_Giovanni_Paolo_II.jpg, License: (CC BY-SA 3.0) https://creativecommons.org/licenses/by-sa/3.0/deed.en.

P. 236: Our Lady of Akita Japan, Author: SICDAMNOME, Source: https://commons.wikimedia.org/wiki/File:Virgin_Mary_of_Akita_Japan.jpg, License: (CC BY-SA 4.0) https://creativecommons.org/licenses/by-sa/4.0/deed.en.

P. 237: Statue of Our Lady of La Salette and the two children, in the church of Corps, Isère, France, Author: Fr. Latreille, Source: https://commons.wikimedia.org/wiki/File:Eglise_de_Corps-statue-82.JPG, License: (CC BY-SA 3.0) https://creativecommons.org/licenses/by-sa/3.0/deed.en.